Software Project Management in Practice

Software Project Management in Practice

Pankaj Jalote

✦ Addison-Wesley

Boston • San Francisco • New York • Toronto • Montreal
London • Munich • Paris • Madrid
Capetown • Sydney • Tokyo • Singapore • Mexico City

The publisher offers discounts on this book when ordered in quantity for special sales. For more information, please contact:

Pearson Education Corporate Sales Division
201 W. 103rd Street
Indianapolis, IN 46290
(800) 428-5331
corpsales@pearsoned.com

Visit Addison-Wesley on the Web at www.awl.com/cseng/

Library of Congress Cataloging-in-Publication Data

Jalote, P.
    Software project management in practice / Pankaj Jalote.
        p. cm.
    Includes bibliographical references and index.
    ISBN 0-201-73721-3 (alk. paper)
    1. Computer software—Development—Management.   I Title.

    QA76.76.D47 J354 2002
    005.1'068—dc21

                                    20010553320

ISBN 0-201-73721-3
Text printed on recycled paper
1 2 3 4 5 6 7 8 9 10—CRS—0605040302
First printing, February 2002

*Dedicated to the project managers of Infosys,
and to software project managers across the world.*

Contents

Preface

The genesis of this book dates back to 1996. For my sabbatical, I joined Infosys as the head of quality, with the charter of improving the processes for project execution. Seeing the problems faced by project managers, I felt that software project management must be the toughest job on the planet. And I thought that delivering high-quality software within budget and on schedule must be an oxymoron.

The situation, I now realize, is not quite that hopeless. By using sound project management processes, project managers in some organizations are successfully executing projects.

Infosys, one such global organization, has successfully executed more than 500 projects last year alone. It has about 10,000 employees spread across 25 cities in more than a dozen countries around the globe, and it has been assessed at the highest maturity level (level 5) of the CMM. Its revenues and profits have grown at about 75% per year for the past five years. The level of customer satisfaction can be judged by the fact that despite the company's huge growth about 85% of its revenue comes from repeat orders from existing customers.

I have used my experience and knowledge of Infosys processes to cull out and describe in this book the key project management practices that have been used to successfully execute project after project. The beauty of these practices is that despite being highly effective, they are not complex; rather, they are grounded in common sense and are supported by simple measurements and analyses.

In describing project management processes at Infosys, the book offers a unique combination of two value propositions. First, it provides the complete set of processes employed for project management in a highly successful organization. The use of these processes is illustrated with real examples and a running case study. Second, because the processes satisfy the requirements of the Capability

Maturity Model (CMM), this book demystifies the way projects are managed in a high-maturity organization, and it provides the benefits that the CMM offers to project management without the need of a detailed understanding of the CMM.

The book is written primarily for project managers and for professionals who plan to become project managers. By using the methods described in this book they can systematically improve the planning and execution of their projects. It can also be very useful for an organization that wants to reach a high maturity level. If project managers start using the methods described here, they will lay the foundations for high maturity in the organization.

Because most chapters begin with an overview before describing the details of the Infosys method, this book can also be used as a text in a software project management course. In a general software engineering course, it can serve as a supplementary text, providing a view of how a software project is managed in a business environment.

Chapter 1 contains a brief introduction to Infosys and the relationship of the CMM and project management. The remainder of the book is divided into two parts. Part I, consisting of Chapters 2 through 9, focuses on project planning and covers topics such as planning infrastructure, process planning, effort and schedule estimation, quality planning, risk management, measurement planning, and configuration management. Part II, consisting of Chapters 10 through 12, focuses on project execution and completion and covers reviews, project monitoring and control, and project closure.

To the extent possible, each chapter has been kept independent and stand-alone and has been organized as follows. The relevant concepts and background material are given in the first section, followed by a discussion of methods used by Infosys. Next come examples of the use of these methods in real projects and in the case study. Each chapter ends with a summary that lists the key takeaways from the chapter and describes which aspects of CMM are satisfied by the methods discussed in the chapter.

Although this book draws on my earlier book *CMM in Practice* (Addison-Wesley, 2000), it has a different focus and substantially different contents. Whereas *CMM in Practice* considers the entire software process and focuses on implementation of the CMM in an organization, this book focuses exclusively on project management.

Many people helped to make this book a reality. Because the book has its origins in *CMM in Practice*, my thanks to all the people who helped in that project. In addition, I would like to again express my gratitude to Infosys and its directors, whose cooperation and help made this book possible. My sincere thanks to members of the quality department at Infosys for providing information whenever needed, and to the many people who shared with me their experiences, which find their way into mini-cases throughout the book (although with the names changed). My special thanks to Naresh Agarwal for his help with the main case study, and to Sanjay Joshi for his help in bringing a sharper focus to the chapters. And finally, my thanks to my wife, Shikha, and my daughters, Sumedha and Sunanda, for bearing with me and my odd hours once again.

Any comments about the book, or any inaccuracies that might be present (which are entirely my responsibility), can be sent to me at jalote@iitk.ac.in. For information regarding Infosys, visit www.infy.com or send mail to public-relations@infy.com.

Pankaj Jalote

Chapter 1

Managing Software Projects

Worldwide, some half a million project managers execute about a million software projects each year, producing software worth $600 billion. Many of these projects fail to fulfill customers' quality expectations or fail to deliver the software within budget and on schedule. One analysis suggests that about one-third of projects have cost and schedule overruns of more than 125%.[1]

Why do so many software projects fail? Although there are many reasons, one of the most important is improper management of the project. For example, the major reasons for runaways (projects that are out of control) are unclear objectives, bad planning, new technology, a lack of a project management methodology, and insufficient staff.[2] At least three of these five reasons clearly relate to project management. The other two—insufficient staff and new technology—can be considered as risks whose management is also a part of project management.

Clearly, by using effective project management techniques a project manager can improve the chances of success. But what are these effective techniques?

Let's consider an analogy. Suppose you want to develop a muscular, toned body. To reach your goal, you start looking at exercise routines described in magazines. One article describes how to develop arm strength, giving a set of 10 exercises to be done—not too many by any standard. But then another article, this one on developing thigh strength, also gives 10 exercises, and the evangelist for flat stomachs also feels that doing 10 exercises is not too much. If you want to develop your body overall by following each of these isolated exercise programs, you would find that you have a set of 50 to 100 exercises to do—a clear impossibility for most people, let alone a busy project manager. To achieve your objective, you need a comprehensive training program that is practical and effective.

Similarly, you'll find an abundance of suggestions for performing the various aspects of project management, including effort estimation, risk management, project monitoring, configuration management, and so on. Although each proposed technique solves the problem it is designed to solve, it is not clear how to combine these techniques into a practical and workable process. For effective project management, the need of the hour is a practical, manageable "exercise routine" that will deliver the result. In other words, what is needed is a balanced process that covers the management of the entire project from inception to completion. Unfortunately, there is a paucity of published approaches illustrating how to integrate techniques in this way.

This book fills this gap by describing the set of processes used in a world-class organization to effectively and efficiently manage software projects. The company is Infosys, a software development company that has an enviable track record of project execution; in 2000 alone, Infosys project managers used the processes described here to successfully execute about 500 projects for customers. This book discusses all aspects of Infosys project management—planning, execution, and closure. You'll learn how Infosys project managers estimate, plan for managing risks, collect metrics data, set quality goals, use measurements for monitoring a project, and so on. An interesting aspect of these processes, one that will appeal to busy project managers, is that they are neither complex nor cumbersome, and they use simple metrics.

Infosys has been assessed at level 5 (the highest level) of the Capability Maturity Model (CMM). By extracting project management processes from the set of processes at Infosys, this book also illustrates how projects are managed in a high-maturity organization. Through this illustration, I hope to bring the benefits of the CMM to project managers who have not studied it because of lack of time, because they regard it as being for "process folks" or because they have found it difficult to relate the CMM to project management practices.

This chapter introduces the two topics that form the background for the book: the CMM and Infosys. Because the focus of the book is project management and not the CMM, I restrict the discussion to the project management aspects of the CMM. This chapter also provides an overview of the project management process and the main case study; details of these are discussed in the remainder of the book. First, then, let's briefly discuss the role of processes in project management.

1.1 PROCESSES AND PROJECT MANAGEMENT

A software project has two main activity dimensions: engineering and project management. The engineering dimension deals with building the system and focuses on issues such as how to design, test, code, and so on. The project management dimension deals with properly planning and controlling the engineering activities to meet project goals for cost, schedule, and quality.

If a project is small (say, a team of one or two working for a few weeks), it can be executed somewhat informally. The project plan may be an e-mail specifying the delivery date and perhaps a few intermediate milestones. Requirements might be communicated in a note or even verbally, and intermediate work products, such as design documents, might be scribbles on personal note pads.

These informal techniques, however, do not scale up for larger projects in which many people may work for many months—the situation for most commercial software projects. In such projects, each engineering task must be done carefully by following well-tried methodologies, and the work products must be properly documented so that others can review them. The tasks in the project must be carefully planned and allocated to project personnel and then tracked as the project executes. In other words, to successfully execute larger projects, formality and rigor along these two dimensions must increase.

Formality requires that well-defined processes be used for performing the various tasks so that the outcome becomes more dependent on the capability of the processes. Formality is further enhanced if quantitative approaches are employed in the processes through the use of suitable metrics.

What is a process? Technically, a *process* for a task comprises a sequence of steps that should be followed to execute the task. For an organization, however, the processes it recommends for use by its engineers and project managers are much more than a sequence of steps; they encapsulate what the engineers and project managers have learned about successfully executing projects. Through the processes, the benefits of experience are conferred to everyone, including newcomers in the organization. These processes help managers and engineers emulate past successes and avoid the pitfalls that lead to failures.

For a project, the engineering processes generally specify how to perform engineering activities such as requirement specification, design, testing, and so on. The project management processes, on the other hand, specify how to set milestones, organize personnel, manage risks, monitor progress, and so on. This book focuses on the project management process.

When you consider project management processes, you must ask the question whether project managers will use them. I have often heard process designers complain that project managers don't follow the process and that they resist changes. My experience with project managers at Infosys and other organizations is that they actually want to use processes but only if they're reasonable and will help the project managers execute their projects better. Project managers do, however, resent processes that seem to be unnecessarily bureaucratic and add little value to their work. The trick, then, is to have *lightweight* processes—those that help project managers plan and control their projects better and that give them the flexibility to handle various situations.

In response to the question "Why should project managers follow processes?" S.D. Shibulal—founder, director, and the current head of customer delivery at Infosys—sums it up nicely in a few key points:

- Processes represent collective knowledge. Using them increases your chances of success.

- A process may have some extra steps, but you will not always know beforehand which ones are not needed, and hence you will increase your risks by taking shortcuts.

- Without processes, you cannot predict much about the outcome of your project.

- You and the organization cannot learn effectively without having defined processes. And learning and improvement are imperative in today's knowledge-based world.

- Processes lower your anxiety level. The checklists inevitably cover 80 percent of what needs to be done. Hence, your task reduces to working out the remaining 20 percent.

1.2 PROJECT MANAGEMENT AND THE CMM

Once it is accepted that use of effective processes can help in executing a project successfully, a question immediately arises: What are the desirable characteristics of these processes? The CMM for software is a framework that tries to answer this question.

The CMM for software is a framework that was developed by the Software Engineering Institute (SEI) at Carnegie Mellon University by observing the best practices in software and other organizations. Hence, the CMM reflects the collective process experience and expectations of many companies. It specifies desired characteristics of processes without prescribing specific processes. Thus, different processes can fulfill the requirements of the CMM. It can be used to evaluate the software process of an organization and to identify deficiencies.

The CMM is one of the most popular frameworks for software process improvement (the other commonly used framework is ISO 9001[3,4,5]). The foundations of the CMM were laid down in Watts Humphrey's *Managing the Software Process*,[6] and the framework itself is described completely in the SEI's *The Capability Maturity Model: Guidelines for Improving the Software Process*.[7] A "new edition" of the CMM, called CMM-I, has been released. But because the focus of this book is not on the models and because there is still little experience available with CMM-I, I discuss only the CMM for software and only the project management aspects, even though the CMM also covers organizational and process management issues. I do not discuss the assessment procedure, a brief description of which is given in my book *CMM in Practice*,[8] and a detailed description given in *CMM Based Appraisal for Internal Process Improvement*, by S. Masters.[9]

1.2.1 Overview of the CMM

One objective of the CMM is to distinguish mature processes from immature, or ad hoc, processes. Immature software processes imply that projects are executed without many guidelines, and the outcome of a project depends largely on the capability of the team and the project leader. On the other hand, with mature processes, a project is executed by following defined processes. In this case, the outcome of the project is less dependent on people and more on the processes. It follows, then, that the more mature the processes, the more predictable the results and the more well controlled the projects.

The range of results that can be expected in a project when it is executed using a process is its *process capability*. The actual result achieved in a project executed using the process is its *process performance*. Clearly, the process performance depends on the process capability. To consistently improve process performance on projects, you must enhance the process capability; the process itself must become more mature.

The path to higher maturity includes some well-defined plateaus referred to as *maturity levels* by the CMM. Each maturity level specifies certain characteristics for processes, with higher maturity levels having more advanced characteristics that are found in more mature software processes. Hence, the CMM framework describes the key elements of software processes at different levels of maturity. Consequently, it also specifies the path that a software process follows in moving from immature processes to highly mature processes. This path includes five maturity levels, as shown in Figure 1.1.[7]

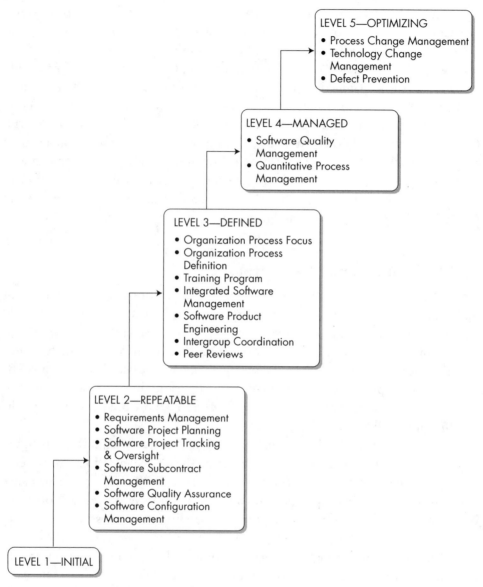

Figure 1.1 Maturity levels in the CMM

In level 1, the *initial* level, a project is executed in a manner that the team and project manager see fit. The *repeatable* level (level 2) applies when established project management practices are employed, although organization-wide processes may not exist. At the *defined* level (level 3), organization-wide processes have been defined and are regularly followed. At the *managed* level (level 4), quantitative understanding of the process capability makes it possible to quantitatively predict and control the process performance on a project. At the *optimizing* level (level 5), the process capability is improved in a controlled manner and the improvement is evaluated quantitatively.

Each maturity level (except level 1) is characterized by *key process areas* (KPAs), which specify the areas on which the organization should focus to elevate its processes to that maturity level. Figure 1.1 also shows the KPAs for the different levels. For an organization to achieve a maturity level, it must satisfy all the KPAs at that maturity level as well as the KPAs at all lower maturity levels.

Maintaining processes at higher levels of maturity is a challenging task requiring commitment from the organization and a proper work culture. Of the 900 assessments conducted between 1996 and June 2000 whose assessment results were provided to the SEI, only 3% of the organizations were at level 5, and another 5% were at level 4.[10] The rest were at level 3 or below, with 38% at level 2 and 18% at level 3.

1.2.2 KPAs for Project Management

Each KPA specifies goals that the processes of the organization must meet to satisfy that KPA. In addition, each KPA specifies a group of activities, called *key practices*, that collectively satisfy the goals of that KPA. In many senses, the goals for each KPA capture its essence. They specify the objectives that the CMM has set for the processes relating to the KPA. To illustrate the KPAs associated with project management, we briefly discuss here the goals of these KPAs. These goals are taken from the CMM,[7] with some minor changes in the wording of some goals.

Table 1.1 lists all the goals for KPAs at level 2, showing clearly that the level 2 focus is almost exclusively on project management. Under these goals, you create and document a project plan, evaluate the ongoing project performance against the plan, and take actions when the actual performance significantly deviates from the plan. Requirements are properly documented, and changes to requirements are properly managed. All work products are controlled, and changes to products are properly managed through a planned configuration management plan. Reviews and audits are performed to ensure that planned processes and standards are being followed. If some parts of the project are subcontracted to other vendors, the subcontracted work is also monitored properly.

Table 1.2 details the goals of three of the seven KPAs at level 3. The other KPAs focus on organizational and process management issues. A project in a

Table 1.1 Goals for KPAs at Level 2 (Repeatable)

KPA	Goals
Requirements Management (RM)	• Software requirements are controlled to establish a baseline for software engineering and management activities. • Software plans, products, and activities are kept consistent with requirements.
Software Project Planning (SPP)	• Estimates are documented for use in planning and tracking the project. • Project activities and commitments are planned and documented. • Affected groups and individuals agree to their commitments related to the project.
Software Project Tracking and Oversight (SPTO)	• Actual results and performances are tracked against the software plans. • Corrective actions are taken and managed to closure when actual results and performance deviate significantly from the software plans. • Changes to commitments are agreed to by the affected groups and individuals.
Software Subcontract Management (SSM)	• The prime contractor and the subcontractor agree to their commitments. • The prime contractor tracks the subcontractor's actual results against its commitments. • The prime contractor and the subcontractor maintain ongoing communication. • The prime contractor tracks the subcontractor's actual performance against its commitments.
Software Quality Assurance (SQA)	• Software quality assurance activities are planned. • Adherence of software products and activities to the applicable standards, procedures, and requirements is verified objectively. • Affected groups and individuals are informed of software quality assurance activities and results. • Noncompliance issues that cannot be resolved within the project are addressed by senior management.
Software Configuration Management (SCM)	• Software configuration management activities are planned. • Selected software work products are identified, controlled, and available. • Changes to identified software work products are controlled. • Affected groups and individuals are informed of the status and content of software baselines.

level 3 organization uses a tailored version of the standard process and reuses assets, data, and experience from past projects for planning. The various groups that contribute to the project cooperate smoothly through well-defined interfaces and mechanisms. Reviews are properly carried out to identify defects in work products, and sufficient support for conducting reviews and follow-up activities is provided.

Table 1.2 Goals of Three KPAs at Level 3 (Defined)

KPA	Goals
Integrated Software Management (ISM)	• The project's defined software process is a tailored version of the organization's standard software process. • The project is planned and managed according to the project's defined software process.
Intergroup Coordination (IC)	• All affected groups agree to the customer's requirements. • All groups agree to the commitments between different groups. • The groups identify, track, and resolve intergroup issues.
Peer Reviews (PR)	• Peer review activities are planned. • Defects in the software work products are identified and removed.

Table 1.3 shows the goals for the two KPAs at level 4. At level 4, the capability of the organization's process is understood in quantitative terms. The process capability is used to set quantitative goals for a project. Data on project performance are collected on an ongoing basis and are compared with data on past performance; if significant deviations are observed, proper corrective actions are applied to bring the project back in control. A key aspect of level 4 is the use of statistical process control techniques on an ongoing basis so that each activity can be evaluated and corrective action taken if needed.

The three KPAs at level 5 focus on improving the capability of the process. Of the three KPAs, the Defect Prevention KPA is the one that most directly affects project management. This KPA requires that defects be prevented proactively by systematically analyzing the causes of defects and then eliminating those causes. If

Table 1.3 Goals for KPAs at Level 4 (Managed)

KPA	Goals
Quantitative Process Management (QPM)	• The quantitative process management activities are planned. • The process performance of the project's defined software process is controlled quantitatively. • The process capability of the organization's standard software process is known in quantitative terms.
Software Quality Management (SQM)	• The project's software quality management activities are planned. • Measurable goals for software product quality and their priorities are defined. • Actual progress toward achieving the quality goals for the software products is quantified and managed.

defects can be prevented from entering the software, the effort spent in removing them can be reduced, thereby improving quality and productivity.

1.3 PROJECT MANAGEMENT AT INFOSYS

Infosys executes hundreds of projects each year. Full responsibility for executing a project rests with the project manager, who must make sure that the project team delivers high-quality software to the customer on time and within cost. To help the project manager fulfill this responsibility, support from the organization is necessary. This section provides a brief background on Infosys and its support for managing projects.

1.3.1 Background: Infosys

Infosys is a software house headquartered in Bangalore, India. Its stated mission is "to be a globally respected corporation that provides best-of-breed software solutions delivered by best-in-class people." It employs the global delivery model, in which the customer can be located anywhere in the world and customer fulfillment can be provided from anywhere. In this model, the customer is sought anywhere in the world where it provides the most value to the company. For customer fulfillment, a combination of processes, technology, and management is employed to segregate the work so that value can be added in the most optimum locations and then reaggregated for delivery to the customer.

Infosys currently employs about 10,000 people, with about 15 development centers in four countries and offices in more than a dozen countries. The company was founded in 1981 by seven software professionals with an equity base of only $300. Today, Infosys has a market capitalization of more than $8 billion (based on market rates in June 2001), and its revenue was more than $400 million in 2000 (revenue in 1994 was $9.5 million). Its customers are spread across the globe and include major corporations—more than 60 of them being Fortune 1000 companies—that are engaged in diverse businesses such as banking, retailing, manufacturing, telecommunications, financial services, insurance, and transportation.

Infosys is a highly respected company that has been rated as the best managed and most respected company in India and one of Asia's leading information technology (IT) companies. It has bagged many awards, including the Ramakrishna Bajaj award, which is modeled after the Malcolm Balridge award. It can be safely said that Infosys is one of the best software services corporations in the world.

Infosys provides a top-notch infrastructure so that its project managers can better serve the needs of its worldwide customers. The company has provided audio conferencing facilities to almost every group so that project managers can interact easily with customers and with group members located in different sites. Similarly, a state-of-the-art video conferencing facility is used for interaction among the company's various locations as well as for virtual meetings. Its main campus in Bangalore is now one of the largest software service facilities in the world, with work-related facilities such as a library, extensive computing and networking facilities, training facilities, discussion rooms, projection facilities, and so on, as well as recreational facilities such as an art gallery, a health club, and facilities for tennis, basketball, and so on.

Process orientation and improvement are a part of the Infosys work culture, and processes are defined for most tasks that are performed regularly. For process definition and improvement, Infosys first adopted the ISO 9000 framework and got its ISO certification in 1993. To further improve the software process, Infosys then adopted the CMM framework. It was first assessed at level 4 in December 1997, and then at level 5 in December 1999. In its pursuit of continuous improvement, Infosys now employs the Malcolm Balridge framework for all-around improvement and building leadership excellence in all areas of operation.

1.3.2 SEPG Support to Projects

The quality department at Infosys contains the software engineering process group (SEPG). The SEPG is responsible for coordinating all the process activities, including process definition, process improvement, and process deployment. It also manages all information and data related to the use of processes (such as the process database and the process capability baseline, which are discussed further in Chapter 2).

Although the responsibility for all aspects of delivery, including quality, belongs to the project team, the SEPG facilitates the project team in following the right processes. The SEPG also forms an independent channel for monitoring and reporting to senior management on process and quality issues. Because "processes won't stick by themselves,"[6] the SEPG helps to ensure that the defined processes are implemented and become standard practice.

To this end, in addition to offering training on processes, the SEPG provides a member who is associated with a project as a *software quality adviser*. The quality adviser assists in defining and following processes, ensures that the processes are followed, aids in analyzing the data, and provides any needed process training. Because the adviser is well versed on processes, guidelines, and so on, the adviser's main help comes during project planning. The adviser also reviews the project plan to ensure that it contains all the key elements.

In addition to providing consulting and help with processes and metrics, the Infosys SEPG schedules and manages regular independent audits (see Chapter 11) to ensure that the defined processes and standards are being followed.

1.3.3 Senior Management Involvement in Projects

Infosys prides itself in providing value to its customers through delivery excellence. Everything at Infosys, including its organizational structure, is driven by the aim of serving customers efficiently and effectively and quickly tapping new business opportunities.

For delivery of customer services, Infosys has many *business units*. Within a business unit, a *team*, headed by a *project manager*, executes a project. The project manager is responsible for all aspects of project execution, from determining the requirements to final installation of the software. The project manager reports to a *business manager*, who in turn generally reports to the *business unit head*.

To handle situations that cannot be resolved by the project manager, senior management involvement in projects is essential. At Infosys, the business manager regularly interacts with the project manager and monitors the project through status reports and milestone reports (discussed in Chapter 11). In addition to regular monitoring, the business manager also helps to resolve issues and problems that cannot be handled by the project team and are *escalated* to his level (escalation is discussed in Chapter 8). The business manager also interacts with customers to ensure that they are satisfied and that any issues are promptly raised and addressed.

In addition, other senior people also review projects periodically by regularly taking part in internal audits (discussed in Chapter 11). Through two systems—called PRISM (project review by senior management) and IPM (integrated project management)—milestone reports and project plans are available for senior management to review. All senior managers are expected to review some projects periodically through this system and to give feedback to the project leaders.

Overall, senior management maintains involvement in the project primarily by monitoring to ensure that the project objectives are met and that the customer is fully satisfied.

1.3.4 Training for Project Managers

Because project managers have the main responsibility for satisfying the customer, they need to master not only executing the technical aspects of a project but also interacting with customers, eliciting requirements, managing the team, and so on. Clearly no one is likely to possess all the skills needed, so it's crucial to train people to develop the necessary skills. Infosys has implemented a variety of programs to help people transition from being engineers to being project leaders.

All fresh entrants undergo a three- to four-month *induction training program.* In addition to training in engineering and technology, this program contains one- or two-day programs in business etiquette, written communication, public speaking, body language, and so on.

Later, when engineers are ready to become *module leaders* (those who manage the development of a system module, especially in larger projects) or project managers, they attend a series of technical and soft-skills training programs. Included in the former is a five-day project management course that focuses on all aspects of project management: planning, monitoring, controlling, and so on. A two-week course on requirements specification and management teaches how to elicit requirements, how to document them, how to verify them, and so on. The five-day residential soft-skills training program includes modules on appraisals and team management, customer focus and customer management, leadership, social and business etiquette for different countries, and so on.

Other regularly offered programs focus on various aspects of management; project leaders take these courses when their schedules permit. Also, team-building workshops are conducted by professionals.

1.3.5 The Project Management Process

For a project team to successfully execute a project, it must perform hundreds of tasks, many of them interdependent. Effectively managing this process is extremely important for success. At Infosys, the set of activities executed by a project manager is specified in the *project management* process. It is fairly standard, having three main stages:

- Project planning
- Project execution
- Project closure

In the *project planning* stage, the project manager reviews contractual commitments and creates a plan to meet them. Creating a project plan involves defining a life-cycle process to be followed, estimating the effort and schedule, preparing a detailed schedule of tasks, and so on. It also includes planning for quality and configuration management as well as risk management. In this phase, the major activities of the project manager are as follows:

- Perform startup and administrative tasks.
- Create a project plan and schedule.
  - Define the project objectives.
  - Identify a suitable standard process for project execution.
  - Tailor the standard process to meet project requirements.
  - Define a process for managing changes in requirements.
  - Estimate the effort.
  - Plan for human resources and team organization.
  - Define the project milestones and create a schedule.
  - Define the quality objectives and a quality plan to achieve them.
  - Make a defect prevention plan.
  - Identify risks and make plans to mitigate them.
  - Define a measurement plan for the project.
  - Define a training plan for the project.
  - Define project-tracking procedures.
- Perform a review of the project plan and schedule.
- Obtain authorization from senior management.
- Define and review the configuration management plan.
- Orient the project team to the project management plan.

In addition to the project manager, this phase involves the customer, an SEPG representative, and the business manager for the project. The entry criterion is that the contract or project authorization is available. The exit criterion is that the project plan has been documented and group reviewed (see Chapter 10).

The second phase, *project execution,* involves executing the project plan, tracking the status of the project, and making corrections whenever project performance strays from the path laid down in the project plan. In other words, it involves tracking and controlling the implementation of the project process. This phase is the longest in the project management process, incorporating periodic tasks such as monitoring project status and quality and taking any needed corrective steps. In this phase, the project manager performs these main activities:

- Execute the project as per the project plan.
- Track the project status.
- Review the project status with senior management.
- Monitor compliance with the defined project process.
- Analyze defects and perform defect prevention activities.
- Monitor performance at the program level.
- Conduct milestone reviews and replan if necessary.

Other members of the team also participate in this stage. The entry criterion is that the project plan is complete and approved, and the exit criterion is that all work products delivered are accepted by the customer.

The last stage of the project management process, *project closure,* involves a systematic wind-up of the project after customer acceptance. The main goal here is to learn from the experience so that the process can be improved. Post-project data analysis constitutes the main activity; metrics are analyzed, process assets (materials, such as templates and guidelines, used to aid in managing the process itself) are collected for future use, and lessons are recorded. Because learning from the project is the main goal, this is a group activity that involves the project manager, the SEPG, and other members of the team. The entry criterion is that the customer has accepted the work products. The exit criterion is that a postproject meeting has been conducted. The main outputs of this phase are the project closure report and the collected process assets.

The remainder of this book discusses the various elements of this management process. Part I includes separate chapters devoted to key planning activities, such as process definition and tailoring, risk management, effort and schedule estimation, quality planning, and configuration management planning. The other tasks in the planning phase (such as human resource planning, project organization, tools to be used, project tracking procedures, and so on) are discussed briefly in Chapters 7 and 8. Part II includes chapters on project monitoring and controlling and on project closure.

1.4 OVERVIEW OF THE ACIC CASE STUDY

ACIC Corporation (name changed to protect confidentiality) is a multibillion-dollar financial institution. To keep up with the times, several years ago it started slowly

Web-enabling its applications, and it wanted to start an on-line service for opening and tracking accounts. Because Infosys had successfully built some e-services for ACIC earlier in a project called Synergy (name changed), ACIC employed Infosys to analyze the problem. This work was executed in *time and material* (T&M) mode— that is, the customer paid for the effort spent by Infosys in doing the analysis. Based on the analysis output, Infosys made a successful bid for the Web project, giving rise to the ACIC case study that runs throughout this book. The project successfully released the new service in time, and the software has been in operation without any problem. (This case study is different from the WAR project case study discussed in my earlier book.[6])

The ACIC project illustrates the various project planning and monitoring tasks undertaken in executing a project at Infosys. Many of the outputs related to management of the ACIC project are given in the relevant chapters. These include the following:

- The data from the Synergy project, which was used by the ACIC project manager during planning (Chapter 2)
- The project's process plan (Chapter 3)
- An analysis of the impact of a requirement change request (Chapter 3)
- Effort estimates and the high-level schedule, along with a description of how they were obtained (Chapter 4)
- The quality plan containing quality goals and plans for achieving them, including plans for defect prevention and reviews (Chapter 5)
- The risk management plan describing the major risks, their risk exposure and impact, their prioritization, and the risk mitigation plans for the high-priority risks (Chapter 6)
- The measurement and tracking plan (Chapter 7)
- The complete project management plan, including the team management plan and the customer communication and escalation plan (Chapter 8)
- The complete configuration management plan (Chapter 9)
- Project tracking documents, including the defect log, the issues log, the status report, and the milestone report (Chapter 11)
- Details of defect prevention, including defect analysis results and the impact on the project of the defect prevention plan (Chapter 11)
- The complete closure report, which includes the metrics data on quality, productivity, cost of quality, defect removal efficiency, and so on (Chapter 12)

1.5 SUMMARY

Software project management is perhaps the most important factor in the outcome of a project. Without proper project management, a project will almost certainly fail. Many organizations have evolved effective project management processes. This book describes these processes for one such organization, Infosys, which has been assessed at level 5 of the CMM and whose project managers have successfully executed hundreds of projects.

Here are the key takeaways from this chapter:

- Processes for the various aspects of project management should not be looked at in isolation. In a balanced process, the practices integrate smoothly.

- Processes of an organization should encapsulate its best practices so as to help new projects replicate past successes and avoid failures.

- At the top level, the project management process consists of three phases: planning, execution, and closure.

- For effective execution of projects, project managers should be supported through the help of an SEPG in executing processes; senior management monitoring and issue resolution; and good training.

- Many key process areas at all maturity levels of the CMM for software focus directly on project management.

1.6 REFERENCES

1. L.H. Putnam and W. Myers. *Industrial Strength Software: Effective Management Using Measurement.* IEEE Computer Society Press, 1997.

2. R.L. Glass. *Software Runaways: Lessons Learned from Massive Software Project Failures.* Prentice Hall PTR, 1998.

3. International Standards Organization. *ISO 9001, Quality Systems—Model for Quality Assurance in Design/Development, Production, Installation, and Services.* 1987.

4. International Standards Organization. *ISO 9000-3, Guidelines for the Application of ISO9001 to the Development, Supply and Maintenance of Software.* 1991.

5. U.K. Dept. of Trade and Industry and British Computer Society. *TickIT: A Guide to Software Quality Management System Construction and Certification Using EN29001.* 1992.

6. W. Humphrey. *Managing the Software Process.* Addison-Wesley, 1989.

7. Carnegie Mellon University/Software Engineering Institute. *The Capability Maturity Model: Guidelines for Improving the Software Process.* Addison-Wesley, 1995.

8. P. Jalote. *CMM in Practice: Processes for Executing Software Projects at Infosys.* Addison-Wesley, 2000.

9. S. Masters. *CMM Based Appraisal for Internal Process Improvement (CBA-IPI): Method Description. Technical Report, Software Engineering Institute, CMU/SEI-96-TR-007,* 1996.

10. Software Engineering Institute. Maturity Profile Report, http://www.sei.cmu.edu/activities/sema/profile.html.

Part I

PROJECT PLANNING

Chapter 2

The Project Planning Infrastructure

At the end of his tenth project plan review meeting, Dinesh, the head of delivery at Infosys at the time, was not very happy. In review after review of project plans, Dinesh had noted that each project manager was working in a world of his own, valiantly struggling to create optimum processes to execute his project and to produce estimates that he could meet—this even though Dinesh knew that similar projects had been executed earlier by other teams whose experience and data could considerably ease the project manager's pain. Not only were the project managers investing their planning effort in reinventing the wheel, but also they were "planning" to make the same mistakes as the project managers before them. Dinesh realized that the answer to this predicament lay in creating an institutional memory that would be accessible to all project managers.

The million dollar question was how to build this institutional memory and use it to mold an infrastructure for project planning. What were its elements? How should past experience be systematically recorded and made available for reuse? How could Infosys keep the infrastructure current?

This chapter discusses the key elements of the planning infrastructure at Infosys: the process database, the process capability baseline, and the process assets. In later chapters you will see how these elements are used in project planning.

The *process database* (PDB) captures the performance data of completed projects. The *process capability baseline* (PCB) summarizes the performance across projects. It thereby specifies quantitatively the range of results that have been obtained by following the processes, and therefore the range of results to be expected if the same processes are followed. *Process assets* are documents such as checklists, templates, methodologies, and lessons learned—materials that capture past experience and help project managers and engineers use the processes effectively. These components are usually present in high-maturity organizations, although their use in these organizations differs.[1]

2.1 THE PROCESS DATABASE

The process database is a permanent repository of the process performance data from projects; it can be used for project planning, estimation, analysis of productivity and quality, and other purposes.[2] The PDB consists of data from completed projects, with each project providing one data record. As you can imagine, to populate the PDB, data must be collected, analyzed, and then organized for entry. Here we focus on how the data are represented in the PDB at Infosys; Chapter 7 explains how the data are collected.

2.1.1 Contents of the PDB

To use the information in the PDB during planning, project managers often find information about similar projects particularly useful. To allow for similarity checking, you should capture in the PDB general information about the project, such as languages used, platforms, databases used, tools used, size, and effort. With this type of information, a project manager can search and find information on all projects that, for example, focused on a particular application domain, used a particular database management system (DBMS) or language, or targeted a specific platform.

To help in project planning, you should capture data about the effort, defects, schedule, risk, and so on. If the total effort spent in a project is known, along with the size and distribution of effort in different phases, this data can be used for estimating effort in a new project.

Thus, the data captured in the PDB at Infosys can be classified as follows:

- Project characteristics
- Project schedule
- Project effort
- Size
- Defects

Data on project characteristics consists of the project name, the names of the project manager and module leaders (so that they can be contacted for further information or clarification), the business unit (to permit analysis based on business unit), the process deployed (to allow separate analyses of different processes), the application domain, the hardware platform, the languages used, the DBMS used, a brief statement of the project goals, information about project risks, the duration of the project, and team size.

The schedule data is primarily the project's expected and actual start and end dates. The data on project effort includes data on the initial estimated effort and the total actual effort, and the distribution of the actual effort among various stages, such as project initiation, requirements management, design, build, unit testing, and other phases. Chapter 7 discusses how to capture the effort data.

The size of the software developed may be in terms of lines of code (LOC), the number of simple, medium, or complex programs, or a combination of these measures. Even if function points are not used for estimation, you can obtain a uniform metric for productivity by representing the final size in function points, which is usually obtained by converting the measured size of the software in LOC to function points using published conversion tables.[3] The size of the final system in function points is also captured.

The data on defects includes the number of defects found in the various defect detection activities, and the number of defects injected in different stages. Hence, you record the number of defects of different origins found in requirements review, design review, code review, unit testing, and other phases. Chapter 7 explains how projects record defect data.

In addition, notes are recorded, including notes on estimation (for example, the criteria used for classifying programs as simple, medium, or complex) and notes on risk management (for example, how risk perception changed during the project).

2.1.2 A Sample Entry

Let's look at a sample PDB entry for a project, which we will refer to with the pseudonym Synergy. In the Synergy project an application was built that formed the precursor to that of the case study (the ACIC project). The case study will refer to this PDB entry during planning.

Data for the four major tables are shown (the example uses expressive names, but codes are used in the actual database for various phases and quality activities). In this example, the data are fairly complete; in other situations, however, the data may not be complete. Such data cannot always be discarded because the information may still be useful.[4] Hence, such data may also be captured in the PDB.

Table 2.1 gives the general information on the project, including start and end dates (estimated and actual), estimated effort (actual effort is not put in this

Table 2.1 General Data about a Project

General Characteristics

Field Name	Value for Synergy
ProcessCategory	Development
LifeCycle	Full
BusinessDomain	Brokerage/Finance
ProcessTailoringNotes	Added group review for high-impact documents. First program of each developer was group reviewed.
PeakTeamSize	12
ToolsUsed	VSS for document CM, VAJ for source code
EstimatedStart	20 Jan 2000
EstimatedFinish	5 May 2000
EstimatedEffortHrs	3,106
EstimationNotes	Use case point approach was one method used for estimation.
ActualStart	20 Jan 2000
ActualFinish	5 May 2000
First Risk	Working through link on customer DB
Second Risk	Additional requirements
Third Risk	Attrition
RiskNotes	Worked in shifts; agreed to take enhancements after acceptance of this product; team building exercises were done.

table because it can be computed from the effort table), peak team size, information about the risk, tools used, and other items. In addition, other information—
for example, about the client—is stored in this table.

The second table captures the information about effort. For different stages
in the process, it includes data on the effort spent in the activity and the effort
spent in rework after the task. Rework effort is captured because it helps in calcu-
lating and understanding the cost of quality. Table 2.2 shows the Synergy effort
data in person-hours. Estimated effort for the phases is also given. (The total effort
spent in life-cycle stages is 2,950 person-hours, and in review, 223 person-hours;
the total estimated effort is 3,012 person-hours.)

The third table contains information about defects. It is desirable to know
not only when the defect was detected but also when it was injected. Hence, you

Table 2.2 Effort Data

Effort by Stage

Stage	TaskEffort	Review Effort	Estimated
Requirements analysis	0	0	0
Design	414	32	367
Coding	1147	76	1182
Independent unit testing	156	74	269
Integration testing	251	30	180
Acceptance testing and installation	183	0	175
Project management	237	8	357
Configuration management	30	3	38
Project-specific training	200	0	218
Others	332	0	226

should record the number of defects found for each injection stage and detection stage combination. The detection stages consist of various reviews and testing, whereas the injection stages involve requirements, design, and coding. If you can separate the defects detected by stage according to their injection stages, then you can compute removal efficiencies of the defect detection stages. This information can be useful for identifying potential improvement areas. Table 2.3 shows the defect data for the Synergy project.

The final table contains information about the size of the project. Different languages may be used in a project, so this table may have multiple entries. Multiple units of size may also be used, so the table captures the unit. Generally, if the size is given in LOC, size in function points can also be computed by using conversion

Table 2.3 Defect Data for the Synergy Project

	Requirement Review	Design Review	Code Review	Unit Testing	System Testing	Acceptance Testing
Requirements	0	0	0	1	1	0
Design		14	3	1	0	0
Coding			21	48	17	6

Table 2.4 Size Data for the Synergy Project

Size

LangCode	OSCode	DBMSCode	HWCode	MeasureCode	ActualCode Size
Java	Windows	—	PC	LOC	8,082
Persistent Builder	Windows NT	DB2	Client MC	LOC	12,185

tables as needed. This information is used to calculate productivity in terms of function points. Because size is a critical factor in determining productivity, other factors, such as the operating system and hardware used, are also captured. Table 2.4 shows the values for this table for Synergy.

2.2 THE PROCESS CAPABILITY BASELINE

Whereas the PDB contains data for each project, the process capability baseline represents a snapshot of the *capability* of the process at some point in time in quantitative terms. The capability of a process is essentially the range of outcomes that can be expected by a project if the process is followed.[5] The capability of a stable process can be determined from past performance of the process. If baselines are regularly established, trends in the process capability can easily be obtained—a key reason for having a PCB.

The first issue that must be resolved is what the PCB should contain—that is, what types of "outcomes" the PCB should include. The PCB at Infosys contains the process performance stated primarily in terms of productivity, quality, schedule, and effort and defect distributions. It specifies the following:

- Delivered quality
- Productivity
- Schedule
- Effort distribution
- Defect injection rate
- In-process defect removal efficiency

• Cost of quality

• Defect distribution

This information can be used in project planning. For example, a project manager can use productivity and the estimated size to estimate the effort for the project and can use the distribution of effort to predict the effort for various phases and to make staffing plans. Similarly, you can use the defect injection rate to predict the total number of defects and can use the distribution of defects to predict the defect levels for various defect detection activities. Overall defect removal efficiency or quality can be used to forecast the number of defects that may crop up after the software is delivered and to plan for maintenance.

The PCB also serves an important role in overall process management in the organization. For example, you can easily measure process improvements by analyzing the trends in the PCB over time. You can also improve the planning of improvement initiatives by using information on distribution of effort and defects, defect injection rates, removal efficiencies, and other measures.

Because a baseline indicates the capability of a process, you must create a separate baseline for each process in the organization. At Infosys, separate processes are defined for maintenance, reengineering, and development projects; a separate baseline is therefore defined for each of these processes. Even these processes are too broad, however, and they provide only general guidelines. If projects of a certain type are executed frequently, a PCB for that type of project is created. This focused baseline gives a much tighter range, in terms of expected results, for that type of project.

The PCB given in Table 2.5 is applicable for development projects and for projects done in a third-generation language (3GL). The PCB for maintenance projects, for example, differs not only in terms of actual figures in the PCB but also in the information included (to suit the maintenance process). (The numbers used in this PCB have been sanitized to protect confidentiality.)

The interpretation of this PCB is straightforward. The PCB states that for development projects, the average productivity is about 12 function points per person-month, with the range being from 4 to 31 function points. The average quality of these projects is 0.02 defects per function point, with the range being between 0.00 and 0.094. The PCB also gives the average and range for other parameters, such as defect injection rate and total defect removal efficiency. Overall defect injection rate is given with respect to size as well as effort, so effort as well as size estimates can be used for estimating defects. The cost of quality includes the cost of

Table 2.5 Process Capability Baseline for Development Process

Sequence Number	Parameter	Remarks	General Baseline, Development Projects
1	Delivered Quality	Delivered Defects /FP (Delivered Defects = Acceptance Defects + Warranty Defects)	0.00–0.094 Delivered Defects/FP (avg: 0.021)
		Quality expressed in terms of effort	0.00–0.012 Delivered Defects/ Person-hour (avg: 0.003)
2	Productivity	For Third-Generation Languages	4–31 FP/person-month (avg: 12)
		For Fourth-Generation Languages	10–129 FP/person-month (avg: 50)
3	Schedule Adherence		81% of projects delivered within ±10% of the agreed schedule
4	Effort		
4.1	Build Effort	Build effort for a medium program	Min–Mean–Max 2–4–6 person days
4.2	Effort Distribution		Min–Mean–Max
		Req. Analysis + Design	1–15–29%
		Build (Code + Code review + UT)	22–41–60%
		Coding	14–33–52%
		Review	1–4–11%
		Unit Testing	1–5–14%
		Integration Testing + System Testing	1–9–20%
		Acceptance Testing & Warranty	1–8–23%
		Project Mgmt + Config. Mgmt	1–10–20%
		Training	1–7–14%
		Others	1–10–26%
5	Defects		
5.1	Defect Injection Rate	Overall LC defect injection rate in terms of size	0.02–1.12 Defects/FP (avg: 0.33)
		Overall LC defect injection rate in terms of effort	0.00–0.1516 Defects/person-hour (avg: 0.052)
		Defect injection rate in the coding phase (in terms of effort)	0.02–0.57 Defects/person-hour (avg: 0.155)

Table 2.5 Process Capability Baseline for Development Process (continued)

Sequence Number	Parameter	Remarks	General Baseline, Development Projects
5.2	Defect injection distribution	Requirements and Design	Approx. 30%
		Coding	Approx. 70%
5.3	In-process Defect Removal Efficiency	For the entire life cycle	78–100% (avg: 94%)
6	Cost of Quality	(Review effort + rework effort + test effort + training effort) as a percentage of total effort	32%
7	Defect Detection Distribution	% of Total Defects Min–Mean–Max	
		Req. Spec Review + HLD Review + Detail Design Review	2–13–20%
		Code review + Unit Testing	21–53–83%
		Integration Testing + System Testing	3–28–56%
		Acceptance Testing	1–6–17%

all activities that help prevent or remove defects. For effort, defect, and defect injection rates, it also specifies a distribution among the various stages.

2.3 PROCESS ASSETS AND THE BODY OF KNOWLEDGE SYSTEM

As discussed in Chapter 1, a process encapsulates an organization's experience in form of successful "recipes." Process descriptions, however, usually contain the sequence of steps to be executed, identify who executes them, specify the entry and exit criteria for major steps, and so on. To facilitate the use of processes, guidelines, checklists, and templates often provide useful support. Together, these materials are called *process assets*.

Guidelines usually give rules and procedures for executing a step. For example, a step in the project planning process is "Estimate effort." To execute this step, a project manager needs guidelines. *Checklists* are usually of two types: activity checklists and review checklists. As the name suggests, an *activity* checklist is a list of the activities that constitute a process step. The purpose of *review* checklists is to draw the attention of reviewers to the defects that are likely to be found in an output. *Templates* essentially provide the structure of the document in which the output of a process or step can be captured. Figure 2.1 shows the relationship between the process and these assets.

The main purpose of these process assets is to facilitate the use of processes by saving effort, thereby improving productivity. For example, using a template to create a document can be much easier and less time-consuming than creating it from scratch. These assets also help improve the quality of the project, first by providing proper guidelines and activity checklists and thereby minimizing the number of defects injected, and then by aiding reviews and thereby catching the injected defects early.

In short, to derive full benefits from a process-oriented approach for project execution, it's crucial to capture and use process assets. At Infosys, all guidelines, checklists, and templates are available online and are regularly updated. Table 2.6 shows a sample of these materials relating to project management.

In addition to these generic assets (which are part of the Infosys quality management system), a project manager may want to reuse some of the outputs of a past project that was similar in some respects. Reusing artifacts can save effort and increase productivity. To promote this goal, process assets from projects can also

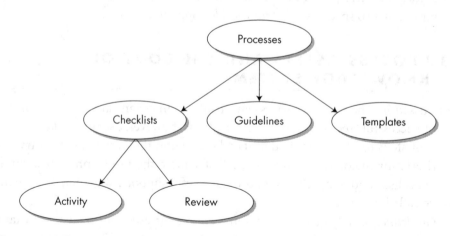

Figure 2.1 Process assets

Table 2.6 Guidelines, Checklists, and Templates for Project Management

Guidelines	Checklists	Templates/Forms
Effort and schedule estimation guidelines	Requirements analysis checklist	Requirements specification document
Group review procedure	Unit test and system test plan checklists	Unit test plan document
Process tailoring guidelines	Configuration management checklist	Acceptance test plan document
Defect estimation and monitoring guidelines	Status report checklist	Project management plan
Guidelines for measurements and data analysis	Requirement review checklist	Configuration management plan
Risk management guidelines	Functional design review checklist	Metrics analysis report
Guidelines for requirement traceability	Project plan review checklist	Milestone status report
Defect prevention guidelines	Code review checklist for C++	Defect prevention analysis report

be collected when projects terminate. The assets that are typically collected, and made available through a separate system, include the following:

- Project management plan
- Configuration management plan
- Schedule
- Standards, checklists, guidelines, templates, and other aids
- Developed tools and related notes
- Training material
- Other documents that can be reused by future projects

Although process assets attempt to encapsulate experience through checklists, templates, and so on, they cannot always capture the diverse forms of knowledge gained in executing projects. Capturing and reusing different forms of knowledge require proper knowledge management, which has become important in knowledge-based organizations such as solution providers and consulting companies.

Many organizations have developed systems to effectively leverage the collective experience and knowledge of their employees. At Infosys, in addition to the process database and process assets, a system called the body of knowledge (BOK) is used to encapsulate experience.

The Web-based BOK system has its own keyword- or author-based search facility. The knowledge in BOK, which is primarily in the form of articles, is organized by topics. Key topics include the following:

- Computer and communication services
- Requirements specification
- Build
- Tools
- Methodologies and techniques
- Education and research
- Design
- Reviews, inspection, and testing
- Quality assurance and productivity
- Project management

The BOK system contains posted articles relating to lessons learned and best practices. The entries are general and are not tied to a particular project. Using a template set up for this purpose, any member of the organization can submit an entry for inclusion in the BOK. Each submission undergoes a review, which focuses on its usefulness, generality, changes required, and other characteristics. Editorial control is maintained to ensure that entries meet the quality standards. Financial incentives have been provided for employees to submit information to the BOK, and the department that manages the BOK actively pursues new articles. To further the cause, submission to the BOK is one factor considered during employees' yearly performance appraisal.

2.4 SUMMARY

A project manager can plan a project better if past experience on projects is available. The project planning infrastructure can help effectively capture data and lessons learned and make them available to project managers. The main components of the planning infrastructure at Infosys are the process database, the process capability baseline, and the process assets. These elements have the following key characteristics:

- A process database contains the performance data of completed projects. It contains data on risks, effort and effort distribution, defect and defect distribution, size, and other project characteristics.

- The process capability baseline summarizes the process performance across projects, thereby specifying the range of results to be expected if the processes are followed. It contains measures such as quality, productivity, defect removal efficiency, and effort and defect distribution.

- Process assets are documents such as checklists, templates, methodologies, and guidelines. They improve productivity by reducing effort required to do some tasks, and they improve quality by reducing defects or catching them early.

If these elements are not in place in an organization, project managers can take actions to build limited forms of some of these components. A few project managers who get together and collect their experience can build a limited PDB. The key issue here is to perform project closure analysis (discussed in Chapter 12). When you have created a limited PDB, you can also extract some aspects of a PCB. Building a set of process assets is even easier; you simply collect the templates, checklists, and similar materials that are used in projects. Then you review and polish them and make them available.

These infrastructure elements do not directly satisfy requirements of the CMM KPAs dealing with project management. They are, however, necessary for satisfying many of the project-management-related KPAs at levels 3 and 4. The systems discussed in this chapter also satisfy requirements of some other KPAs of the CMM. For example, existence of a process database is explicitly required by the CMM at level 3, as is the management of process assets. The process capability baseline is needed by both the KPAs at level 4.

2.5 REFERENCES

1. P. Jalote. *Use of Metrics in High Maturity Organizations,* SEPG2K Conference, Seattle, 2000.

2. W. Humphrey. *Managing the Software Process.* Addison-Wesley, 1989.

3. C. Jones. *Applied Software Measurement: Assuring Productivity and Quality,* second edition. McGraw Hill, 1996.

4. R. Grady and D. Caswell. *Software Metrics: Establishing a Company-wide Program.* Prentice Hall, 1987.

5. Carnegie Mellon/Software Engineering Institute. *The Capability Maturity Model: Guidelines for Improving the Software Process.* Addison-Wesley, 1995.

Chapter 3

Process Planning

Ravi, like many project managers, had studied the waterfall model of software development as the primary software life-cycle process. He was all set to use it for an upcoming project, his first assignment. However, Ravi found that the waterfall model could not be used because the customer wanted the software delivered in stages, something that implied that the system had to be delivered and built in parts and not as a whole.

The situation in many other projects is not very different. The real world rarely presents a problem in which a standard process, or the process used in a previous project, is the best choice. To be the most suitable, an existing process must be tailored to the new problem.

This chapter describes the Infosys development process and process tailoring. A development process, even after tailoring, generally cannot handle change requests. To accommodate change requests without losing control of the project, you must supplement the development process with a requirement change management process. This chapter also describes the requirement change management process used at Infosys.

3.1 THE INFOSYS DEVELOPMENT PROCESS

During project planning, a project manager must decide what process should be used for engineering the software. This is a crucial issue because much of the engineering activity will be governed by this decision. It is like going on a long driving trip—the planned route determines the course you will drive.

Several process models for software development exist. The most common ones include the waterfall model (a description of this model and its limitations can be found in Boehm's *Software Engineering Economics*[1]), iterative enhancement,[2] prototyping,[3] and spiral.[4] The most widely used model is the waterfall model, which organizes the phases in a linear sequence, although most implementations adapt this model to minimize its shortcomings.

At a macro level, a standard process can give the optimum organization of phases for a class of projects and makes a good starting point for process definition. However, a standard process cannot be suitable for all situations; the best process may be a variation on a standard process. Hence, to decide which process to use, the project manager must select the base process and also decide how it must be tailored to obtain a process that will suit the project. The rest of this section discusses the standard development process used at Infosys and explains how it is tailored by project managers.

3.1.1 The Standard Process

The standard development process used at Infosys resembles the waterfall model, although the traditional phases have been broken into smaller phases, or stages, to allow parallel execution of some phases. For example, planning for system testing is defined as a separate phase from system testing itself, a practice that allows teams to conduct the system test planning phase in parallel with coding, even though system testing takes place only after coding is finished.

The phases in the process include requirements analysis, high-level design, detailed design, build, unit testing, integration planning, integration, system test planning, system testing, documentation, acceptance and installation, and warranty support. Figure 3.1 depicts the phases and the dependencies between them. Details of the stages are omitted here, although they are described in my earlier book.[5]

The formal description of this process specifies the entry and exit criteria, inputs and outputs, participants, activities, and other information for each phase (stage). The process descriptions are generally brief, specifying the list of activities to be undertaken in that phase.

This overall process remains the same even for a project using an object-oriented approach, although some of the phases are done differently in such a project. The difference lies mostly in the analysis and design phases, although the guidelines and standards for some of the later phases are also different.

This basic process is also used by projects that do iterative development or prototyping or perform only some stages of the life cycle. In these situations this

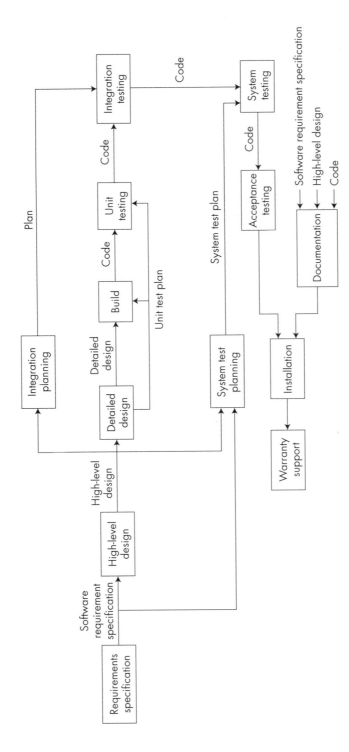

Figure 3.1 The Infosys development process

standard process is adjusted to suit the project. These adjustments are done through process tailoring, which is discussed next.

3.1.2 Process Tailoring

No defined process—whether an organization's standard process or the process used in a previous project—will apply to all situations and all projects. A defined process must be tailored to suit the needs of the current project.

Tailoring is the process of adjusting a previously defined process of an organization to obtain a process that is suitable for the particular business or technical needs of a project.[5,6] You can view tailoring as adding, deleting, or modifying the activities of a process so that the resulting process is better suited to achieving the project's goals.

Uncontrolled tailoring effectively implies creating a process from scratch. To allow effective reuse of previously defined processes, tailoring guidelines are provided. These guidelines define the conditions and the types of changes that should be made to a standard process. In essence, they define a set of *permitted deviations* to the standard process in the hope that the optimal process can be defined for a project. Figure 3.2 illustrates the role of tailoring guidelines.

To illustrate the need for tailoring, let's take an activity in the build phase of the development process—*Do code review.* Code review adds a great deal of value in many cases, but sometimes its added value is not commensurate with the effort required. Also, the review could be done by either a group (following the group review procedure) or by one person. The standard development process does not

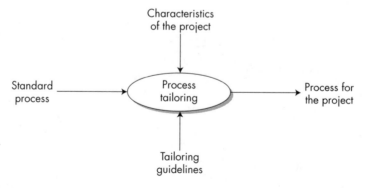

Figure 3.2 Process tailoring

specify how code review should be performed. Tailoring guidelines can help a project manager by advising that the activity *Do code review* be performed only for certain types of programs (such as complex programs or external interfaces) and by suggesting the optimal form of the review (group review or one-person review).

The Infosys tailoring approach is similar to the table-based approach proposed by Ginsberg and Quinn,[7] in which the project manager specifies the process element, the tailorable attribute, the options for each attribute, and the reasons for selecting a particular option. A project manager performs tailoring at two levels: summary and detailed.

Summary-Level Tailoring In *summary-level tailoring*, depending on the project characteristics, the project manager applies overall guidelines for tailoring the standard process. That is, it provides some general rules regarding certain types of detailed activities. To perform this step, the project manager first identifies certain characteristics of the project. For development projects, the following characteristics are used for tailoring:

- Experience and skill level of the team and the project manager
- Peak team size
- Clarity of the requirements
- Project duration
- Application criticality

The experience level of the team is considered high if a majority of team members have more than two years of experience with the technology being deployed in the project; otherwise, it is considered low. Application criticality is considered high if the effect of the application on a customer's business or Infosys's business is significant; otherwise, it is low. Duration of the project is considered particularly short if the project must be delivered in less than three months.

Summary tailoring guidelines are provided for different values of these characteristics. The summary guidelines are generally review-related, effort-related, schedule-related, resources-related, or formality-related. Review-related guidelines typically specify when reviews should be done and what type of review should take place. Similarly, the effort-related guidelines suggest steps to be taken for the project that may affect the effort. These general guidelines set the context for detailed process tailoring and defining a suitable process for the project.

Detailed Tailoring   *Detailed tailoring* covers execution of activities, their review, and documentation needs. Tailoring guidelines may specify an activity as optional, in which case the project manager can decide whether or not to execute the activity. Similarly, preparation of some documents may be optional, in which case the project manager decides whether or not the project needs the document. For review, the general alternatives are *Do group review, Do one-person review,* or *Do not review.* In addition, a project manager may add some new activities or may repeat some activities.

When detailed tailoring is finished, the sequence of activities to be performed in the process for the project is defined. These definitions are then used to plan and schedule activities and form the basis of project execution. The tailoring performed is highlighted in the project plan, so the process definition and tailoring also are reviewed when the plan is reviewed.

3.1.3 Example: Tailoring for Short-Duration Projects

We illustrate the concept of tailoring by showing the summary-level tailoring for short-duration projects. Infosys observed that the duration of software projects has decreased over the years, and there is increased demand for projects of very short duration. Clearly, such projects require processes to be tailored to allow maximum parallelism and very tight project monitoring and control. The process tailoring depends on the clarity of the requirements, the experience level of the team or the project leader, the size of the team, and so on. Table 3.1 shows tailoring guidelines prepared by project managers of such projects for one combination of values.

Because the shortness of the schedule is the main characteristic, schedule-related guidelines suggest the use of a technique called timeboxing and mini-milestones. In *timeboxing,* several-week duration cycles are planned, and a working system is delivered after each cycle. To keep tight control on the timeboxes, *mini-milestones*—milestones within the cycle—are also set. At mini-milestones, a limited milestone analysis (see Chapter 11) is done. Most of the other guidelines are self-explanatory.

A project manager who must execute a short-duration project can use these guidelines to tailor the development process. For example, the project manager may plan to use iterative delivery with short iterations, perform limited milestone analysis but more frequently, define a change management process that defers most change requests to the next iteration, and so on. In addition, while performing

Table 3.1 Tailoring Guidelines for a Short-Duration Project

Values	Summary Guidelines	Why?
Size of team >= 5, duration < 3 months, low requirements clarity, new technology, experienced project leader	Scheduling-related	
	• Plan for mini-milestones	Identifies problems very early and gives better control of project.
		Schedule-related risk is decreased because the visibility into the schedule is more frequent.
		Effort slippage is likely to be controlled early in the project.
	• Try to timebox the deliverables	Schedule is potentially reduced because it ensures deliverable system at fixed intervals and discourages feature creep.
		Schedule-related risk is reduced.
	Effort-related	
	• Apply appropriate adjustment factors to base estimate as defined in estimation guidelines.	All project constraints are accommodated in effort estimate to project a realistic timeline.
	• Give optimistic, pessimistic, and probable estimates. • Revise and renegotiate estimates at the end of design stage.	Reduces risk related to improper estimation and "quick" commitments.
	Resource allocation-related	
	• Assign skilled resources for the tasks.	Productivity will improve.
		Schedule-related risk decreases.
	• Get expert help for performance- related issues.	Rework and delays due to performance tuning are minimized.
	Formality-related	
	• Identify all stakeholders and their objectives and prioritize them.	Helps in focusing on clear objectives.
		Reduces schedule-related risk because the important success factors are identified, agreed to, and addressed.
	• Regularly report status on risk mitigation activities to senior management.	Schedule-related risk is reduced because mitigation is done proactively.
	• Define formal requirement change management process and educate team to strictly follow it.	Minimizes impact of requirement changes on the schedule.

detailed tailoring to define the project's process, the project manager may reduce the documentation for each cycle by, for example, reducing the scope of the templates used for reporting status.

The summary guidelines shown in Table 3.1 are for a project whose duration is less than three months, has a peak team size of more than five, is working with new technology, and has an experienced project leader. During detailed tailoring, the project manager chooses options based on the summary guidelines and suitability to the project. If, however, the tailoring guidelines are not sufficient to allow you to select the right process for the project, you may have to modify the process beyond what was allowed by the tailoring guidelines. Such deviations represent potential risks and hence are highlighted in the project management plan, which is reviewed and approved.

3.2 REQUIREMENT CHANGE MANAGEMENT

Requirements change. And changes in requirements can come at any time during the life of a project (or even after that). The later in the life cycle the requirements change, the more severe the impact on the project. Instead of wishing that changes will not happen or hoping that somehow the initial requirements will be "so good" that no changes will be required, it is better to prepare to handle change requests as and when they come. Uncontrolled changes to requirements can have an adverse effect on the cost, schedule, and quality of the project. Requirement changes can account for as much as 40% of the total cost.[8]

Ravi realized the need for a change management process the hard way. In an effort to please the customer, he readily agreed to make the changes the customer requested. With no control on change requests, the project experienced them at an increasing frequency. In the end, after 60-hour weeks for the team members and an effort escalation of more than 100%, Ravi barely finished the project. What's worse, he found that the customer was still not satisfied because he thought that more changes would have made the product better.

In another project, Mary, a seasoned project manager, recorded each change request her customer made on the phone or through e-mail and informed the customer of the impact of the request on effort and schedule. Not only did the frequency of change requests decrease with time, but also the customer transferred many requests to the next release. The final result? The project was completed in time, and the happy customer actually paid for the extra effort that was incurred in implementing the change requests.

This section discusses the requirement change management process used at Infosys. This process defines the set of activities that are performed when there are new requirements or changes to existing requirements (we will call both of these changes in the requirements). Given the experience of project managers such as Ravi and Mary, the change management process is routinely used by project managers, and specifying it as part of the project management plan is treated less as a planning exercise and more as means for clarifying the process to customers and getting their buy-in.

3.2.1 The Change Management Process

During project planning, a project manager decides which process is to be followed for handling change requests. The planned process is discussed with the customer so that both the customer and the vendor are in agreement about how to manage changes. Generally, the process specifies how the change requests will be made, when formal approvals are needed, and so on. When a request for a requirements change comes in, the requirements change management process must be executed.

Because change requests have cost implications, it is necessary to have a clear agreement on payment. Frequently, with customer approval, projects build a buffer into their estimates for implementing change requests (typically a small percentage of the total project effort). Such a budget provision simplifies the administrative aspects of implementing approved change requests.

The commonly used change management process at Infosys has the following steps.

1. Log the changes.

2. Perform an impact analysis on the work products.

3. Estimate the effort needed for the change requests.

4. Reestimate the delivery schedule.

5. Perform a cumulative cost impact analysis.

6. Review the impact with senior management if thresholds are exceeded.

7. Obtain customer sign-off.

8. Rework work products.

You maintain a change request log to keep track of the change requests. Each entry in the log contains a change request number, a brief description of the change, the effect of the change, the status of the change request, and key dates. You assess the effect of a change request by performing impact analysis. Impact analysis involves identifying work products that need to be changed and evaluating the quantum of change to each; reassessing the project's risks by revisiting the risk management plan; and evaluating the overall implications of the changes for the effort and schedule estimates. The outcome of the analysis is reviewed and approved by the customer. The change requests are incorporated in the requirements specification document, usually as appendixes. Sometimes the relevant portions of the document are also modified to reflect the changes. Monitoring of approved change requests and ensuring their proper implementation are handled by the configuration management process, which is discussed in Chapter 9.

A change might be classified as minor if the total effort involved in implementing it does not exceed a predetermined value—say, two person-days. Minor changes typically become part of the project effort, utilizing the buffer in the planned estimate. Major changes usually have a larger impact on effort and schedule and must be formally approved by the client. Senior management gains visibility in the changes through status and milestone reporting, which are discussed in Chapter 11.

3.2.2 Examples

To specify the changes and the output of the change management process, projects generally use a simple template. Each change is assigned a unique reference number that is specified in the template's *request number* field. The *change specification field* gives a brief description of the requested change. The category of the change (for example, design change, contract change, functionality change, performance change) and the nature of the change are specified as *change category*. The summary of the *impact analysis* is recorded, along with brief information regarding work products that will be affected, the effort involved, and the implications for the schedule. The status of the change request—what is being done with it—is recorded in the *status field*. The date of the change request might also be recorded, along with the date the change was approved, if approval is needed. Generally, the projects customize this template to suit their needs.

Figure 3.3 shows a filled-in template for a change request for the ACIC project. The various components in the template are self-explanatory. This example is of a major change request that has an impact on effort as well as schedule. The result of the impact analysis states the impact on these dimensions. The anal-

---

Request No: 3   **Date:** 11th August 2000

Change Specification

This change request is to allow the client screens to change the resolution automatically, depending on the monitor. This is required as the monitors of ACIC are of resolution 1600 * 1200, while the monitors of the business partner, who will also use the application, have a resolution of 800 * 600.

Impact Analysis

    Change Category: Major enhancement as it affects all screens.

    Solution: The Layout manager and setting the constraints for each of the components has to be changed. Because of Applet implementation, the code has to be changed so that the screens automatically adjust to the resolution of the monitor.

    On Effort: Total number of screens is 40. Implementing the solution for a screen will take about 12 hours. Hence, total estimated effort to implement this change is 480 person-hours (about 53 person-days).

    On Schedule: As we have an average team size of about 5.5, the impact on the overall schedule of implementing this change request will be about 10 days.

Status

Analysis approved by customer. Will be incorporated immediately. Project schedule will be changed; dates for milestones will also be changed, where needed.

Prepared by: xxxxxx   **Reviewed by:** xxxxx

Figure 3.3 Impact analysis of a change request in the ACIC project

ysis report also states that the customer has approved the impact analysis (including the changes in effort and schedule).

Figure 3.4 gives another example of a change request. In the example, the detailed contents of the impact analysis are not important for the purposes of understanding requirements change management.

Note that although the impact of a change request is specified, and approved, by using the template, the actual tracking of implementation of a change request is handled by the configuration management process, which is discussed in Chapter 9.

One danger of requirement changes is that, even though each change is not large in itself, over the life of the project the cumulative impact of the changes is large. Hence, in addition to studying the impact of and tracking individual changes, you must monitor the cumulative impact of changes. For cumulative

---

Project XYZ

Request No: 11   **Date:** 23 Feb 1998

Change Spec. IS-41 Analyzer—IS-41 Analyzer support for CDMA

Impact Analysis

No particular change in configuration module and analyzers for CDMA.
The TDMA code can be reused as is. Scripts can also be reused. Netconfig and analyzer
classes can be reused. The impacted modules are as follows: cgaapp module: Has to trigger
analysis for IS-41 also, separately. cdmaroi module: (a) TRIS41ROI has to be copied as
TRCDMAIS 41ROI; (b) There is a pure virtual method in TRCDMAROI for setting the
ActualCallModelManager. It needs to be redefined. silver06guiapp++ module: IS-41 has to
be added in the resource list.

On Schedule   Nil
On Effort   5
Status   Will be incorporated in the new CDMA package.

Figure 3.4 Another Change Request Example

changes, a *change log* is used. To facilitate this analysis, the log is frequently maintained as a spreadsheet. The example in Figure 3.5 illustrates how cumulative
changes are maintained. For details of each request, the relevant change request
can be accessed by using the change request number and date.

   From a spreadsheet of this type, you can immediately see the total cost of the
requirement changes made so far. As mentioned earlier, Infosys project managers
sometimes plan some buffer for handling change requests. As long as the cumulative effort for all change requests is less than this buffer, nothing special needs to
be done. If the cumulative effort of all changes exceeds this buffer, however, further changes can have an adverse effect on total cost and scheduling. In this situation, the project manager must revise the estimates and get them approved.

3.3 PROCESS PLANNING FOR THE ACIC PROJECT

Because the ACIC project is a development project, the standard Infosys development process is followed. However, it is tailored to accommodate the requirements
of the Rational Unified Process (RUP) methodology because using RUP is a commitment to the customer. RUP is an iterative approach to development. The Info-

Chg. Req. No.	Date of Change Req.	Change Specs	Effort (person-days)	Status
1	18 Feb	Specify usage statistics	3	Closed, Feb 22
2	During demo	Blocking of users	2	Open
3	During demo	Force logout of users	2	Open
4	18 Feb	Archival of knowledge users	5	Closed, Feb 27
5	During demo	Cloning of window	1	Open
6	During demo	Saving off an expanded tree and retrieving the same on demand	10	Open
7	During demo	Ability to start from a specific node	2	Open
8	During demo	Listing of all nodes while deleting	1	Open
9	18 Feb	Annotations (creating/ deleting/approving/ modifying/and so on)	10	Open
10	23 Feb	PFNETCONFIG—Packed format netconfig support	10	Open
11	23 Feb	IS-41 Analyzer—IS-41 Analyzer support for CDMA	5	Closed, March 1
		TOTAL	51	

Figure 3.5 Tracking the cumulative effect of changes

sys tailoring guidelines allow the different phases to be executed iteratively as long as the specification, design, coding, and testing activities are executed in each iteration. In addition to doing iterative development, the following key modifications were made to the standard process to accommodate RUP.

- Only those use cases that are taken up in a particular iteration will be elaborated at that point.
- The logical object model and the physical object model will be developed incrementally in the first few iterations.

- The physical database design may be refined in later iterations.
- A unit test plan will be developed in each iteration.
- Defects will be logged iteration-wise.

In addition, the standard traceability matrix mechanism will not be used for requirement traceability. Instead, requirements will be traced using the Requisite Pro tool, which is part of the development environment.

For requirement change management, the standard process will be used. Although impact analysis will be done for each request, a reestimation will be done if a request is expected to take more than 2% of the total effort. The process planning outputs are captured in the project management plan, which is given in Chapter 8.

3.4 SUMMARY

The main process planning issue in a project is designing the development process to be used for building the software to satisfy the customer. This process is supported with a change management process to accommodate requirement changes.

Following are the key process planning lessons learned from the Infosys approach:

- When you plan the project's process, start with a standard process. The waterfall model, broken into smaller phases, can serve as a suitable base.
- To define the optimum process for a project, tailor the standard process to suit the project constraints. First, set the context for tailoring using key project characteristics. Then do detailed tailoring of activities. Tailoring guidelines can help.
- Have a separate requirement change management process that assesses the impact of each change request and also keeps track of the cumulative impact. With respect to CMM, the process planning methods described here satisfy some requirements of the Software Project Planning KPA of level 2. The tailoring approach satisfies some requirements of the Integrated Project Management KPA at level 3. The requirements change management method satisfies some requirements of the Requirement Management KPA of level 2.

3.5 REFERENCES

1. B.W. Boehm. *Software Engineering Economics.* Prentice Hall, 1981.

2. V.R. Basili and A. Turner. Iterative enhancement, a practical technique for software development. *IEEE Transactions on Software Engineering,* 1(4), 1975.

3. H. Gomma and D.B.H. Scott. Prototyping as a tool in the specification of user requirements. *Proceedings of the 5th International Conference on Software Engineering,* pp. 333–341, 1981.

4. B.W. Boehm. A spiral model of software development and enhancement. *IEEE Computer,* May 1988.

5. P. Jalote. *CMM in Practice: Processes for Executing Software Projects at Infosys.* Addison-Wesley, 2000.

6. W. Humphrey. *Managing the Software Process.* Addison-Wesley, 1989.

7. M.P. Ginsberg and L.H. Quinn. *Process Tailoring and the Software Capability Maturity Model.* Technical Report, Software Engineering Institute, CMU/ SEI-94-TR-024, 1995.

8. B.W. Boehm. Improving software productivity. *IEEE Computer,* Sept. 1987.

Chapter 4

Effort Estimation and Scheduling

In early 2000, the newspapers and TV in India reported with jubilation the successful test flight of a newly built light combat aircraft. But the detailed reports also indicated a somber side: The prototype delivery was more than five years late, and the project had cost more than 10 times its initial estimated cost. Many projects across the world suffer a similar fate. It seems as if the estimated cost and time are never enough to execute a project. Improper estimation is the bane of project management in many engineering disciplines, and software engineering is no different, as the poor record of software projects unambiguously illustrates.

In a services business, improper estimation hurts even more. Asked to identify the one thing he wants from projects, Nandan Nilekeni, the managing director of Infosys, answers, "No surprises." No surprises on the customer satisfaction front, and no surprises on the revenue and profit front. More often than not, the cause of surprises that come late in a project on these two fronts is improper estimation of effort or schedule.

There are no quick and ready-made solutions for the estimation problem. Project managers, however, can improve their estimation by using tested guidelines that are based on past experience and data. This chapter discusses the approaches used by Infosys project managers for estimating effort and schedule. It includes examples from real projects and the estimates for the ACIC case study.

4.1 ESTIMATION AND SCHEDULING CONCEPTS

Before we discuss the approach taken at Infosys, this section describes some concepts relating to estimation and scheduling. Effort estimation usually takes place in the early stages of a project, when the software to be built is being understood. It may be redone later when more information becomes available.

Highly precise estimates are generally not needed. Reasonable estimates in a software project tend to become a self-fulfilling prophecy—people work to meet the schedules (which are derived from effort estimates). Indeed, in software projects, one cannot even precisely answer the question, "Is this estimate accurate?" because the only way to ascertain the accuracy of an estimate is to compare it with the actual effort expended. Because of the general principle of human psychology reflected in the maxim "work expands to fill the available time," one cannot say that just because the actual effort expended matches the estimated effort, the estimates are "accurate." Hence, the goal for a project manager is to obtain *reasonable* estimates so that the goals are met and the project personnel are not burned out. The range of reasonableness is not very wide, and it depends on human factors, but it is probably wide enough to give sufficient leeway for estimation.

Effort estimation can rely on a hunch or on previous experience, but a more scientific and desirable approach is to use an estimation model.

4.1.1 Effort Estimation Models

A software *estimation model* defines the project characteristics whose values (or their estimates) it needs and the ways these values are used to compute the effort. An estimation model does not—and cannot—work in a vacuum; it needs inputs to produce the effort estimate as output. At the start of a project, when the details of the software itself are not known, the hope is that the estimation model will require values of characteristics that can be measured at that stage.

The size of the software is the predominant factor in determining how much effort is needed to build it. But the ultimate size is not known when the project is being conceived, and the software does not exist. Hence, if size is to be used for the effort estimation model, it must be estimated for the initial estimation.

A common approach is to use a simple equation to obtain an estimate of the overall effort from the size estimate. This equation can be determined through regression analysis of past data on effort and size.[1,2] Then, once the overall effort for the project is known, the effort for various phases or activities can be determined as a percentage of the total effort.

Many models have been proposed that use this *top-down approach* to estimation,[1,3] with the COCOMO model being the most famous.[1,4] Models using function points (instead of LOC) as size units have also been built.[5,6] In these models, you can accommodate other factors that affect the effort by refining the estimates based on these factors. This is the approach taken in the COCOMO model.[1] Another approach is to adjust the size of the system based on these parameters, as is done in function points.[7]

In the *bottom-up approach*, on the other hand, you obtain the estimates first for parts of the project and then for the overall estimate.[1] That is, the overall estimate of the project is derived from the estimates of its parts. One bottom-up method calls for using some type of *activity-based* estimation. In this strategy, the major activities are first enumerated, and then the effort for each activity is estimated. From these estimates, the effort for the overall project is obtained.

The bottom-up approach lends itself to direct estimation of effort; once the project is partitioned into smaller tasks, it is possible to directly estimate the effort required for them. Although size does play a role in determining the effort for many activities in a project, a key advantage of this approach is that it does not require explicit size estimates for the software. Instead, it requires a list of project tasks, which might be easier to prepare in some situations. A risk of bottom-up methods is that you may omit some important activities in the list of tasks. When effort is directly estimated for tasks, it may prove difficult to directly estimate the effort required for some overhead tasks, such as project management, that span the project and are not as clearly defined as coding or testing.

Both the top-down and the bottom-up approaches require information about the project: size (for top-down approaches) and a list of tasks (for bottom-up approaches). In many ways, these approaches are complementary.[1] Both types of estimates are more accurate if more information about the project is available or as the project proceeds. For example, estimating the size is much more difficult when very high level requirements are given but becomes considerably easier when design is finished, and even easier and more accurate when code is developed. Thus, the accuracy of estimates depends on the point at which effort is estimated, with accuracy increasing as more information about the project becomes available.[4]

4.1.2 Estimating Schedule

Once the effort is known or fixed, various schedules (or project *duration*) are possible, depending on the number of *resources* (people) put on the project. For example, for a project whose effort estimate is 56 person-months, a total schedule of 8 months is possible with 7 people. A schedule of 7 months with 8 people is also possible, as is a schedule of approximately 9 months with 6 people.

As is well known, however, manpower and months are not fully interchangeable in a software project.[8] For instance, in the example here, a schedule of 1 month with 56 people is not possible even though the effort "matches" the requirement. Similarly, no one would execute the project in 28 months with 2 people. In other words, once the effort is fixed, you can gain some flexibility in setting the schedule by appropriately staffing the project. But this flexibility is not unlimited, a fact corroborated by data that shows that no simple equation between effort and schedule fits the empirical data.[9]

"Stretching" the schedule is easy; you simply apply fewer people (although the project may not be very valuable if completed over a long duration). Compressing the schedule, however, is not easy. A clear example is given earlier: You cannot compress the schedule of a 56 person-month project to 1 month regardless of the resources you apply. And, generally speaking, compressing the schedule beyond what is "normal" increases the effort; by having more resources than optimally needed, you might end up wasting them, doing more rework, and so on.

Some approaches discuss the effect of schedule compression on total effort. However, to assess that effect you must first define the normal schedule for a project.

One method to determine the *normal* (or *nominal*) schedule is to use a suitable function to determine it from the effort. In turn, one method for determining the function is to study the patterns in data from completed projects. For example, you can obtain a scatter plot of effort and schedule for completed projects and then fit a regression curve through this scatter plot. This curve is generally nonlinear because the schedule does not grow linearly with effort. You can then use the equation for the curve to determine the schedule for a project whose effort has been estimated. Many models follow this approach, and Boehm's book summarizes the various models.[1]

4.2 EFFORT ESTIMATION

At Infosys, estimation generally takes place after analysis. That is, when a project manager estimates the effort, the requirements are well understood. The business processes are organized to support this approach. For example, the requirement phase is sometimes executed as a separate project from the software development project.

At Infosys, multiple estimation approaches have been proposed, some of which are discussed here. A project manager can choose any of the estimation approaches that suit the nature of the work. Sometimes, a project manager may estimate using multiple methods, either to validate the estimate from its primary method or to reduce the risks, particularly where past data of similar projects are limited.

4.2.1 The Bottom-up Estimation Approach

Because the types of projects undertaken at Infosys vary substantially, the bottom-up approach is preferred and recommended. The company employs a task unit approach,[1] although some of the limitations of this strategy have been overcome through the use of past data and the process capability baseline (see Chapter 2).

In the *task unit* approach, the project manager first divides the software under development into major programs (or units). Each program unit is then classified as simple, medium, or complex based on certain criteria. For each classification unit, the project manager defines a *standard* effort for coding and self-testing (together called the *build effort*). This standard build effort can be based on past data from a similar project, from the internal guidelines available, or some combination of these.

Once the number of units in the three categories of complexity is known and the estimated build effort for each program is selected, the total effort for the build phase of the project is known. From the build effort, the effort required for the other phases and activities is determined as a percentage of the coding effort. From the process capability baseline or the process database, the distribution of effort in a project is known. The project manager uses this distribution to determine the effort for other phases and activities. From these estimates, the total effort for the project is obtained.

This approach lends itself to a judicious mixture of experience and data. If suitable data are not available (for example, if you're launching a new type of project), you can estimate the build effort by experience after you analyze the project and when you know the various program units. With this estimate available, you can obtain the estimate for other activities by working with the effort distribution data obtained from past projects. This strategy even accounts for activities that are sometimes difficult to enumerate early but do consume effort; in the effort distribution for a project, the "other" category is frequently used to handle miscellaneous tasks.

The procedure for estimation can be summarized as the following sequence of steps:

1. Identify programs in the system and classify them as simple, medium, or complex (S/M/C). As much as possible, use either the provided standard definitions or definitions from past projects.

2. If a project-specific baseline exists, get the average build effort for S/M/C programs from the baseline.

3. If a project-specific baseline does not exist, use project type, technology, language, and other attributes to look for similar projects in the process database. Use data from these projects to define the build effort of S/M/C programs.

4. If no similar project exists in the process database and no project-specific baseline exists, use the average build effort for S/M/C programs from the general process capability baseline.

5. Use project-specific factors to refine the build effort for S/M/C programs.

6. Get the total build effort using the build effort of S/M/C programs and the counts for them.

7. Using the effort distribution given in the capability baseline or for similar projects given in the process database, estimate the effort for other tasks and the total effort.

8. Refine the estimates based on project-specific factors.

This procedure uses the process database and process capability baseline, which are discussed in Chapter 2. As mentioned earlier, if many projects of a type are being executed, you can build a project-specific capability baseline. Such baselines are similar to the general baselines but use only data from specific projects. These baselines have been found to be the best for predicting effort for another project of that type. Hence, for estimation, their use is preferred.

Because many factors can affect the effort required for a project, it is essential that estimates account for project-specific factors. Instead of classifying parameters into different levels and then determining the effect on the effort requirement, the approach outlined here lets the project manager determine the impact of project-specific factors on the estimate. Project managers can make this adjustment using their experience, the experience of the team members, or data from projects found in the process database.

Note that this method of classifying programs into a few categories and using an average build effort for each category is followed for overall estimation. In detailed scheduling, however—in which a project manager assigns each unit to a member of the team for coding and budgets time for the activity—characteristics of a unit are taken into account to give more or less time than the average.

4.2.2 The Top-Down Estimation Approach

Like any top-down approach, the Infosys approach starts with an estimate of the size of the software in function points. The function points can be counted using standard function point counting rules. Alternatively, if the size estimate is known in terms of LOC, it can be converted into function points.

In addition to the size estimate, a top-down approach requires an estimate of productivity. The basic approach is to start with productivity levels of similar projects (data for which is available in the process database) or with standard productivity figures (data for which is available in the process capability baseline), and then to adjust those levels, if needed, to suit the project. The productivity estimate is then used to calculate the overall effort estimate. From the overall effort estimate, estimates for the various phases are derived by using the percentage distributions. (These distributions, as in the bottom-up approach, are obtained from the process database or the capability baseline.)

To summarize, the overall approach for top-down estimation involves the following steps:

1. Get the estimate of the total size of the software in function points.

2. Using the productivity data from the project-specific capability baseline, from the general process capability baseline, or from similar projects, fix the productivity level for the project.

3. Obtain the overall effort estimate from the productivity and size estimates.

4. Use effort distribution data from the process capability baselines or similar projects to estimate the effort for the various phases.

5. Refine the estimates, taking project-specific factors into consideration.

Like the bottom-up estimation, the top-down approach allows the estimates to be refined using project-specific factors. This allowance, without actually defining these factors, acknowledges that each project is unique and may have some characteristics that do not exist in other projects. It may not be possible to enumerate these characteristics or formally model their effects on productivity. Hence, it is left to the project manager to decide which factors should be considered and how they will affect the project.

4.2.3 The Use Case Points Approach

The use case points approach employed at Infosys is based on the approach from Rational and is similar to the function points methods. This approach can be applied if use cases are used for requirement specification. The basic steps in this approach are as follows.

1. Classify each use case as simple, medium, or complex. The basis of this classification is the number of transactions in a use case, including secondary scenarios. A *transaction* is defined to be an atomic set of activities that is either performed entirely or not at all. A simple use case has three or fewer transactions, an average use case has four to seven transactions, and a complex use case has more than seven transactions. A simple use case is assigned a factor of 5, a medium use case a factor of 10, and a complex use case a factor of 15. Table 4.1 gives this classification and factors.

2. Obtain the total *unadjusted use case points* (UUCPs) as a weighted sum of factors for the use cases in the application. That is, for each of the three complexity classes, first obtain the product of the number of use cases of a particular complexity and the factor for that complexity. The sum of the three products is the number of UUCPs for the application.

3. Adjust the raw UUCP to reflect the project's complexity and the experience of the people on the project. To do this, first compute the technical complexity factor (TCF) by reviewing the factors given in Table 4.2 and rating each factor from 0 to 5. A rating of 0 means that the factor is irrelevant for this project; 5 means it is essential. For each factor, multiply its rating by its weight from the table and add these numbers to get the TFactor. Obtain the TCF using this equation:

$$TCF = 0.6 + (0.01 * TFactor)$$

Table 4.1 Use Case Complexity and Factors

Use Case Type	Description	Factor
Simple	3 or fewer transactions	5
Medium	4–7 transactions	10
Complex	>7 transactions	15

Table 4.2 Technical Factors and Weights

Sequence Number	Factor	Weight
1	Distributed system	2
2	Response or throughput performance objectives	1
3	End-user efficiency (online)	1
4	Complex internal processing	1
5	Code must be reusable	1
6	Easy to install	0.5
7	Easy to use	0.5
8	Portable	2
9	Easy to change	1
10	Concurrent	1
11	Includes special security features	1
12	Provides direct access for third parties	1
13	Special user training facilities required	1

4. Similarly, compute the environment factor (EF) by going through Table 4.3 and rating each factor from 0 to 5. For experience-related factors, 0 means no experience in the subject, 5 means expert, and 3 means average. For motivation, 0 means no motivation on the project, 5 means high motivation, and 3 means average. For the stability of requirements,

Table 4.3 Environmental Factors for Team and Weights

Sequence Number	Factor	Weight
1	Familiar with Internet process	1.5
2	Application experience	0.5
3	Object-oriented experience	1
4	Lead analyst capability	0.5
5	Motivation	1
6	Stable requirements	2
7	Part-time workers	−1
8	Difficult programming language	−1

0 means extremely unstable requirements, 5 means unchanging requirements, and 3 means average. For part-time workers, 0 means no part-
time technical staff, 5 means all part-time staff, and 3 means average. For
programming language difficulty, 0 means easy-to-use programming language, 5 means very difficult programming language, and 3 means average. The weighted sum gives the EFactor, from which the EF is obtained
by the following equation:

$$EF = 1.4 + (-0.03 * EFactor)$$

5. Using these two factors, compute the final use case points (UCP) as
follows:

$$UCP = UUCP * TCF * EF$$

For effort estimation, assign, on an average, 20 person-hours per UCP for
the entire life cycle. This will give a rough estimate. Refine this further as follows.
Count how many factors are less than 3 and how many factors are greater than 3. If
the total number of factors that have a value less than 3 are few, 20 person-hours
per UCP is suitable. If there are many, use 28 person-hours per UCP. In other
words, the range is 20 to 28 person-hours per UCP, and the project manager can
decide which value to use depending on the various factors.

4.2.4 Effectiveness of the Overall Approach

The common way to analyze the *effectiveness* of an estimation approach is to see
how the estimated effort compares with the actual effort. As discussed earlier, this
comparison gives only a general idea of the accuracy of the estimates; it does not indicate how optimal the estimates are. To gain that information, you must study the
effects of estimates on programmers (for example, whether they were "stretched" or
were "underutilized"). Nevertheless, a comparison of actual effort expended and
estimated effort does give an idea of the effectiveness of the estimation method.

For completed projects, as discussed in Chapter 3, the process database includes information on the estimated effort as well as the actual effort. Figure 4.1
shows the scatter plot of estimated effort and actual effort for some of the completed development projects.

As the plot shows, the estimation approach works quite well; most of the
data points are close to the 45-degree line in the graph (if all estimates match the
actual effort, all points will fall on the 45-degree line). The data also show that

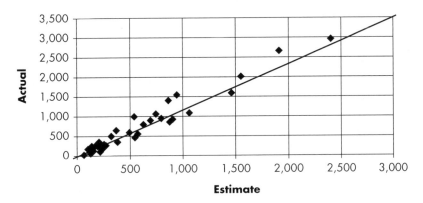

*Figure 4.1 **Actual versus estimated effort***

more than 50% of the projects are within 25% of the estimated effort. Neverthe-less, the data indicate that the estimates are usually lower than the actual effort; note that most of the points are above the 45-degree line rather than below it. That is, people tend to underestimate more often—something that afflicts the software industry in general. On average, the actual effort was 25% higher than the esti-mate. Overall, although there is room for improvement, the estimation approach is reasonably effective.

4.2.5 Effort Estimate of the ACIC Project

Here we illustrate the estimation approach by showing its application on the ACIC project. Two other examples can be found in my earlier book.[10] The ACIC project employs the use-case-driven approach. Hence, the main decomposition is in terms of use cases and not in terms of modules. To classify the use cases, the project manager used the classification criteria. Table 4.4 lists the 26 use cases along with their complexity.

To estimate the build effort for different types of use cases, the ACIC project manager used the data from the Synergy project, whose process database entry is given in Chapter 3. The Synergy project had 21 simple, 11 medium, and 8 complex use cases. The detailed build data for the different use cases was used to estimate the average build efforts. (The total build effort was about 143 person-days. With average build efforts of 1 person-day, 5 person-days, and 8 person-days, respec-tively, for average, medium, and complex use cases, the total comes to 140, a num-ber that is reasonably close to actual.) Table 4.5 shows the average build effort for each type of use case and the total build effort.

Table 4.4 Use Cases in the ACIC Project

Use Case Number	Description	Complexity
1	Navigate Screen	Complex
2	Update Personal Details	Medium
3	Add Address	Medium
4	Update Address	Complex
5	Delete Address	Complex
6	Add Telephone Number	Medium
7	Update Telephone Number	Complex
8	Delete Telephone Number	Complex
9	Add E-mail	Medium
10	Update E-mail	Medium
11	Delete E-mail	Medium
12	Update Employment Details of a Party	Medium
13	Update Financial Details of a Party	Medium
14	Update Details of an Account	Medium
15	Maintain Activities of an Account	Complex
16	Maintain Memos of an Account	Simple
17	View History of Party Details	Complex
18	View History of Account Details	Complex
19	View History of Option Level and Service Options	Simple
20	View History of Activities and Memos	Simple
21	View History of Roles	Complex
22	View Account Details	Simple
23	View Holdings of an Account	Complex
24	View Pending Orders of an Account	Complex
25	Close/Reactivate Account	Simple
26	Make Intelligent Update to Business Partners of ACIC	Complex

To estimate the effort distribution among the stages, the project manager used the distribution found in the Synergy project. Because the earlier project did not have a requirements phase, the distribution had to be modified. Table 4.6 gives the estimate for each phase and for the total.

Table 4.5 Build Effort for the ACIC Project

Use Case Type	Effort (per use case, in person-days)	Number of Units	Total Build Effort (person-days)
Simple use cases	1	5	5
Medium use cases	5	9	45
Complex use cases	8	12	96
Total			146

In this project, in addition to estimating in this bottom-up manner, the project manager employed the use case point methodology. As described earlier, first the UUCPs are determined from the use cases by assigning 5 points to each simple use case, 10 points to each medium-complexity use case, and 15 to each complex use case. The number of simple, medium, and complex use cases were 5, 9, and 12, respectively, so this translates to

$$UUCP = 5 * 5 + 9 * 10 + 12 * 15 = 295$$

To take into account the various factors, first the ACIC project manager assigned weights to the factors related to the complexity of the technology and

Table 4.6 Estimated Effort for the ACIC Project

Activity	Estimated Effort	
	Person-days	% of Total Effort
Requirements	50	10
Design	60	12
Build	146	29
Integration testing	35	7
Regression testing	10	2
Acceptance testing	30	6
Project management	75	15
Configuration management	16	3
Training	50	10
Others	40	6
Estimated effort	501	100%

obtained the technology complexity factor. He chose the following values of the factors (in the order given in Table 4.3): 4, 3, 5, 3, 4, 5, 5, 0, 4, 1, 2, 0, and 5, resulting in a TFactor of 40 (8 + 3 + 5 + 3 + 4 + 2.5 + 2.5 + 0 + 4 + 1 + 2 + 0 + 5) and a TCF of 1.0. Next, he computed the environmental factor. He assigned the following weights to the environmental factors: 3, 1, 3, 4, 5, 5, 0, and 3; the resulting EFactor was 22 (4.5 + 0.5 + 3 + 2 + 5 + 10 + 0 − 3) and an EF of 0.74. From these, he calculated the total use case points as

$$UCP = 295 * 1.0 * 0.74 = 218.3$$

Using the standard effort figure of 20 person-hours per UCP, he got the effort estimate as

$$218 * 20 = 4,360 \text{ person-hours} = 499 \text{ person-days (at 8.75 hrs/day)}$$

or

$$513 \text{ person-days (at 8.5 hrs/day)}$$

These estimates were amazingly close to the earlier estimate, increasing the confidence of the project manager in the estimation. (As it turns out, the estimates for this project were indeed highly accurate, as you will see in the closure report given in Chapter 12. Furthermore, at all the milestones, the effort overrun, as compared to planned, was minuscule, as you will see in a milestone analysis given in Chapter 11.)

In this project, as mentioned earlier, the iterative process of RUP was used. Because the phases of design, analysis, and build were spread over many iterations, a phase-wise effort estimate, by itself, would not have provided a direct input for planning. For planning, the project manager had to estimate the effort for the various iterations. To obtain this, he started with the overall estimate as determined earlier. The estimate for requirements was broken into project initiation and inception phases. The effort for design, build, and test was broken into elaboration and construction, based on the use cases chosen in the various iterations and the guidelines given in the RUP methodology. The project management, CM, and other costs remained the same. Table 4.7 shows the distribution of effort by iterations.

Table 4.7 Distribution of Effort by Iterations in the ACIC Project

Iteration	Estimated Effort	
	Person-days	**% of Total Effort**
Project initiation	25	5
Inception phase	24	5
Elaboration phase: Iteration 1	45	9
Elaboration phase: Iteration 2	34	7
Construction phase: Iteration 1	27	5
Construction phase: Iteration 2	24	5
Construction phase: Iteration 3	21	4
Transition phase	110	22
Project closure	10	2
Project management	75	15
Configuration management	16	3
Training	50	10
Others	40	8
Total estimated effort	501 person-days	100%

4.3 SCHEDULING

The scheduling activity at Infosys can be broken into two subactivities: determining the overall schedule (the project duration) with major milestones, and developing the detailed schedule of the various tasks.

4.3.1 Overall Scheduling

As discussed earlier in the chapter, you can gain some flexibility in determining the schedule by controlling the staffing level, but this flexibility is limited. Because of this possible flexibility, building strict guidelines for scheduling may not be desirable; strict guidelines forfeit the advantage of the flexibility to be passed to the project or the customer. Furthermore, the project schedule is usually determined in the larger context of business plans, which impose some schedule requirements. Whenever possible, you should exploit your schedule flexibility to satisfy such requirements. One method is to use scheduling guidelines more for checking the feasibility of the schedule than for determining the schedule itself.

Figure 4.2 shows the scatter plot of the schedule and effort for some of the completed development projects at Infosys, along with a nonlinear regression curve fit for the scatter plot.

The equation of the curve in Figure 4.3 is

$$\text{schedule} = 23.46\,(\text{effort})^{0.313}$$

From the distribution of the points, it is evident that schedule is not a function solely of effort. The determined schedule can, however, be used as a guideline or check of the schedule's reasonableness, which might be decided based on other factors. Similarly, the schedule and effort data from similar projects can be used to check the reasonableness of any proposed schedule.

Project managers often use a rule of thumb, called the *square root check*, to check the schedule of medium-sized projects. The principle is that the proposed schedule should be around the square root of the total effort in person-months; the schedule can be met if $\sqrt{\text{effort}}$ resources are assigned to the project. For example, if the effort estimate is 50 person-months, a schedule of about 7 to 8 months will be suitable with about 7 to 8 full-time resources.

Because of the relationship between schedule and resources, a schedule is accepted only if the head of the business unit to which the project belongs agrees to provide the necessary resources. If the necessary resources are not available, the schedule must be adjusted. Dependencies of the project are also checked before a schedule is accepted. If the project execution depends on external factors (such as

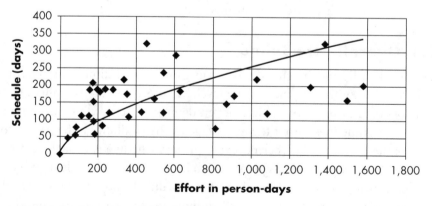

Figure 4.2 Schedule as a function of effort

completion of another project or availability of certain software), the schedule must be adjusted to accommodate these factors.

Once the overall duration of the project is fixed, the schedule for the major milestones must be determined. To determine the milestones, you must first understand the manpower ramp-up that usually takes place in a project. The number of people in a software project tends to follow the Rayleigh curve.[9,11] In the beginning and the end, few people work on the project; the peak team size (PTS) is reached somewhere near the middle of the project. This behavior occurs because only a few people are needed in the initial phases of requirements analysis and design. The human resources requirement peaks during coding and unit testing. Again, during system testing and integration, fewer people are required. In many cases, the staffing level does not change very often, but approximations of the Rayleigh curve are used: assigning a few people at the start, having the peak team during the build phase, and then leaving a few people for integration and system testing. If you consider design, build, and test as three major phases for which requirements are done, the manpower ramp-up in projects typically resembles the function shown in Figure 4.3.

At Infosys, this approach for assigning resources is generally followed. Fewer people are assigned to the starting and ending phases, with maximum people during the build phase. During the build phase, the PTS for the project is usually achieved.

For ease of scheduling, particularly for smaller projects, all the required people are often assigned together around the start of the project. This approach can

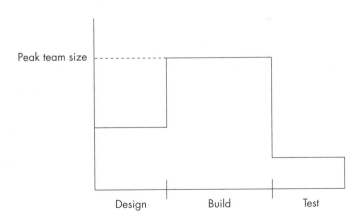

*Figure 4.3 **Manpower ramp-up in a typical project***

lead to some people being unoccupied at the start and toward the end. This slack time is often used for training. Project-level training is generally needed in the technology being used and the business domain of the project, and this training consumes a fair amount of effort, as can be seen in the effort distribution given in the PCB. Similarly, the slack time available in the end can be utilized for documentation and other closure tasks.

The schedule distribution differs from the effort distribution. For these three major phases, the percentage of the schedule consumed in the build phase is smaller than the percentage of the effort consumed because this phase involves more people. Similarly, the percentage of the schedule consumed in the design and testing phases exceeds their effort percentages. The exact schedule depends on the planned manpower ramp-up. Given the effort estimate for a phase, you can determine the duration of the phase when you know the manpower ramp-up.

Generally speaking, design requires about 40% of the schedule (20% for high-level design and 20% for detailed design), build consumes about 40%, and integration and system testing consume the remaining 20%. The manpower ramp-up typically is around 1:2:1 for design, build, and integration and testing, respectively (giving an effort distribution among these phases as 1:4:1). These types of guidelines provide a check for the milestones, which can be set based on other constraints.

It is important to recognize that even a person assigned full time to a project typically performs other tasks that consume time but do not contribute to the project. These tasks include leave, corporate activities, general (not project-specific) training, reviews in other projects, and so on.

4.3.2 The Effectiveness of the Approach

As with effort estimates, one way of checking the schedule estimates is to plot the actual schedule against the estimated schedule and see how close the points are to the 45-degree line. If all the points fall very close to the 45-degree line, the scheduling approach can be considered effective. Figure 4.4 shows this plot for previously completed development projects.

As you can see, the scheduling approach results in schedules that match reasonably well with the actual schedule. Keep in mind, however, that other factors (discussed in section 4.2) may determine whether the estimated schedule is met.

4.3.3 Detailed Scheduling

Once the milestones and the resources are fixed, it is time to set the detailed scheduling. The project manager breaks the tasks into small schedulable activities in a hierarchical manner. For each detailed task, the project manager estimates the time required to complete it and assigns a suitable resource so that the overall schedule is met. In assigning resources, she considers various factors such as leave plans of the team members, their personal growth plans and career paths, their skill sets and experience, training and mentoring needs, the criticality of the task, and the future value that the experience acquired in a task may provide to the project.

At each level of refinement, the project manager checks the effort for the overall task in the detailed schedule against the effort estimate. If necessary, she adjusts the detailed estimates. For example, she will break down the detailed design phase into tasks such as developing the detailed design for each module, review of each detailed design, fixing of defects found, and so on, and she may break down each of these further. Then she schedules these activities and assigns resources for some duration.

If this detailed schedule is not consistent with the overall schedule and effort estimate for detailed design, she must change the detailed schedule. If she finds that the best detailed schedule cannot match the milestone effort and schedule, she must revise the earlier estimates. Thus, scheduling is an iterative process.

Generally, the project manager refines the tasks to a level so that the lowest-level activity can be scheduled to occupy no more than a few days from a single resource. She also adds general activities, such as project management, coordination, database management, and configuration management. These activities have

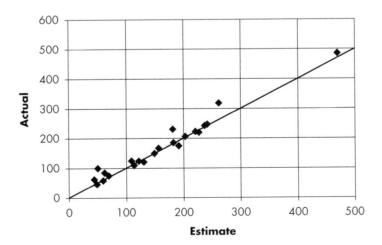

Figure 4.4 ***Actual versus estimated schedule***

less direct effect on the schedule because they are ongoing tasks rather than schedulable activities. Nevertheless, they consume resources and hence are included in the project schedule.

Rarely does the project manager complete the detailed schedule of the entire project all at once. Once the overall schedule is fixed, she may do the detailing for a phase only at the start of that phase.

For detailed scheduling, project managers frequently use Microsoft Project (MSP) or a spreadsheet. For each lowest-level activity, they stipulate the effort, duration, start date, end date, and resources. For each activity, they also specify the activity code (discussed further in Chapter 7), the program code, and the module code. They may also specify dependencies between activities, due either to an inherent dependency (for example, you can conduct a unit test plan for a program only after it has been coded) or to a resource-related dependency (the same resource is assigned two tasks).

A detailed project schedule is never static. Changes may be needed because the actual progress in the project may be different from what was planned, because newer tasks are added in response to change requests, or because of other unforeseen situations. Changes are done as and when the need arises.

The final schedule, as recorded in MSP or some other tool, is the most "live" project plan document. During the project, if plans must be changed and additional activities must be done, after the decision is taken, any changes are reflected in the detailed schedule. Hence, the detailed schedule becomes the main document that tracks the activities and schedule. The detailed schedule is also a key input in project monitoring, which is discussed in Chapter 11.

4.3.4 The Schedule of the ACIC Project

Let's consider the example of the ACIC project. (See my earlier book for the scheduling of a different case study.[10]) As discussed earlier, the effort estimates for the ACIC project were 501 person-days, or about 24 person-months. The customer gave approximately 5.5 months to finish the project (from May 15 to November 3). Because this is more than the square root of effort in person-months, and because requirement gathering had to be finished before the project started, this schedule was accepted. (The resource requirement for this schedule was also estimated and is given in the project management plan in Chapter 8.)

The milestones are determined by using the effort estimate for the phase and an estimate of the number of resources that can be fully occupied in this phase. In the ACIC project, the project manager listed the major activities in each phase and assigned them to resources. From this assignment, he determined the overall schedule and effort for the phase. If the total effort for the phase did not match the effort estimate, he revised the assignment until the total effort matched the effort estimate. Then the overall schedule, as obtained from the assignment of activities, was taken as the schedule for the phase. (The milestones are specified in the project management plan given in Chapter 8.) Table 4.8 shows the high-level schedule of the ACIC project. This schedule is obtained automatically from the final detailed schedule of the project.

In the table, the task ID is the sequence number assigned in the MSP. The task IDs show that the total number of tasks in the final schedule was more than 330 and that each of these high-level tasks had many schedulable activities under it. The first task was the overall project, with a duration of about 140 days and an effort of 560 person-days. (This schedule is from the final schedule of the project,

Table 4.8 High-level Schedule for the ACIC Project

Task ID	Task	Duration (days)	Work (person-days)	Start Date	End Date
1	ACIC development schedule	139.56	559.93	4/3/00	11/3/00
2	Project initiation activities	33.78	24.2	5/4/00	6/23/00
29	Regular activities	87.11	35.13	6/5/00	10/16/00
74	Training	95.11	49.37	5/8/00	9/29/00
99	Organization activities	76.89	12.9	5/22/00	9/15/00
104	Knowledge sharing initiative	78.22	19.56	6/2/00	9/30/00
110	Inception phase activities	26.67	22.67	4/3/00	5/12/00
114	Elaboration Iteration 1	27.56	55.16	5/15/00	6/23/00
157	Elaboration Iteration 2	8.89	35.88	6/26/00	7/7/00
198	Construction Iteration 1	8.89	24.63	7/10/00	7/21/00
228	Construction Iteration 2	6.22	28.22	7/20/00	7/28/00
256	Construction Iteration 3	6.22	27.03	7/31/00	8/8/00
290	Transition phase activities	56	179.62	8/9/00	11/3/00
323	Window resized release of 2.0 code	26.67	39.11	8/14/00	9/22/00
331	Back-end mainframe work for 3.0	4.44	6.44	8/14/00	8/18/00

which incorporated the changes to be done; the final two tasks in this table are the two major changes.)

This high-level schedule is not suitable for assigning resources and detailed planning. During detailed scheduling, these tasks are broken into schedulable activities. In this way, the schedule also becomes a checklist of tasks for the project. As mentioned before, this "exploding" of top-level activities is not done fully at the start but rather takes place many times during the project.

Table 4.9 shows part of the detailed schedule of the construction-iteration 1 phase of the ACIC project. For each activity, the table specifies the module, the program, and the activity code, along with the duration, effort, and so on. The Module and Program columns represent the module and program on which work is being done. Activity Code represents the activity being performed. (The standard organization-wide activity codes are discussed further in Chapter 7.)

Sometimes, the *predecessors* of the activity (the activities upon which the task depends) are also specified, although they are omitted here. This information helps in determining the critical path and the critical resources.

For each task, how much is completed is given in the % Complete column. This information is used for activity tracking, which is discussed further in Chapter 11. The detailed schedule also specifies the resource to which the task is assigned.

The activity number has been omitted from Table 4.9. As Table 4.8 indicated, there were more than 330 line items in the final schedule of the ACIC project, the lowest-level tasks being the schedulable tasks.

4.4 SUMMARY

The basic goal of effort estimation is to generate reasonable estimates that will work most of the time. The following are key lessons from the estimation and scheduling approaches used at Infosys:

- Use past data to estimate. Prefer data from similar projects to general process capability data. Use a model to estimate, but allow flexibility for adjusting estimates to accommodate project-specific factors.

- Employ different models in different situations. Bottom-up estimation is effective when project details are known. Use the top-down approach if you can estimate the size and productivity, and the use case approach when using a use-case-based development approach.

Table 4.9 *Portion of the Detailed Schedule for the ACIC Project*

Module	Program	Activity Code	Task	Duration (days)	Effort (days)	Start Date	End Date	% Complete	Resource Initials
—	—	PRS	Requirements	8.89 days	1.33 days	7/10/00 8:00	7/21/00 17:00	100%	BB, BJ
—	—	PDDRV	Design review	1 day	0.9 days	7/11/00 8:00	7/12/00 9:00	100%	BB, BJ, SB
—	—	PDDRW	Rework after design review	1 day	0.8 days	7/12/00 8:00	7/13/00 9:00	100%	BJ, SB
History	UC17	PCD	View history of party details, UC17	2.67 days	1.87 days	7/10/00 8:00	7/12/00 17:00	100%	HP
History	UC7	PCDRV	Code walkthrough, UC17	0.89 days	0.27 days	7/14/00 8:00	7/14/00 17:00	100%	BJ, DD
History	UC19	PCDRV	Code walkthrough, UC19	0.89 days	0.27 days	7/14/00 8:00	7/14/00 17:00	100%	BJ, DD
—	—	PCDRW	Rework after code walkthrough	0.89 days	2.49 days	7/17/00 8:00	7/17/00 17:00	100%	DD, SB, HP, BJ
—	—	PUTRW	Rework after testing	0.89 days	0.71 days	7/18/00 8:00	7/18/00 17:00	100%	BJ, SB, DD, HP
History	UC17	PUT	Test, UC 17	0.89 days	0.62 days	7/18/00 8:00	7/18/00 17:00	100%	SB
History	UC19	PUT	Test, UC 19	0.89 days	0.62 days	7/18/00 8:00	7/18/00 17:00	100%	HP
Configuration	—	PCM	Reconciliation	0.89 days	2.49 days	7/19/00 8:00	7/19/00 17:00	100%	BJ, DD, SB, HP
Management	—	PPMPT	Scheduling and tracking	7.11 days	2.13 days	7/10/00 8:00	7/19/00 17:00	100%	BB
Quality	—	PPMPT	Milestone analysis	0.89 days	0.62 days	7/19/00 8:00	7/19/00 17:00	100%	BB

- For the overall schedule and the high-level milestones, use the existing flexibility to meet proposed dates. Once the overall schedule and milestones are fixed, determine the resource requirement for each phase from the phase-wise effort estimate.

- Detailed scheduling is a dynamic task; take into account people issues while assigning tasks. It is not necessary to completely refine the schedule at the start. You can develop details for the tasks in the overall schedule as the need arises.

- The detailed schedule forms the planned activity list for the project. Capture all activities planned in the project in this document and use it later to track activities.

From the CMM standpoint, a proper effort and schedule estimation method is a requirement for the Software Project Planning KPA at level 2. At level 4, the use of past data for estimation is expected to increase, and the goals of the Quantitative Process Management KPA cannot be satisfied unless a good estimation procedure is in place. The Integrated Software Management KPA at level 3 also assumes that good estimation methods are available to projects for planning. The requirements related to estimation in these KPAs are satisfied by methods discussed in this chapter.

4.5 REFERENCES

1. B. Boehm. *Software Engineering Economics.* Prentice Hall, 1981.

2. S.D. Conte, H.E. Sunsmore, and V.Y. Shen. *Software Engineering Metrics and Models.* Benjamin/Cummings, 1986.

3. V.R. Basili. *Tutorial on Models and Metrics for Software Management and Engineering.* IEEE Press, 1980.

4. B. Boehm. Software engineering economics. *IEEE Transactions on Software Engineering,* 10(1), 1984.

5. C.F. Kemerer. An empirical validation of software cost estimation models. *Communications of the ACM,* 30(5), 1987.

6. J.E. Matson, B.E. Barrett, and J.M. Mellicham. Software development cost estimation using function points. *IEEE Transactions on Software Engineering,* 20(4), 1994.

7. A.J. Albrecht and J.R. Gaffney. Software function, source lines of code, and development effort prediction: A software science validation. *IEEE Transactions on Software Engineering,* 9(6), 1983.

8. F. Brooks, Jr. *The Mythical Man Month, Anniversary Edition.* Addison-Wesley, 1995.

9. L.H. Putnam and W. Myers. *Industrial Strength Software: Effective Management Using Measurement.* IEEE Computer Society Press, 1997.

10. P. Jalote. *CMM in Practice: Processes for Executing Software Projects at Infosys.* Addison-Wesley, 2000.

11. L.H. Putnam. A general empirical solution to the macro software sizing and estimating problem. *IEEE Transactions on Software Engineering,* 4(4), 1978.

Chapter 5

Quality Planning

Until a few years ago, software engineering suffered the same tragic notion of quality that manufacturing companies had much earlier—that quality was something that was done at the end of the assembly/development process, before the product was to be delivered. It was common to see quality-conscious project managers plan for system testing after the development (other project managers did not even plan properly for system testing!) but fail to give any importance to quality control tasks during development. The result? System testing frequently revealed many more defects than anticipated. These defects, in turn, required much more effort than planned for repair, finally resulting in buggy software that was delivered late.

As the situation improved, project managers started planning for reviews and unit testing. But they did not know how to judge the effectiveness and implications of these measures. In other words, projects still lacked clear quality goals, convincing plans to achieve their goals, and mechanisms to monitor the effectiveness of quality control tasks such as unit testing.

With proper use of measurements and past data, it is possible to treat quality in the same way you treat the other two key parameters: effort and schedule. That is, you can set quantitative quality goals, along with subgoals that will help track the project's progress toward achieving the quality goal.

This chapter discusses how project managers at Infosys set the quality goals for their projects and how they develop a plan to achieve these goals using intermediate quality goals to monitor their progress. Before we describe Infosys's approach, we briefly discuss some general concepts of quality management.

5.1 QUALITY CONCEPTS

Ensuring that the final software is of high quality is one of the prime concerns of a project manager. But how is software *quality* defined? The concept of software quality is not easily definable because software has many possible quality characteristics.[1] In practice, however, quality management often revolves around defects. Hence, we use *delivered defect density*—that is, the number of defects per unit size in the delivered software—as the definition of quality. This definition is currently the de facto industry standard.[2] Using it signals that the aim of a software project is to deliver the software with as few defects as possible.

What is a defect? Again, there can be no precise definition of a defect that will be general and widely applicable (is a software that misspells a word considered to have a defect?). In general, we can say a *defect* in software is something that causes the software to behave in a manner that is inconsistent with the requirements or needs of the customer.

Before considering techniques to manage quality, you must first understand the defect injection and removal cycle. Software development is a highly people-oriented activity and hence error-prone. Defects can be injected in software at any stage during its evolution. That is, during the transformation from user needs to software to satisfy those needs, defects can be injected in all the transformation activities undertaken. These injection stages are primarily the requirements specification, the high-level design, the detailed design, and coding.

For high-quality software, the final product should have as few defects as possible. Hence, for delivery of high-quality software, active removal of defects is necessary; this removal takes place through the quality control activities of reviews and testing. Because the cost of defect removal increases as the latency of defects (the time gap between the introduction of a defect and its detection) increases,[3] any mature process will include quality control activities after each phase in which defects can potentially be injected. The activities for defect removal include requirements reviews, design reviews, code reviews, unit testing, integration testing, system testing, and acceptance testing (we do not include reviews of plan documents, although such reviews also help in improving quality of the software). Figure 5.1 shows the process of defect injection and removal.

The task of quality management is to plan suitable quality control activities and then to properly execute and control them to achieve the project's quality goals.

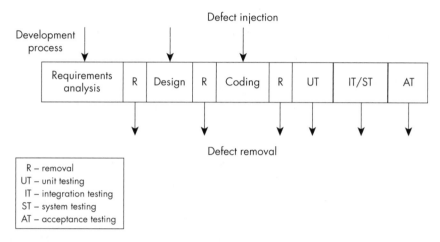

Figure 5.1 Defect injection and removal

5.1.1 Procedural Approach to Quality Management

As noted earlier, you detect defects by performing reviews or testing. Whereas *reviews* are structured, human-oriented processes, *testing* is the process of executing software (or parts of it) in an attempt to identify defects. In the *procedural* approach to quality management, procedures and guidelines for the review and testing activities are established. In a project, these activities are planned (that is, it is established which activity will be performed and when); during execution, they are carried out according to the defined procedures. In short, the procedural approach is the execution of certain processes at defined points to detect defects.

The procedural approach does not allow claims to be made about the percentage of defects removed or the quality of the software following the procedure's completion. In other words, merely executing a set of defect removal procedures does not provide a basis for judging their effectiveness or assessing the quality of the final code. Furthermore, such an approach is highly dependent on the quality of the procedure and the quality of its execution. For example, if the test planning is done carefully and the plan is thoroughly reviewed, the quality of the software after performance of the testing will be better than if testing was done but the test plan was not carefully thought out and the review was done perfunctorily. A key drawback in the procedural approach is the lack of quantitative means for project managers to assess the quality of the software produced; the only factor visible to project managers is whether the quality control tasks are executed.

5.1.2 Quantitative Approaches to Quality Management

To better assess the effectiveness of the defect detection processes, an approach is needed that goes beyond asking, "Has the method been executed?" and looks at metrics data for evaluation. Based on this analysis of the data, you can decide whether more testing or reviews are needed. If controls are applied during the project based on quantitative data to achieve quantitative quality goals, then we say that a *quantitative* quality management approach is being applied.

Quantitative quality management has two key aspects: setting a quantitative quality goal and then managing the software development process quantitatively so that this quality goal is met (with a high degree of confidence).

A good quality management approach should provide warning signs early in the project and not only toward the end, when the options are limited. Early warnings allow for timely intervention. To achieve this goal, it is essential to predict the values of some parameters at various stages so that controlling them during project execution will ensure that the final product has the desired quality. If such predictions can be made, you can use the actual data gathered to judge whether the process has been applied effectively. With this approach, a defect detection process does not terminate with the declaration that the process has been executed; instead, the data from process execution are used to ensure that the process has been performed in a manner that exploited its full potential.

One approach to quantitatively control the quality of the software is to work with *software reliability* models. Most such models use the failure data during the final stages of testing to estimate the reliability of the software. These models can indicate whether the reliability is acceptable or more testing is needed. Unfortunately, they do not provide intermediate goals for the early phases of the project, and they have other limitations. Overall, such models are helpful in estimating the reliability of a software product, but they have a limited value for quality management. (More information is available on reliability models.[4,5,6])

Another well-known quality concept in software is defect removal efficiency. For a quality control (QC) activity, we define the *defect removal efficiency* (DRE) as the percentage of existing total defects that are detected by the QC activity.[5] The DRE for the full life cycle of the project—that is, for all activities performed before the software is delivered—represents the in-process efficiency of the process. If the overall defect injection rate is known for the project, then DRE for the full life cycle also defines the quality (delivered defect density) of the software.

Although defect removal efficiency is a useful metric for evaluating a process and identifying areas of improvement, by itself it is not suitable for quality management. The main reason is that the DRE for a QC activity or the overall process can be computed only at the end of the project, when all defects and their origins are known. Hence, it provides no direct way to control quality during project execution.

Another approach to quantitative quality management is *defect prediction*. In this approach, you set the quality goal in terms of delivered defect density. You set the intermediate goals by estimating the number of defects that may be identified by various defect detection activities; then you compare the actual number of defects to the estimated defect levels.

This approach makes the management of quality closely resemble the management of effort and schedule—the two other major success parameters of a project. A target is first set for the quality of the delivered software. From this target, the values of chosen parameters at various stages in the project are estimated; that is, milestones are established. These milestones are chosen so that, if the estimates are met, the quality of the final software is likely to meet the desired level. During project execution, the actual values of the parameters are measured and compared to the estimated levels to determine whether the project is traveling the desired path or whether some actions need to be taken to ensure that the final software has the desired quality.

The effectiveness of this approach depends on how well you can predict the defect levels at various stages of the project. It is known that the defect rate follows the same pattern as the effort rate, with both following the Rayleigh curve.[5,7,8] In other words, the number of defects found at the start of the project is small but keeps increasing until it reaches a peak (around unit testing time) before it begins to decline again. Because a process has defined points for defect detection, you can also specify this curve in terms of percentages of total defects detected at the various detection stages. And from the estimate of the defect injection rate and size, you can estimate the total number of defects. This approach for defect level prediction is similar to both the base defect model and the STEER approach of IBM's Federal Systems Division.[5]

Yet another approach is to use *statistical process control* (SPC) for managing quality (Chapter 7 includes a brief discussion of SPC). In this approach, you set performance expectations of the various QC processes, such as testing and reviews, in terms of control limits. If the actual performance of the QC task is not within the limits, you analyze the situation and take suitable action. The control limits resemble prediction of defect levels based on past performance but can also be used for monitoring quality activities at a finer level, such as review or unit testing of a module.

When you use a performance prediction approach and the actual number of defects is less than the target, the approach has too many uncertainties for you to say with surety that the removal process was not executed properly. As a result, you must look at other indicators to determine the cause.[5] In other words, if the actual data are out of range, the project manager will look at other indicators to decide what the actual situation is and what action, if any, is needed.

5.2 QUANTITATIVE QUALITY MANAGEMENT PLANNING

Now let's consider how project managers at Infosys use the defect prediction approach for quantitatively managing software quality. (As discussed in Chapters 10 and 11, projects also use SPC at the task level.) As discussed earlier, when you plan for quantitatively managing quality for a project, you face two key issues: first, setting the quality goal, and second, predicting defect levels at intermediate milestones that can be used for quantitatively monitoring progress toward the goal. In addition, if the project goals exceed the capability of existing processes, the project manager must plan suitable enhancements to the quality process. Let's look at how project managers perform these three tasks at Infosys.

5.2.1 Setting the Quality Goal

Project managers at Infosys set quality goals during the planning stages. The *quality goal* for a project generally is the expected number of defects found during acceptance testing. You can set the quality goal according to what is *computed* using past data; in this case, it is implied that you will use the standard process, and hence standard quality results will be expected. Two primary sources can be used for setting the quality goal: past data from similar projects and data from the PCB.

If you use data from similar projects, you can estimate the number of defects found during acceptance testing of the current project as the product of the number of defects found during acceptance testing of the similar projects and the ratio of the estimated effort for this project and the total effort of the similar projects.

If you use data from the PCB, you can use any of several methods to compute this value. If you set the quality target as the number of defects per function point, you estimate size in function points (as discussed earlier), and the expected number of defects is the product of the quality figure and the estimated size. The following sequence of steps is used:

1. Set the quality goal in terms of defects per FP.

2. Estimate the expected productivity level for the project.

3. Estimate the size in FP as (expected productivity * estimated effort).

4. Estimate the number of AT defects as (quality goal * estimated size).

Instead of setting the quality goal in terms of defects per function point, sometimes it is more useful to set the target in terms of the process's defect removal efficiency. In this situation, you can determine the number of defects to be expected during acceptance testing from the defect injection rate, the target in-process removal efficiency, and the estimated size. The sequence of steps is as follows:

1. Set the quality goal in terms of defect removal efficiency.

2. Estimate the total number of defects from the defect injection rate and the estimated size, or by the effort-based defect injection rate and the effort estimate.

3. Estimate the number of AT defects from the total number of defects and the quality goal.

5.2.2 Estimating Defects for Other Stages

Once the project's quality goal is set, you should estimate defect levels for the various quality control activities so that you can quantitatively control the quality. The approach for estimating defect levels for other phases is similar to the approach for estimating the defects in acceptance testing. From the estimate of the total number of defects that will be introduced, you forecast the defect levels for the various testing stages by using the percentage distribution of defects as given in the PCB. Alternatively, you can forecast defects for the various phases based on past data from similar projects.

At a minimum, you estimate the defects uncovered in system and integration testing. System testing is singled out because it is the major testing activity and the final QC activity performed before the software is submitted to the customer.

Estimating defects for system testing and then comparing that number to the actual number of defects found will help you determine whether the system testing has been sufficient and the software is ready for release.

For reviews, instead of making an explicit prediction of the defect levels, you can use norms given in the review baseline to evaluate the effectiveness of a review immediately after it has been executed. These norms are determined based on SPC and allow you to evaluate the effectiveness of each review rather than evaluating the effectiveness of a phase. Chapter 10 discusses quantitatively managing reviews in more detail. Similarly, norms are also provided for unit testing. Monitoring of unit testing is discussed further in Chapter 11.

5.2.3 Quality Process Planning

You can set a quality goal that is higher (or lower) than the quality level of a similar project, or you can aim for the levels achieved by the standard process. You can then determine the expected number of defects for the higher goal by using the quality goal set for the project. Alternatively, after determining the expected number of AT defects, you can set the quality goal by choosing a different number of AT defects as the target.

If the quality goal is based on the data from similar projects and the goal is higher than that of the similar projects, it is unreasonable to expect that following the same process as used in the earlier projects will achieve the higher quality goal. If the same process is followed, the reasonable expectation is that similar quality levels will be achieved. Hence, if a higher quality level is desired, the process must be suitably upgraded. Similarly, if the quality goal is set higher than the quality levels given in the PCB, it is unreasonable to expect that following the standard process will lead to the higher quality level. Hence, a new strategy will be needed— generally, a combination of training, prototyping, testing, reviews, and, in particular, defect prevention. This strategy is explicitly stated in the quality plan for the project. Here we discuss testing and reviews, the two main quality control processes. Defect prevention planning is discussed later in this chapter.

Different levels of testing are deployed in a project. You can modify the overall testing by adding or deleting some testing steps (these steps show up as process deviations in the project management plan). In addition, you can enhance the approach to testing by, for example, performing a group review of the test plans and test results.

The choice of work products to be reviewed is generally made by the project manager. The set of documents reviewed may, in fact, change from project to project. It can be adjusted according to the quality goal. If a higher quality level is set, it is likely to be achieved by having a larger number of programs group reviewed, by including a group review of the test plans, by having a more critical review of detailed designs, and so on. If this approach is selected, it is mentioned as the strategy for meeting the quality goal. To further elaborate on the implications of this type of strategy, you specify in the project plan all documents that will be reviewed and the nature of those reviews.

You can use the data in the process capability baseline to estimate the effects of the proposed process changes on the effort and schedule planned for the project. Frequently, once the process changes are identified, their effects are predicted based on past experience. This tactic is usually acceptable because the changes are generally minor.

5.3 DEFECT PREVENTION PLANNING

Defect prevention (DP) activities are intended to improve quality and improve productivity. It is now generally accepted that some defects present in the system will not be detected by the various QC activities and will inevitably find their way into the final system. Consequently, the higher the number of defects introduced in the software during development, the higher the number of residual defects that will remain in the final delivered system.

This point can be stated in another way. The overall defect removal efficiency of a process is the percentage of total defects that are removed by the various QC activities before the software is delivered. For a stable process, the defect removal efficiency is also generally stable. Hence, the greater the total number of defects in the system, the greater the number of defects in the delivered system. In other words, the higher the defect injection rate, the poorer the quality. Clearly, for a given process and its removal efficiency, the quality of the final delivered software can be improved if fewer defects are introduced while the software is being built. This recognition serves as the quality motivation for defect prevention.

DP also has productivity benefits. As discussed earlier, the basic defect cycle during the building of software is that developers introduce defects and later identify and remove them. In other words, something is introduced that is later removed. Clearly, this defect injection and removal cycle is a waste of effort—it adds no value to the software. In this cycle, developers introduce something only to put in more effort to remove it (and they hope they remove all the errors). It therefore makes sense not to introduce defects in the first place; then the effort required to identify and remove them will not be needed. In other words, if you inject fewer defects, fewer defects must be removed; the effort required to remove defects, in turn, will be reduced, thereby increasing productivity. This concept serves as the cost motivation for DP.

How is DP done? The premise of DP is that there is some cause behind the injected defects. If the cause can be understood, efforts can be made to eliminate defects or minimize their impact. In other words, DP generally entails collecting data on defects found in the past, analyzing the data to find the root causes for the injection of the defects, and then developing solutions that attack the root causes.

Like any other major project task, the DP activities must be planned. You actually analyze defects and find solutions, however, after some amount of defect data from the project is available. To implement DP, a project manager may start with the set of recommendations available at the organization level and then build project-specific recommendations based on analysis of the project's defect data. At Infosys, the following steps are taken for defect prevention activities at the project level:

- Identify a defect prevention team within the project.
- Have a kick-off meeting and identify existing solutions.
- Plan for defect prevention.
  - Set defect prevention goals for the project.
  - See that the DP team is trained on DP and causal analysis, if needed.
  - Define the frequency at which defect prevention activities will be carried out.
- Do defect prevention.
  - At defined points, collate defects data.
  - Identify the most common types of defects by doing Pareto analysis.
  - Perform causal analysis and prioritize the root causes.
  - Identify and develop solutions for the root causes.
  - Implement the solutions.
  - Review the status and benefits of DP at the project milestones.
- Capture learning.
  - In the metrics analysis report and BOK, capture the learning and benefits you have obtained.
  - Submit all outputs of DP as a part of the process assets.

During quality planning, your only activities are the planning activities. The activities under "Do defect prevention" or "Capture learning" are done while the project is executing or when it is finished. Here, we focus primarily on the tasks related to planning. Chapter 11 describes the tasks under "Do defect prevention" in a discussion of project monitoring.

Most of the activities relating to DP planning are self-explanatory. A project manager identifies a team that will perform the DP analysis (obviously, everyone in the project must perform the actual solutions that are to be executed to prevent defects). A kick-off meeting raises the awareness of team members and identifies the solutions that may be available in the organization. If needed, the DP team is trained on DP and causal analysis.

Setting the DP goals is a key planning activity. As mentioned earlier, DP is viewed as a strategy to achieve higher quality and productivity than the standard organization process can achieve. Hence, if a project manager has set quality and productivity goals that are higher than the organization level, as part of her strategy to achieve the goals she may use DP. In general, a project manager sets the DP goal in terms of reduction in the defect injection rate, typically about 10% to 20%. With this rate, its impact on quality and productivity can be estimated.

The other key planning activity is to decide when and how often DP tasks will be performed. Although a project manager can make these decisions, the general guideline at Infosys is that the DP activities should be carried out after about 20% of the programs have been coded, code reviewed, and unit tested, and again when about 50% of them have been coded, reviewed, and unit tested. That is, the first DP exercise is undertaken when the defect data from about 20% of the modules are available. Hopefully, the results of this DP should result in actions that will reduce the defect injection rate for the rest of the project. Then another DP exercise should be done at the 50% mark. In this exercise the project manager can determine whether the solutions are bearing results and whether further actions need to be taken. At this point of development, all the different types of defects should have been seen and their causes understood and acted on. Hence, further analysis will yield little new information.

5.4 THE QUALITY PLAN OF THE ACIC PROJECT

Now let's discuss the quality planning of our case study, the ACIC project. (Other examples, including a different case study, can be found in my earlier book.[9]) To set its goals and defect estimates, the ACIC project manager used the data from the Synergy project, a similar project done earlier for the same client. The defect injection rate in Synergy was 0.036 defects per person-hour (obtained by dividing the total number of defects by total effort—both available in the Synergy process database). The ACIC project manager wanted to do better than Synergy and expected to have a 10% reduction in the defect injection rate, considerably better than the organization norms. At the projected rate, the number of defects injected was expected to be around 501 * 8.75 * 0.033 (the product of effort in person-days, the total hours in one person-day, and the expected defect injection rate). That is, the estimate of the total number of defects injected during the entire life cycle was around 145 defects.

Quality is defined as the defect density during acceptance testing, or the overall defect removal efficiency before acceptance testing. Synergy found 5% of the defects during acceptance testing. The ACIC project aimed to reduce it to 3%, giving the number of defects expected to be found during acceptance testing as 145 * 0.03 = 5 (approximately).

The productivity goal was a slight improvement over what was achieved in Synergy. The goal for the schedule was to deliver on time, and the expected cost of quality was 32%, which was the same as in Synergy and the organization capability baseline. Table 5.1 shows all these goals for the ACIC project.

For the purposes of monitoring and controlling the project, the ACIC project manager wanted estimates of the number of defects detected in the various stages. He could then compare these estimates to the actual number of defects found and use them to monitor the progress of the project. With the estimate of the total number of defects injected, he could obtain these per-stage estimates using defect distribution.

Table 5.1   Goals for the ACIC Project

Goals	Value	Basis for Setting Goals	Organization-wide Norms
Total number of defects injected	145	0.033 defects/person-hour. This is 10% better than Synergy, which was 0.036 defects/person-hour	0.052 defects/person-hour
Quality (acceptance defects)	5	3% or less of total estimated number of defects	6% of estimated number of defects
Productivity (in FP/person-month)	57	3.4% productivity improvement over Synergy	50
Schedule	Delivery on time		10%
Cost of quality	32%	31.5%	32%

To obtain the defect distribution, he had the choice of using the capability baseline data or the Synergy data. Because Synergy did not have a requirements phase, he modified its distribution to suit the current life cycle. Essentially, he reduced the percentage of defects found in unit testing from 45% to 40%, reduced the percentage of defects in acceptance testing to 3% (because that was the quality goal), and increased the percentage of defects in requirements and design review to 20%. These percentages were also consistent with the distribution given in the capability baseline. Table 5.2 shows the estimates of defects to be detected in the various stages.

Because the quality goal was higher than that achieved in Synergy as well as the organization-wide norms, and because the productivity goal was also somewhat higher, the ACIC project manager had to devise a strategy to achieve these goals because following the standard process would not help achieve them. The basic strategy was threefold:

- To employ defect prevention
- To conduct group reviews of specifications and the first program written by programmers
- To use the RUP methodology

Table 5.2 Estimates of Defects to Be Detected

Review/Testing Stage	Estimated Number of Defects to Be Detected	% of Defects to Be Detected	Basis for Estimation
Requirements and design review	29	20%	Similar project (Synergy) and PCB
Code review	29	20%	Similar project (Synergy) and PCB
Unit testing	57	40%	Similar project (Synergy) and PCB
Integration and regression testing	25	17%	Similar project (Synergy) and PCB
Acceptance testing	5	3%	Similar project (Synergy) and PCB
Total estimated number of defects to be detected	143	100%	

Table 5.3 Strategy for Achieving the Higher Goals of the ACIC Project

Strategy	Expected Benefits
Prevent defects using the standard defect prevention guidelines and process; use standards developed in Synergy for coding.	10%–20% reduction in defect injection rate and about 2% improvement in productivity.
Group review program specs for first few and the logically complex use cases. Group review design docs and first-time-generated code.	Improvement in quality because of improvement in overall defect removal efficiency; some benefits in productivity because defects will be detected early.
Introduce RUP methodology and implement the project in iterations. Conduct milestone analysis and defect prevention exercise after each Iteration.	Approximately 5% reduction in defect injection rate and 1% improvement in overall productivity.

That is, as compared with the process used in Synergy, the ACIC process was changed to achieve the higher goals.

Based on data from other projects, the project manager expected defect prevention to reduce the defects by about 10% to 20%. This would reduce the rework effort after testing and reviews, giving approximately a 2% improvement in productivity (based on the rework effort percentage of Synergy). He expected that group review of the program specifications and of the first module coded by programmers would improve the overall defect removal efficiency and also provide some benefits on the productivity front. Based on literature and anecdotes, he expected the use of RUP to benefit quality and productivity. Table 5.3 shows the strategy and expected benefits. Note that although the expected benefits of each strategy item are mentioned separately, it is hard to monitor the effects separately.

Because reviews are a key aspect of the quality process, they were mentioned separately in the quality plan. The plan specified the points in the development life cycle when the review was to be done, the work product to be reviewed, and the nature of the review. Table 5.4 shows these reviews in the ACIC project.

5.5 SUMMARY

Ensuring that the final software has few defects is one of the prime concerns of a project manager. In the procedural approach to quality management, quality control procedures are planned and then properly executed. In the quantitative quality management approach, a quantitative quality goal is set for the project; to achieve this goal, the execution of the process is monitored quantitatively.

Table 5.4 Reviews in the ACIC Project

Review Point	Review Item	Type of Review
End of project planning	Project plan Defect control system set up Project schedule	Group review Software quality adviser review Software quality adviser review
End of project planning	CM plan	Group review
End of 90% of requirements (this should be at the end of the first elaboration iteration)	Business analysis and requirements specification document Use case catalog	Group review
End of 90% design (this should be at the end of the second elaboration iteration)	Design document Object model	Group review
Beginning of each iteration	Iteration plans	One-person review
End of detailed design	Complex and first-time-generated program specs including test cases, interaction diagrams	Group review
After coding of first few programs	Code	Group review
After self-testing of a process	Code	One-person review
End of unit test plan	Unit test plan	One-person review
Beginning of integration test	Integration test plan	Group review

Following are the key lessons from Infosys's approach to quantitative quality management through defect prediction:

- As with managing effort and schedule, you can manage quality by using the number of defects as the metric for quality.

- Set the quality goal for a project in terms of the number of defects during acceptance testing. Use past data on process capability to set this goal.

- Using past data, estimate the defect levels for the various defect detection stages in the process. Compare these estimates to the actual number of defects found during project execution to see whether the project is progressing satisfactorily toward achieving the goal or whether some correction is needed.

- In addition to testing, plan for reviews, clearly specifying the review points, review items, and review types.

- If the quality goal of the project is higher than past performance, it cannot be achieved using the same process as earlier projects. To achieve the higher goals, you must enhance the process.

- Use defect prevention as a strategy to achieve higher quality and productivity goals in a project. For defect prevention, identify the defect prevention team, the points at which defect analysis will be done, and the expected benefits.

The methods described in this chapter satisfy the quality planning requirements of the Software Product Engineering KPA and the planning requirements of the Peer Review KPA at level 3 of the CMM. They also satisfy the quantitative quality planning requirements of the Software Quality Management KPA at level 4. The defect prevention planning satisfies some requirements of the Defect Prevention KPA of level 5.

5.6 REFERENCES

1. International Standards Organization. *Information Technology—Software Product Evaluation—Quality Characteristics and Guidelines for Their Use.* ISO/IEC IS 9126, Geneva, 1991.

2. N.E. Fenton and S.L. Pfleeger. *Software Metrics: A Rigorous and Practical Approach,* second edition. International Thomson Computer Press, 1996.

3. B. Boehm. *Software Engineering Economics.* Prentice Hall, 1981.

4. A.L. Goel. Software reliability models: Assumptions, limitations and applicability. *IEEE Transactions on Software Engineering,* 11, 1985.

5. S.H. Kan. *Metrics and Models in Software Quality Engineering.* Addison-Wesley, 1995.

6. J.D. Musa, A. Iannino, and K. Okumoto. *Software Reliability: Measurement, Prediction, Application.* McGraw Hill, 1987.

7. L.H. Putnam and W. Myers. *Measures for Excellence: Reliable Software on Time, within Budget.* Yourdon Press, 1992.

8. L.H. Putnam and W. Myers. *Industrial Strength Software: Effective Management Using Measurement.* IEEE Computer Society Press, 1997.

9. P. Jalote. *CMM in Practice: Processes for Executing Software Projects at Infosys.* Addison-Wesley, 2000.

Chapter 6

Risk Management

A software project is a complex undertaking. Unforeseen events may have an adverse impact on a project's cost, schedule, or quality. *Risk management* is an attempt to minimize the chances of failure caused by unplanned events. The aim of risk management is not to avoid getting into projects that have risks but rather to minimize the impact of risks in the projects that are undertaken. In words of N.R. Narayana Murthy, CEO of Infosys, "Anything worth doing has risks. The challenge for a leader is not to avoid them but effectively manage them through de-risking strategies." Improper risk management, the result mainly of the common disease of optimism, is the source of many project failures.

Vasu was designated as the project manager of a large project undertaken by a prestigious multinational corporation. The project was to build parts of an integrated system for worldwide human resource management. For the final system, the software Vasu's team was to develop had to be integrated with a system that was being developed by another vendor. For use in the project, the customer provided proprietary tools whose new version was to be released shortly. Vasu's team of 35 people had a little more than a year to deliver the software. Although the project employed a good team and the project manager made reasonable estimates, the system was commissioned six months late, with Infosys footing the bill for the 50% effort escalation in the project.

Why did this project fail? There are two clear reasons. First, the software being developed by the other vendor was not delivered on time, and the interfaces provided to Vasu's team kept changing. Second, a new version of the customer's tools was released during development, requiring the software to be ported to this new version.

Both of these events are clear instances of risks that were not managed properly. These risks were evident at the start, although, as with any risk, it was not certain that they would materialize. When the project started, the project manager, his business manager, and the customer hoped that the other vendor would deliver its software on time and that the new version of the tools would not affect the project.

In hindsight, Vasu thinks that if a steering team—comprising the project managers of the two projects and a customer representative—had been set up to ensure proper coordination between the two projects and their deliveries, delays could have been minimized. For the second risk, he thinks that the software should have been developed first with the earlier version of the tools. Then it should have been migrated to the new versions later through a separate project. The first solution would have required minimal extra effort, and the cost implications are minor. The second one has clear cost implications for the customer. Perhaps to avoid displeasing the customer, this risk was not highlighted and its mitigation not planned.

This chapter discusses the general concept of risks and risk management before turning to Infosys's approach for risk assessment and risk control—the two major steps in risk management.

6.1 CONCEPTS OF RISKS AND RISK MANAGEMENT

Risks are those events or conditions that *may* occur, and whose occurrence, if it does take place, has a harmful or negative effect on a project. Risks should not be confused with events and conditions that require management intervention or action. A project manager must deal with and plan for those situations that are likely to occur but whose exact nature is not known beforehand; such situations, however, are not risks. For example, it is almost certain that defects will be found during software testing, so a reasonable project must plan to fix these defects when they are found. Similarly, it is almost certain that some change requests will come, so project management must be prepared for changes and plan accordingly to handle such normal events.

A risk, on the other hand, is a probabilistic event—it may or may not occur. For this reason, we frequently have an optimistic tendency to simply not see risks or to wish that they will not occur. Social and organizational factors also may stigmatize risks and discourage clear identification of them.[1] This kind of attitude gets the project in trouble if the risk events materialize, something that is likely to happen in a large project. Not surprisingly, then, risk management is considered first among the best practices for managing large software projects.[2]

Risk management aims to identify the risks and then take actions to minimize their effect on the project. Risk management is a relatively new area in software management. It first came to the forefront with Boehm's tutorial on risk management.[3] Since then, several books have targeted risk management for software.[4,5]

Before we discuss risks in the software context, let's examine the concept a bit more with the aid of an example. Consider a computer show for which an important goal is to provide uninterrupted computer services. For this goal, one clear risk is electric power failure. The power may or may not fail. If it does fail, even for a second, the computer services will be affected substantially (the machines will have to reboot, data will be lost, and so on). If this case is unacceptable (that is, if the cost of the power failure is high), a universal power supply (UPS) can be deployed to minimize its consequences. If it is suspected that the power may go out for a long period, a backup generator may be set up to minimize the problem. With these risk management systems in place, if the power does go out, even for a long period, the show-related goal will not be compromised.

The first thing to note from this example is that risk management entails *additional cost.* Here, the cost for the UPS and the generator is extra because these components would not be needed if the risk of power failure did not exist (for example, if the electric supply company guaranteed continuous power). Hence, risk management can be considered cost-effective only if the cost of risk management is considerably less than the loss incurred if the risk materializes.[5] (Actually, the cost of risk management should be less than the *expected value* of the loss, a concept defined shortly.) For example, if the loss due to power failure is low, the cost of a UPS is not justified—a situation that prevails, for example, in homes.

Second, it is not easy to measure the value of risk management, particularly in hindsight. If the power fails for one-half hour during the show, the value provided by the UPS and generator might be calculated as the "savings" achieved by having the computers running while the power was out. Suppose, however, that the power supply does not fail even for a second and therefore the UPS and generator are not used. Does this mean that the expenditure on these components was a waste? No, because the power *could have* failed. If the risk does not materialize, the value of using risk management cannot be directly measured in terms of value or output produced. Because risk events likely occur infrequently, the chances are high that risk management systems will not be used during the project. It is this probabilistic nature of risks and the inability to always realize the direct value of risk mitigation efforts that make it difficult to manage risk.

From this example, it is clear that the first step in risk management is to identify the possible risks (power failure in this example) and to assess the consequences (loss of face or clients). Once you have done risk assessment, you can develop a risk management plan (for example, having a UPS). Overall, then, risk management has two key components: risk assessment and risk control. Each component involves different tasks, as shown in Figure 6.1.[3]

The purpose of the risk assessment task is to identify the risks, analyze them, and then prioritize them. In prioritizing risks, you identify the risks that should be managed. In other words, prioritization determines where the extra effort of risk management should be spent to get the maximum benefit. For this effort, two factors are important. First is the chance of a risk occurring; a more likely risk is a natural candidate for risk management. Second is the effect of the risk; a risk whose impact is very high is also a likely candidate.

One way to prioritize risks, therefore, is to estimate the probability of its occurrence and its consequences when it does occur. The product of these values, the *expected value* of the loss for the risk, can be used for prioritization. This expected value is called *risk exposure*. If Prob(R) is the probability of a risk R occurring and if Loss(R) is the total loss incurred if the risk materializes, then risk exposure, RE, for the risk is given by the following equation[3]:

$$RE\ (R) = Prob(R)\ x\ Loss(R)$$

Once the risks have been prioritized, you must decide what to do about them. Which ones will be managed is a management decision. Perhaps only the top few need to be handled in a project.

One approach is to take preventive or avoidance actions so that the perceived risk ceases to be a risk. For example, if new hardware is a risk, it could be avoided by implementing the project with proven hardware. Such actions, however, are not

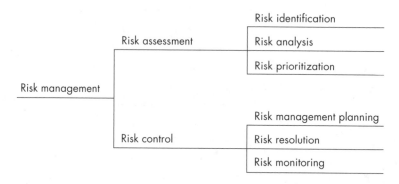

Figure 6.1 Risk management activities

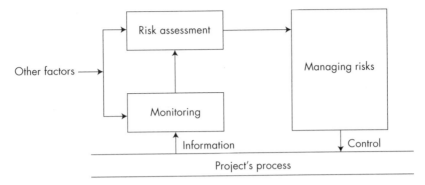

Figure 6.2 Risk management and project execution

always feasible—for example, if working with new hardware is a requirement from the customer. In such situations, the risks to the project must be handled properly.

For each risk that will be handled, you must devise and then execute risk management plans. Because risk perception changes with time, you must also monitor both the risk and the execution of the plans to minimize its consequences. In a project, risk perceptions may evolve naturally, or the risk management plans put into action may reduce the risk. In either case, it is important to continually gauge the status of risks and their management plans.

Risk management can be integrated in the development process itself, as is done in the spiral model of software development.[6] If you treat risk management as a separate process, you must understand its relationship with project execution, depicted in Figure 6.2. As shown in the figure, risk assessment and monitoring take information from project execution, along with other factors, to identify risks to be managed. The risk management activities, on the other hand, affect the project's process for minimizing the consequences of the risk.

The remainder of this chapter describes how project managers at Infosys manage risks using simple, effective techniques. The activities for risk management are combined into two tasks: risk assessment and risk control. We discuss each separately.

6.2 RISK ASSESSMENT

In a project at Infosys, risk assessment consists of the two traditional components: risk identification and risk prioritization. The risk identification activity focuses on enumerating possible risks to the project. The basic activity is to try to envision all situations that might make things in the project go wrong. The risk prioritization activity considers all aspects of all risks and then prioritizes them (for the purposes of risk management). Although the two are distinct activities, they are often carried out simultaneously. That is, a project manager may identify and analyze the risks together.

6.2.1 Risk Identification

For a project, any condition, situation, or event that can occur and would jeopardize the success of the project constitutes a risk. Identifying risks is therefore an exercise in envisioning what can go wrong. Methods that can aid risk identification include checklists of possible risks, surveys, meetings and brainstorming, and reviews of plans, processes, and work products.[5] Checklists of frequently occurring risks are probably the most common tool for risk identification. SEI has also provided a taxonomy of risks to aid in risk identification.[7]

At Infosys, the commonly occurring risks for projects have been compiled from a survey of previous projects. This list forms the starting point for identifying risks for the current project. Frequently, the risks in the current project will appear on the list.

A project manager can also use the process database to get information about risks and risk management on similar projects. Evaluating and thinking about previously encountered risks also help identify other risks that may be pertinent to this project but do not appear on the list.

Project managers can also use their judgment and experience to evaluate the situation to identify potential risks. Another alternative is to use the project management plan review and discussion meetings to elicit views on risks from others.

6.2.2 Risk Prioritization

The identified risks for a project merely give the possible events that can hinder it from meeting its goals. The consequences of various risks, however, may differ. Before you proceed with managing risks, you must prioritize them so that management energies can be focused on the highest risks.

Prioritization requires analyzing the possible effects of the risk event in case it actually occurs. That is, if the risk materializes, what will be the loss to the project? The loss could include a direct loss, a loss due to lost business opportunity or future business, a loss due to diminished employee morale, and so on. Based on the possible consequences and the probability of the risk event occurring, you can compute the risk exposure, which you can then use for prioritizing risks.

Table 6.1 Risk Categories

Probability	Range
Low	0.0–0.3
Medium	0.3–0.7
High	0.7–1.0

This approach requires a quantitative assessment of the risk probability and the risk consequences. Usually, little historical data are available to help you make a quantitative estimate of these parameters. Because risks are probabilistic events, they occur infrequently, and that makes it difficult to gather data about them. Furthermore, any such data must be interpreted properly because the act of managing the risks affects them. This fact implies that risk prioritization will be based more on experience than on hard data from the past. In this situation, categorizing both the probabilities and the consequences can serve to separate high-priority risk items from lower-priority items.[5] At Infosys, the probability of a risk occurring is categorized as low, medium, or high. Table 6.1 gives the probability range for each of these categories.

To rank the effects of a risk on a project, you must select a unit of impact. To simplify risk management, Infosys project managers rate the risk impact on a scale of 1 to 10. Within this scale, the risk effects can be rated as low, medium, high, or very high. Table 6.2 gives the range for the consequences for each of these ratings.

With these ratings and ranges for each rating in hand, the following simple method for risk prioritization can be specified:

1. For each risk, rate the probability of its happening as low, medium, or high. If necessary, assign probability values in the ranges given for each rating.

2. For each risk, assess its impact on the project as low, medium, high, or very high. If necessary, assign a weight on a scale of 1 to 10.

Table 6.2 Impact Categories

Level of Consequences	Range
Low	0.0–3.0
Medium	3.0–7.0
High	7.0–9.0
Very high	9.0–10.0

3. Rank the risks based on the probability and effects on the project; for example, a high-probability, high-impact item will have higher rank than a risk item with a medium probability and high impact. In case of conflict, use your judgment (or assign numbers to compute a numeric value of risk exposure).

4. Select the top few risk items for mitigation and tracking.

The main objective of risk management is to identify the top few risk items and then focus on them. For this purpose, using classification works well. Clearly, a risk that has a high probability of occurring and that has high consequences is a risk with high risk exposure and therefore one with a high priority for risk management.

When you work with classifications, a problem in prioritization can arise if the risk probability and risk effects ratings are either (high, medium) or (medium, high). In this case, it is not clear which risk should be ranked higher. An easy approach to handle this situation is to mitigate both the risks. If needed, you can differentiate between these types of risks by using actual numbers.

This approach for prioritizing risks helps focus attention on high risks, but it does not help you in making a cost-benefit analysis of risk mitigation options. That is, by stating the consequences in terms of a scale rather than in terms of money value, this method does not allow you to calculate the expected loss in financial terms. Hence, you cannot analyze whether a certain risk mitigation strategy, costing a certain amount, is worth employing. Such an analysis is generally not needed, however, because the focus of risk management is usually on managing risks at the lowest cost and not on whether risk management itself is beneficial. On the other hand, if you must make a decision about whether a risk should be managed or whether it is financially smarter to leave it unmanaged, you must understand the financial impact of the risk.

6.3 RISK CONTROL

Once a project manager has identified and prioritized the risks, the question becomes what to do about them. Knowing the risks is of value only if you can prepare a plan so that their consequences are minimal—that is the basic goal of risk management. You minimize the effects of risk in the second step of risk management: *risk control*. Essentially, this step involves planning the risk mitigation followed by executing the plan and monitoring the risks.

6.3.1 Risk Management Planning

Once risks are identified and prioritized, it becomes clear which risks a project manager should handle. To manage the risks, proper planning is essential. The main task is to identify the actions needed to minimize the risk consequences, generally called *risk mitigation steps*. As with risk identification, you refer to a list of commonly used risk mitigation steps for various risks and select a suitable risk mitigation step. The list used at Infosys appears in Table 6.3. This table is a starting point not only for identifying risks but also for selecting risk mitigation steps after the risks have been prioritized. As with identification, you are not restricted to the steps mentioned in Table 6.3. You can use the process database to identify the risks and the risk mitigation steps.

Most of the risks and mitigation steps in Table 6.3 are self-explanatory. As you can see, the top few risks are concerned with manpower and requirements. Many of the items here are similar to those in the top risk lists given in Boehm[3] and Hall.[5] Selecting a risk mitigation step is not just an intellectual exercise. The risk mitigation step must be executed (and monitored). To ensure that the needed actions are executed properly, you must incorporate them into the project schedule. In other words, you must update the project schedule—which lists the various activities and specifies when they will occur—to include the actions related to the chosen risk mitigation steps.

6.3.2 Risk Monitoring and Tracking

Risk prioritization and consequent planning are based on the risk perception at the time the risk analysis is performed. The first risk analysis takes place during project planning, and the initial risk management plan reflects the view of the situation at that time. Because risks are probabilistic events, frequently depending on external factors, the *threat* due to risks may change with time as factors change. Clearly, then, the *risk perception* may also change with time. Furthermore, the risk mitigation steps undertaken may affect the risk perception.

This dynamism implies that risks in a project should not be treated as static and must be reevaluated periodically. Hence, in addition to monitoring the progress of the planned risk mitigation steps, you must periodically revisit the risk perception for the entire project. The results of this review are reported in each milestone analysis report (see Chapter 11); you report the status of the risk mitigation steps along with the current risk perception and strategy. To prepare this report, you make a fresh risk analysis to determine whether the priorities have changed.

Table 6.3 Top Ten Risks and Their Risk Mitigation Steps

Sequence Number	Risk Category	Risk Mitigation Steps
1	Shortage of technically trained manpower	• Make estimates with a little allowance for initial learning time. • Maintain buffers of extra resources. • Define a project-specific training program. • Conduct cross-training sessions.
2	Too many requirement changes	• Obtain sign-off for the initial requirements specification from the client. • Convince the client that changes in requirements will affect the schedule. • Define a procedure to handle requirement changes. • Negotiate payment on actual effort.
3	Unclear requirements	• Use experience and logic to make some assumptions and keep the client informed; obtain sign-off. • Develop a prototype and have the requirements reviewed by the client.
4	Manpower attrition	• Ensure that multiple resources are assigned on key project areas. • Have team-building sessions. • Rotate jobs among team members. • Keep extra resources in the project as backup. • Maintain proper documentation of each individual's work. • Follow the configuration management process and guidelines strictly.
5	Externally driven decisions forced on the project	• Outline disadvantages with supporting facts and data and negotiate with the personnel responsible for forcing the decisions. • If inevitable, identify the actual risk and follow its mitigation plan.
6	Not meeting performance requirements	• Define the performance criteria clearly and have them reviewed by the client. • Define standards to be followed to meet the performance criteria. • Prepare the design to meet performance criteria and review it. • Simulate or prototype performance of critical transactions. • Test with a representative volume of data where possible. • Conduct stress tests where possible.

Table 6.3 Top Ten Risks and Their Risk Mitigation Steps (continued)

Sequence Number	Risk Category	Risk Mitigation Steps
7	Unrealistic schedules	• Negotiate for a better schedule. • Identify parallel tasks. • Have resources ready early. • Identify areas that can be automated. • If the critical path is not within the schedule, negotiate with the client. • Negotiate payment on actual effort.
8	Working on new technology (hardware and software)	• Consider a phased delivery. • Begin with the delivery of critical modules. • Include time in the schedule for a learning curve. • Provide training in the new technology. • Develop a proof-of-concept application.
9	Insufficient business knowledge	• Increase interaction with the client and ensure adequate knowledge transfer. • Organize domain knowledge training. • Simulate or prototype the business transaction for the client and get it approved.
10	Link failure or slow performance	• Set proper expectations with the client. • Plan ahead for the link load. • Plan for optimal link usage.

6.4 EXAMPLES

This section includes two risk management plans: one for the ACIC project and one from another project (here called XYZ). As you will see, the risk management plans tend to be small—usually a table that fits on a page. The activities mentioned in the mitigation plan become part of project activities and may even be explicitly scheduled.

6.4.1 The ACIC Project

The ACIC project manager chose to work with numbers for risk prioritization and analysis. As shown in Table 6.4, the top risk items have impact ratings that range from 8 to 3. The risk mitigation steps are also shown for each risk. For example, the second risk is working with the RUP methodology. That is, the project incurs a risk because the methodology is new to the project personnel. Furthermore, it

Table 6.4 Risk Management Plan for the ACIC Project

Sequence Number	Risks	Probability	Impact	Risk Exposure	Mitigation Plan
1	We will need support from the database architect and the customer's database administrator.	0.5	8	4	Plan carefully for the time required from each of these groups and give enough prior notice. Have an onsite coordinator work closely with these groups.
2	Because RUP is being used for the first time, the understanding of the team may not be complete.	0.9	3	2.7	Work closely with experts in the Infosys R&D lab. Keep the customer in the loop throughout the project and escalate for any schedule or effort deviations. Train the team on RUP methodology.
3	Personnel attrition: Team members might leave on short notice.	0.3	7	2.1	Assign tasks so that more than one person is aware of the units and use cases in the project.
4	Working with the customer's mainframe DB2 over the link: Link may not be as efficient as it is expected.	0.1	8	0.8	Do extra code reviews, desk checking, etc. to minimize the reliance on the link. Escalate as soon as the link goes down.

seems that other projects have not used RUP. One of the risk mitigation plans is the most obvious one: to plan for training in the RUP methodology. In addition, it is suggested that the people from the R&D labs be consulted because they have knowledge of RUP and related concepts, that the customer be kept in the loop continuously, and that any problems be escalated quickly.

Note that once these options are accepted as the risk mitigation steps, they influence the detailed schedule of the project; the schedule must include time for appropriate training and proof-of-concept building activities. This need will arise with many risk mitigation steps. Because they represent actions and because the detailed project schedule represents most of the actions to be taken in the project, the risk mitigation steps will frequently change the detailed project schedule, adding to the project's overall effort requirement.

6.4.2 The XYZ Project

This project used the rating system for its risk management. Table 6.5 shows the various ratings and the risk mitigation steps. This risk management plan is a part of the project management plan for the project and has been extracted from it.

The method for performing the risk analysis at a milestone is essentially the same as described earlier, except that more attention is given to the risks listed in the project plan (that is, greater emphasis is placed on the output of earlier risk analyses for the project). During this risk analysis, project managers may reprioritize risks. In the XYZ project, when an analysis was done at a milestone about three months after the initial risk management plan was made, the risk perception had changed somewhat. Table 6.6 gives some of the risks for which the exposure had changed.

Based on the experience in the project to date, the project manager decided that the consequences of change reconciliation were considerably less dire. This situation might have arisen because, for example, the reconciliation problems encountered had been less difficult than expected. Similarly, the perception of the risk of manpower attrition had increased—again, perhaps because of experience with team members and perhaps the fact that people were leaving in the middle of the project was now perceived as a greater problem than at the start of the project. Whenever risks are analyzed, the risk mitigation plans may also change, depending on the current realities of the project and the nature of risks. In this project, there was no change in the risk mitigation plans.

6.5 SUMMARY

A risk for a project is a condition whose occurrence is not certain but that can adversely affect the project. Risk management requires that risks be identified and prioritized and, for the top few risks, that actions be taken to minimize their impact. The cost of risk mitigation may seem wasted when the risks do not materialize, but they must be incurred to minimize the loss in case the risk materializes.

Table 6.5 Risk Management Plan for the XYZ Project

Sequence Number	Risk	Proba-bility	Conse-quences	Risk Exposure	Mitigation Plan
1	Failure to meet the high performance	High	High	High	• Indicate expected performance to clients through requirements prototypes. • Use tips from body of knowledge database to improve performance. • Make team aware of the requirements. • Update the review checklist to look for performance pitfalls. • Study and improve performance constantly. • Follow guidelines from earlier performance studies. • Test application for meeting performance expectations during integration and system testing.
2	Lack of availability of persons with the right skills	Medium	Medium	Medium	• Train resources. • Review prototype with customer. • Develop coding practices.
3	Complexity of application requirements	Medium	Medium	Medium	• Ensure ongoing knowledge transfer. • Deploy persons with prior experience with the application.
4	Manpower attrition	Medium	Medium	Medium	• Train a core group of four people. • Rotate onsite assignments among people. • Identify backups for key roles.
5	Unclear requirements	Medium	Medium	Medium	• Review a prototype. • Conduct a midstage review.

Table 6.5 Risk Management Plan for the XYZ Project (continued)

Sequence Number	Risk	Proba-bility	Conse-quences	Risk Exposure	Mitigation Plan
6	Difficulty of reconciliation configuration of changes done in onsite maintenance during off-shore development	Medium	Low	Medium	• Create a management plan and adhere to well-defined reconciliation approach. • Reconcile once per month (first Tuesday or next working day). • Do not reconcile changes done after a cut-off date.

Table 6.6 Risk Evolution in the XYZ Project

Sequence Number	Risk	Current Probability	Current Consequences	Current Risk Exposure
2	Manpower attrition	High	High	High
3	Difficulty of reconciliation of changes created in onsite maintenance during off-shore development	Low	Low/medium	Low

Following are some of the key lessons from the Infosys approach to risk management:

- To help you identify risks, a list of commonly occurring risks is a good starting point. In addition, look ahead and try to visualize everything that can go wrong in the project.
- For risk prioritization, a simple and effective mechanism is to classify the probabilities of risks and their impacts into categories such as low, medium, and high, and then manage the risks that have high probabilities and impact.
- For the top few risks, plan the risk mitigation steps, and ensure that they are properly executed during the project.
- Monitor and reevaluate the risks periodically, perhaps at milestones, to see whether the risk mitigation steps are having an effect and to revisit risk perception.

With respect to the CMM, the Project Planning KPA of level 2 requires that a project have a risk management plan. Proper processes for risk management and monitoring are a requirement for the Integrated Software Management KPA at CMM level 3.

6.6 REFERENCES

1. R.N. Charette. Large-scale project management is risk management. *IEEE Software,* July 1996.

2. N. Brown. Industrial-strength management strategies. *IEEE Software,* July 1996.

3. B. Boehm. *Tutorial: Software Risk Management. IEEE Computer Society,* 1989.

4. R. Charette. *Software Engineering Risk Analysis and Management.* McGraw Hill, 1989.

5. E.M. Hall. *Managing Risk: Methods for Software Systems Development.* Addison-Wesley, 1998.

6. B. Boehm. A spiral model of software development and enhancement. *IEEE Computer,* May 1988.

7. M. Carr et al. *Taxonomy-based Risk Identification.* Technical Report, CMU/ SEI-93-TR-006, 1993.

Chapter 7

Measurement and Tracking Planning

A project management plan is merely a document that can be used to guide the execution of a project. Unless the actual performance of the execution is tracked against the plan, the plan has limited value. And for project tracking, the value of certain key parameters must be measured during the project. Tracking is a difficult task, and, as with other tasks, if you want to perform it properly you must plan for it. During planning, you must decide on issues such as how the tasks, the effort, and the defects will be tracked, what tools will be used, what reporting structure and frequency will be followed, and so on.

This chapter discusses how measurements are made in projects at Infosys. It also describes project tracking planning and the selection of thresholds for performance variation, which are used to trigger management actions. Actual project tracking is discussed in Chapters 10 and 11.

7.1 CONCEPTS IN MEASUREMENT

The basic purpose of measurements in a project is to effectively control the project. This section discusses some concepts related to metrics and measurement and the basic metrics that you should measure for controlling a project. One approach for process control is statistical process control. This section also discusses some concepts relating to SPC and the way SPC can be used for software.

7.1.1 Metrics and Measurements

Software metrics can be used to quantitatively characterize various aspects of the software process or software products. *Process metrics* quantify attributes of the software process or the development environment, whereas *product metrics* are measures for the software products.[1,2] Product metrics remain independent of the process used to produce the product. Examples of process metrics include productivity, quality, resource metrics, defect injection rate, and defect removal efficiency. Examples of product metrics include size, reliability, quality (quality can be viewed as a product metric as well as a process metric), complexity of the code, and functionality.

The use of metrics necessarily requires that measurements be made to obtain data. For any metrics program, you must clearly understand the goals for collecting data as well as the models that are used for making judgments based on the data. In general, which metrics to use and which measurements to take will depend on the project and organization goals; you can use a framework, such as the goal-question-metric paradigm, to determine the metrics that need to be measured.[3,4] In practice, however, a few metrics suffice for most situations, and special metrics are needed only for special situations. Schedule, size, effort, and defects are the basic measurements for projects and form a stable metrics set.[5,6]

Schedule is one of the most important metrics because most projects are driven by schedules and deadlines. It is, however, the easiest to measure because calendar time is usually used. Effort is the main resource consumed in a software project. Consequently, tracking of effort is a key activity during monitoring; it is essential for evaluating whether the project is executing within budget. That is, this data is needed to make statements such as "The cost of the project is likely to be about 30% more than projected earlier" or "The project is likely to finish within budget."

Because defects have a direct relationship to software quality, tracking of defects is critical for ensuring quality. A large software project may include thousands of defects that are found by different people at different stages. Often the person who fixes a defect is not the same person who finds or reports it. Generally, a project manager will want to remove most or all of the defects found before the final delivery of the software. In such a scenario, defect reporting and closure cannot be done informally. The use of informal mechanisms may lead to defects being found but later forgotten, so defects end up not being removed or extra effort must be spent in finding the defect again. Hence, at the very least, defects must be logged and their closure tracked. For this procedure, you need information, such as the manifestation of the defect, its location, and the names of the person who found it and the person who closed it. Once each defect found is logged (and later closed), analysis can focus on how many defects have been found so far, what percentage of defects are still open, and other issues. Defect tracking is considered one of the best practices for managing a project.[7]

Merely logging defects and tracking them is not sufficient to support other desirable analyses. To understand what percentage of defects are caught where, you also need to record information about the phases at which defects are detected. To understand the defect removal efficiency of various quality control tasks and thereby improve their performance, you must know not only where a defect is detected but also where it was injected. In other words, for each defect logged, you should also provide information about the phase in which the defect was introduced.

Size is another fundamental metric because many data (for example, delivered defect density) are normalized with respect to size. Without size data, you cannot predict performance using past data. Also, without normalization with respect to a standard measure of size, you cannot benchmark performance for comparison purposes. The two common measures for size are lines of code (LOC) and function points. If you use lines of code as a measure, productivity differs with the programming language. Function points provide uniformity.

7.1.2 Process Monitoring through Statistical Process Control

Statistical process control has been used with great success in manufacturing, and its use in software is also increasing.[8] Here we briefly discuss some general concepts of SPC; for more information, you can consult any textbook on statistical quality control.[9,10] In Chapters 10 and 11 you will see how SPC concepts are used for project monitoring.

A *process* is used to produce output, and the quality of the output can be defined in terms of certain quality *characteristics.* A number of factors affect the variability in the value of these characteristics. These factors can be classified into two categories: natural (or inherent) causes of variability, and assignable (or special) causes. Natural causes are those that are always present and each of which contributes to the variability. It's not practical to control these causes unless the process itself is changed. Assignable causes, on the other hand, are those that occur once in a while, have a larger influence over variability in the process performance, and can be controlled. Figure 7.1 illustrates the relationship between causes and quality characteristics.

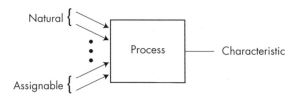

Figure 7.1 Assignable and natural causes

A process is said to be under *statistical control* if the variability in the quality characteristics is due to natural causes only. The goal of SPC is to keep the production process in statistical control.

Control charts are a favorite tool for applying SPC. To build a control chart, the output of a process is considered to be a stream of numeric values representing the values of the characteristic of interest. Subgroups of data are taken from this stream, and the mean values for the subgroups are plotted, giving an X-bar chart. A *lower control limit* (LCL) and an *upper control limit* (UCL) are established. If a point falls outside the control limits, the large variability is considered to be due to assignable causes. Another chart, called an R-chart, plots the range (the difference between the minimum and maximum values) of the chosen subgroups. Control limits are established for the R-chart, and a point falling outside these control limits is also considered as having assignable causes.

By convention, LCL and UCL are frequently set at 3-sigma around the mean, where sigma is the standard deviation for data with only normal variability (that is, variability due to natural causes). With these limits, the probability of a *false alarm*—in which a point with natural variability falls outside the limits—is only 0.27%.

When the production process does not yield the same item repeatedly, as is the case with software processes, forming subgroups may not make sense; individual values are therefore considered. For such processes, XMR charts[9,10] can be used. In an XMR chart, a moving range of two consecutive values is considered as the range for the R-chart. For the X-bar chart, the individual values are plotted; the control limits are then determined using the average moving range.

Note that control limits are different from specification limits. *Specification limits* specify, based on the requirements, the performance that is desired from the process. Control limits, on the other hand, based on actual data from the process, determine the actual performance capability of the process—that is, what the process actually is capable of delivering. Clearly, if the control limits are within the specification limits (the specification limits are wider than the control limits), the process is capable of delivering output that will meet the specifications most of the time. On the other hand, if the specification limit is within the control limits, the probability of the process producing an outcome that does not satisfy the requirements increases. Based on the relationship between the specification limit and the control limit, the capability of a process can be defined formally.[9,10]

You use the control charts to continuously monitor the performance of the process and identify an out-of-control situation. Separately, you decide what action will be taken when a point representing an output falls outside the control limit. Generally, two types of actions are performed:

- Rework the output so that it has acceptable characteristics—that is, take corrective action.
- Conduct further analysis to identify the assignable causes and eliminate them from the process—that is, take preventive actions.

To employ control charts for software processes, you must first identify the processes to which SPC can be applied. One choice is the overall process, whose output is the software product to be delivered. The characteristics that can be studied for the output of this process include productivity, delivered defect density, and defect injection rate, among others. You can obtain the values of most of these characteristics for the output of the overall process only after the project ends, so SPC for the overall process has limited value for project monitoring and control. Its value lies primarily in understanding and improving the capability of the process.

To control a project, you can deploy SPC for "mini-processes" that are executed during the course of the project, such as the review process or testing process. Under SPC, as soon as the process is executed, its results can be analyzed. If required, you can then apply control in the form of corrective or preventive actions. Through corrective actions, the out-of-limit output is made acceptable; preventive actions help to improve execution of the remainder of the project. Chapters 10 and 11 discuss the use of SPC for monitoring projects.

Given the possibility of a large variation in performance in software processes, it is not an easy task to identify points having only natural variability so that you can determine the control limits. Hence, to compute the control limits from past performance data, you must use your judgment to determine which data points should be excluded. Furthermore, past data should not be used blindly, and discerning management must always support its use. For example, you cannot assume that a process has failed just because the performance is out of the range computed from past data.[2,11] A more suitable approach is to use the performance range to draw attention to a deviation and then analyze the reasons for the deviation.

7.2 MEASUREMENTS

Any quantitative control of a project depends critically on the measurements made during the project. To perform measurements during project execution, you must plan carefully regarding what to measure, when to measure, and how to measure. Hence, measurement planning is a key element in project planning. This section discusses the way standard measurements are done in projects at Infosys. Project managers may add to these measurements if their projects require it.

7.2.1 Collecting Effort Data

To help a project manager monitor the effort, each employee records in a *weekly activity report* (WAR) system the effort spent on various tasks. This online system, developed in-house, stores all submitted WARs in a centralized database. Each person submits his WAR each week. On submission, the report goes to the individual's supervisor for approval. Once it is approved, the WAR submission is final and cannot be changed. Everyone submits a WAR, including the CEO, and if a WAR is not submitted within a given time period, leave is deducted.

A WAR entry consists of a sequence of records, one for each week. Each record is a list of items, with each item containing the following fields:

- Program code
- Module code
- Activity code
- Activity description
- Hours for Monday through Sunday

The *activity code* characterizes the type of activity. The *program code* and *module code* permit separation of effort data with respect to modules or programs, a consideration that is important for component-level monitoring. To support analysis and project comparisons, it is important to standardize the activities against which effort is reported. Having a standardized set of activity codes helps to achieve this goal. Table 7.1 shows the activity codes used in Infosys projects. (These are different from the ones given in my earlier book because the codes were changed with the introduction with a new Web-based WAR system.)

In the activity codes, a separate code for rework effort is provided for many phases. This classification helps in computing the cost of quality. With this level of refinement, you can carry out a phase-wise analysis or a subphase-wise analysis of the effort data. The program code and module code, which are specified by the project, can be used to record effort data for different units in the project, thereby facilitating unit-wise analysis.

To facilitate project-level analysis of planned versus actual effort spent, the WAR system is connected to the Microsoft Project (MSP) depiction of the project. Project staff can begin submitting WARs for a project only after the MSP for the project has been submitted (once the MSP is submitted, the system knows which people are supposed to be working on the project). Planned activities are defined as those listed in the MSP and assigned to an authorized person in the project. Unplanned activities are all other project activities.

When entering the WAR for a week, the user works with a screen that is divided into two sections: planned activities and unplanned activities. All activities that are assigned in the MSP to a particular person for this week show up in her planned activities section for that project. The user cannot add or modify activities that show up in this section. She can enter only the hours spent each day for the different activities provided. To log the time spent on activities not listed in the planned section, the user can enter a code, its description, and the hours spent each day on these activities in the unplanned section for the project.

7.2.2 Logging and Tracking Defects

In an Infosys project, defect detection and removal proceed as follows. A defect is found and recorded by a submitter. The defect is then in the state "submitted." Next, the project manager assigns the job of fixing the defect to someone, usually the author of the document or code in which the defect was found. This person does the debugging and fixes the reported defect, and the defect then enters the "fixed" state. A defect that is fixed is still not closed. Another person, typically the submitter, verifies that the defect has been fixed. After this verification, the defect can be marked "closed." In other words, the general life cycle of a defect has three states: submitted, fixed, and closed (see Figure 7.2). A defect that is not closed is also called open.

Table 7.1 Activity Codes for Effort

Activity Code	Description
PAC	Acceptance
PACRW	Rework after acceptance testing
PCAL	Project catch-all
PCD	Coding and self unit testing
PCDRV	Code walkthrough/review
PCDRW	Rework after code walkthrough
PCM	Configuration management
PCOMM	Communication
PCSPT	Customer support activities
PDBA	Database administration activities
PDD	Detailed design
PDDRV	Detailed design review
PDDR	Rework after detailed design review
PDOC	Documentation
PERV	Review of models and drawings
PERW	Rework of models and drawings
PEXEC	Execution of modeling and drafting
PHD	High-level design
PHDRV	High-level design reviews
PHDRW	Rework after high-level design review
PIA	Impact analysis
PINS	Installation/customer training
PIT	Integration testing
PITRW	Rework after integration testing
PPI	Project initiation
PPMCL	Project closure activities
PPMPT	Project planning and tracking
PRES	Research on technical problems
PRS	Requirement specification activities
PRSRV	Review of requirements specifications

Table 7.1 Activity Codes for Effort (continued)

Activity Code	Description
PRSRW	Rework after requirements review
PSP	Strategic planning activities
PST	System testing
PSTRW	Rework after system testing
PTRE	Project-specific trainee activities
PUT	Independent unit testing
PUTRW	Rework after independent unit testing
PWTR	Waiting for resources
PWY	Effort during warranty

A defect control system (DCS) is used in projects for logging and tracking defects. The system permits various types of analysis. Table 7.2 shows the information that is recorded for each defect logged in to the system.

To determine the defect injection stage requires analysis of the defect. Whereas defect detection stages consist of the review and testing activities, defect injection stages include the stages that produce work products, such as design and coding. Based on the nature of the defect, some judgments can be made about when it might have been introduced. Unlike the defect detection stage, which is known with certainty, the defect injection stage is more ambiguous; it is estimated from the nature of the defect and other related information. Using stage injected and stage detected information, you can compute the defect removal efficiencies, percentage distributions, and other metrics.

Sometimes it is desirable to understand the nature of defects without reference to stages, but rather in terms of the defect category. Such a classification can help you to understand the distribution of defects across categories. For this reason, the type

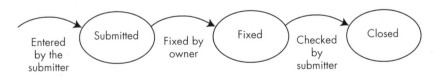

*Figure 7.2 **Life cycle of a defect***

Table 7.2 Recording Defect Data

Data	Description	Mandatory/ Optional
Project code	Code of the project for which defects are captured	M
Description	Description of the defect	M
Module code	Module code	O
Program name	Name of program in which the defect was found	O
Stage detected	Stage in which the defect was detected	M
Stage injected	Stage at which the defect was injected/origin of defect	M
Type	Classification of the defect	M
Severity	Severity of the defect	M
Review type	Type of review	O
Status	Current status of the defect	M
Submitter	Name of the person who detected the defect	M
Owner	Name of the person who owns the defect	M
Submit date	Date on which the defect was submitted to the owner	M
Close date	Date on which the submitted defect was closed	M

of defect is also recorded. Table 7.3 shows the types of defects possible, along with some examples. A project can also define its own type classification.

Finally, the severity of the defect is recorded. This information is important for the project manager. For example, if a defect is severe, you will likely schedule it so that it gets fixed soon. Also, you might decide that minor or unimportant defects need not be fixed for an urgent delivery. Table 7.4 shows the classification used at Infosys.

From this information, various analyses are possible. For example, you can break down the defects with respect to type, severity, or module; plot trends of open and closed defects with respect to modules, severity, or total defects; determine the weekly defect injection rate; determine defect removal efficiency; determine defect injection rates in different phases, and so on. In Chapter 11 you will see some uses of this data for monitoring the quality dimension and for preventing defects. That chapter also describes an example of the defect data entered in the case study.

Table 7.3 Defect Types

Defect Type	Example
Logic	Insufficient/incorrect errors in algorithms used; wrong conditions, test cases, or design documents
Standards	Problems with coding/documentation standards such as indentation, alignment, layout, modularity, comments, hard-coding, and misspelling
Redundant code	Same piece of code used in many programs or in the same program
User interface	Specified function keys not working; improper menu navigation
Performance	Poor processing speed; system crash because of file size; memory problems
Reusability	Inability to reuse the code
Design issue	Specific design-related matters
Memory management defects	Defects such as core dump, array overflow, illegal function call, system hangs, or memory overflow
Document defects	Defects found while reviewing documents such as the project plan, configuration management plan, or specifications
Consistency	Failure to updating or delete records in the same order throughout the system
Traceability	Lack of traceability of program source to specifications
Portability	Code not independent of the platform

Table 7.4 Defect Severity

Severity Type	Explanation for Categorization
Critical	Defect may be very critical in terms of affecting the schedule, or it may be a *showstopper*—that is, it stops the user from using the system further.
Major	The same type of defect has occurred in many programs or modules. We need to correct everything. For example, coding standards are not followed in any program. Alternatively, the defect stops the user from proceeding in the normal way but a workaround exists.
Minor	This defect is isolated or does not stop the user from proceeding, but it causes inconvenience.
Cosmetic	A defect that in no way affects the performance of the software product—for example, esthetic issues and grammatical errors in messages.

7.2.3 Measuring Schedule

Measuring schedule is straightforward because you use calendar time. The detailed activities and the schedule are usually captured in the MSP schedule, so the estimated dates and duration of tasks are given in the MSP. Knowing the actual dates, you can easily determine the actual duration of a task.

7.2.4 Measuring Size

If the bottom-up estimation technique is used, size is estimated in terms of the number of programs of different complexities. Although this metric is useful for estimation, it does not permit a standard definition of productivity that can be meaningfully compared across projects. The same problem arises if lines of code (LOC) are used as a size measure; productivity differs with the programming language. To normalize and employ a uniform size measure for the purposes of creating a baseline and comparing performance, function points are used as the size measure.

The size of delivered software is usually measured in terms of LOC through the use of regular editors and line counters. This count is made when the project is completed and ready for delivery. From the size measure in LOC, as discussed before, size in function points is computed using published conversion tables.[12]

7.3 PROJECT TRACKING

The main goal of tracking is for project managers to get visibility into the project execution so that they can determine whether any action needs to be taken to ensure that the project goals are met. Because meeting the established project goals is the basic motive, all aspects of project execution that can affect the attainment of the goals must be monitored, and this monitoring must be planned. At Infosys, project managers typically plan for the following tracking:

- Activities tracking
- Defect tracking
- Issues tracking

Activities tracking looks at which planned activities have been completed. If the granularity of an activity is small, then at the lowest level you consider it to be in one of two states: not done or fully done. For higher-level tasks, you can compute the percentage completed from the state of the lowest-level tasks and their estimates.

Defect tracking is done in connection with defect logging, as discussed earlier.

Issues tracking ensures that clarifications and other problems that have the potential to delay the project do not go out of control. Chapter 11 explains how these tracking activities are performed at Infosys. During planning, project managers specify what type of tracking they plan to do and what tools or methods they will use.

In addition, to keep track of the project's status along the effort, schedule, and quality dimensions, project managers also plan for the following:

- Activity-level monitoring
- Status reports
- Milestone reports

Activity-level monitoring ensures that each activity has been done properly. You monitor activities quantitatively through the use of statistical process control. Based on past performance, you establish limits for key performance parameters of certain tasks. Then you compare actual performance of an activity to the established limits. If the performance is not within acceptable limits, you might take certain actions. At Infosys, reviews and unit testing, discussed in Chapters 10 and 11, are the two main activities that employ this approach.

Status reports are usually prepared weekly to help you to take stock of what has happened and what needs to be done. At project milestones, you conduct a more elaborate exercise to quantitatively check the actual versus estimated data along the effort, schedule, and defect dimensions. In addition, you monitor risks, training, reviews, customer complaints, and so on. The milestone analysis plays an important role in controlling the project. To ensure that the milestone analysis is done often enough to allow timely intervention, if the milestones required by the customer are too far apart, you plan internal milestones so that a milestone analysis is done every three to five weeks.

At milestones, you analyze actual versus estimated for effort, schedule, and defects. If the deviation is significant, some corrective action is called for. To differentiate the normal from the significant, you specify the acceptable deviation limits; to set these limits, you employ concepts of control charts. Control limits have been defined at Infosys for effort and schedule deviation (between the actual and estimated). These values, originally based on judgment and experience, are now based on past data and are computed in the same manner as other control limits. The earlier limits

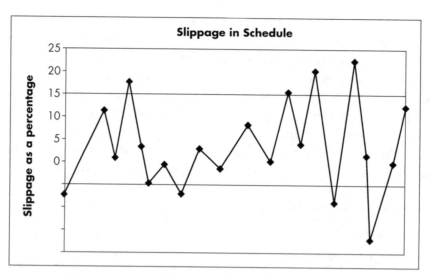

Figure 7.3 Control chart for schedule deviation

were 35% for effort deviation and 15% for schedule; with improvements in the process, these limits have been reduced to 20% and 10%, respectively. Figures 7.3 and 7.4 give the control charts showing the deviation in schedule and effort.

If the deviation at the milestone exceeds these limits, it may imply that the project may run into trouble and might not meet its objectives; under time pres-

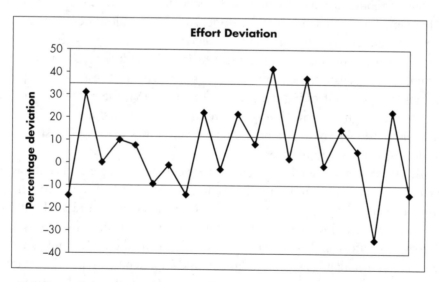

Figure 7.4 Control chart for effort deviation

sure, the project team might therefore start taking undesirable shortcuts. This situation calls for project managers to understand the reasons for the variation and to apply corrective and preventive actions if necessary.

These limits are based on past data and experience. You must set your project's own limits, which may be higher than the organization's limits, during planning.

7.4 THE ACIC MEASUREMENT AND TRACKING PLAN

In the ACIC project the standard metrics of size, effort, defect, and schedule were measured. The plan was to use line counters for size, the WAR system for effort, a defect control system called BugsBunny for defects, and MSP for schedule.

The project manager planned to use MSP for activity tracking and to have regular meetings to monitor the status of the various activities. The issues were classified into onsite, customer, business manager, and support services and tracked separately. Customer feedback—complaints as well as compliments—was logged.

Status reports were sent weekly to the business manager as well as the customer. The deviation limits for the first five milestones were set to 10% for effort and schedule and 20% for defects. For the rest of the milestones, the limits were set to 5% for effort and schedule and 20% for defects. Milestone reports were also sent to the business manager and the customer.

The final outcome of tracking and measurement planning is included in the project management plan of the ACIC project, given in Chapter 8.

7.5 SUMMARY

During project planning, you must decide how you plan to monitor the progress of the project. Progress monitoring is essential to ensure that the project is progressing toward the goals and to allow you to take corrective actions if the situation warrants. Project monitoring usually requires measurements.

Following are some of the lessons from the measurement and tracking planning at Infosys:

- Plan to measure size, schedule, effort, and defects. These suffice for most software projects.

- Classify effort in a few categories, and collect effort data using an automated system with activity codes for each category. To avoid inaccuracies due to poor memory recall, log effort data frequently.

- Log defects and track them to closure. For a defect, also record its type, detection stage, injection stage, and severity to support analyses such as defect removal efficiency, delivered quality, and defect injection rate.

- For performance analysis at milestones, establish acceptable limits for performance variation from planned for effort, schedule, and defects. During project execution, if the performance goes beyond these limits, management intervention may be warranted.

Although project tracking and measurement are required by the Software Project Tracking and Oversight KPA at level 2, by the Integrated Project Management KPA at level 3, and both the KPAs at level 4, the CMM does not explicitly state the need for planning for these measurements. Given that there is a general underlying principle in the CMM that major activities to be performed must be planned, planning for measurement is implied by these KPAs.

7.6 REFERENCES

1. S.D. Conte, H.E. Dunsmore, and V.Y. Shen. *Software Engineering Metrics and Models.* Benjamin/Cummings, 1986.

2. S.H. Kan. *Metrics and Models in Software Quality Engineering.* Addison-Wesley, 1995.

3. V.R. Basili and D.M. Weiss. A methodology for collecting valid software engineering data. *IEEE Transactions on Software Engineering,* 10(6), 1984.

4. V.R. Basili, G. Caldiera, and H.D. Rombach. Goal question metric paradigm. In *Encyclopedia of Software Engineering, John J. Marciniak, editor.* John Wiley and Sons, 1994.

5. R. Grady and D. Caswell. *Software Metrics: Establishing a Company-wide Program.* Prentice Hall, 1987.

6. Carnegie Mellon University/Software Engineering Institute. *The Capability Maturity Model: Guidelines for Improving the Software Process.* Addison-Wesley, 1995.

7. N. Brown. Industrial-strength management strategies. *IEEE Software,* July 1996.

8. W.A. Florac and A.D. Carleton. *Measuring the Software Process: Statistical Process Control for Software Process Improvement.* Addison-Wesley, 1999.

9. D.C. Montgomery. *Introduction to Statistical Quality Control, third edition.* John Wiley and Sons, 1996.

10. D.J. Wheeler and D.S. Chambers. *Understanding Statistical Process Control, second edition.* SPS Press, 1992.

11. W. Humphrey. *Managing the Software Process.* Addison-Wesley, 1989.

12. C. Jones. *Applied Software Measurement: Assuring Productivity and Quality, second edition.* McGraw Hill, 1996.

Chapter 8

The Project Management Plan

The project management plan (PMP) document is the culmination of all planning activities undertaken by project managers. The outputs of the various planning activities appear in this document, which becomes the baseline document guiding the overall execution of the project. It should not be confused with the detailed project schedule, which represents only the schedule and assignment of activities.

Documenting the planning outputs enables the project plan to be reviewed for deficiencies. At Infosys, project plans are usually reviewed by a group that includes project managers, members of the SEPG, and senior management. In many instances, a project plan review has revealed glaring shortcomings that, if not corrected, could have spelled trouble for the project. A thorough review of the management plan is one of the best ways to nip potential problems in the bud—a huge value to project managers, particularly those who are less experienced.

The document also serves an important communication purpose. It gives senior management an overall view of the project goals and commitments and describes how the project will be managed to meet them. It gives the project team a comprehensive view of the project and the roles of the individual team members.

Although we have discussed most of the planning activities, so far we have not discussed the team and communication issues, which are covered in this chapter. Here, we also discuss the structure of the template used at Infosys to document the plan and examine the project management plan of the ACIC project.

8.1 TEAM MANAGEMENT

Software development is a team effort. High quality and productivity result when the team members contribute effectively and remain motivated, and the overall team functions smoothly and efficiently. Team management goes beyond engineering and project management issues into the domain of people issues. It is an important aspect of the project, and ignoring it can spell trouble for the project and the project manager.

8.1.1 Team Structure

At Infosys, a hierarchical team structure is usually employed; a team is headed by a project manager, who reports to the business manager or the account manager (or both). In addition, a typical team consists of developers (DVs), the configuration controller (CC), and the database administrator; all these members report to the project manager. A large project may also have module leaders, each of whom reports to the project manager and has some developers under him. Also, a defect prevention team is formed from the existing team members; this team is responsible for performing the tasks related to defect prevention.

As discussed earlier, an SEPG member known as the software quality adviser (SQA) is also associated with each project. The SQA interacts extensively with the project manager (and with the configuration controller) but does not report to the project manager. Instead, the SQA has an independent reporting channel.

The assignment of roles is a complex task. The project manager's objective is to get a balanced, self-reliant team that helps to further the careers and skill development of the team members. Hence, in determining the team structure, the project manager must factor in the personal and growth needs of the team members as well as the project needs. Following are some of the people factors that a project manager takes into account:

- Skills, background, and experience of the team members
- Personal aspirations and career paths of the members
- Mentoring and people development needs

The initial team structure is documented in the PMP along with the roles and responsibilities of each team member. A team member may have multiple responsibilities. During the course of the project, particularly a long project, the team organization may be changed based on the performance of people in the different roles, personal aspirations, motivation levels, and so on.

8.1.2 Communication

A team that will work together for a few months toward a common goal must jell well and must have good intrateam communication. The team communication can be broadly divided into two categories: communication relating to the project and de-stressing communication. A good people-oriented project manager plans for both.

One way to keep the team members informed about the progress and problems in the project is to give them access to the project status reports and associated customer and business manager comments. In addition to these formal reports, depending on the size of the team and the project duration, Infosys project managers use any of the following methods to enhance team communication:

- Project-specific bulletin boards for announcements, notices, status reports, and so on
- Project mailing list
- Project Web site for publishing documents, home pages of team members, relevant technical articles and notes, and training material for self-learning
- Project meetings for briefings and issue resolution
- Best practice sessions and presentations by team members on their work

Moreover, because deadlines are usually short and everyone is under time pressure, stress tends to build up. Communication aimed at de-stressing is extremely important to ensure continued motivation. Many project managers plan events that enable this "fun" communication. Here are examples of the methods used:

- Project parties (supported by a budget from the organization for all teams)
- Birthday parties
- Events such as quizzes and games with prizes
- Informal, free-wheeling "crib" sessions

8.1.3 Team Development

Project teams often include many junior people. It is the responsibility of the team and the project manager to enhance the personal development of these team members. Helping the growth of individual team members also benefits the project and the organization. As the skills and abilities of the team members improve, they become more productive later in the project and can take on more responsibility. And, of course, they become better equipped to handle their tasks in future projects. Toward this end, project managers use methods such as these:

- Job rotation
- Mentoring of junior members by more experienced team members
- Reviews, appraisals, and feedback
- Regular recognition of contribution at the project level
- Coaching, training, and the like to help people having trouble

8.2 CUSTOMER COMMUNICATION AND ISSUE RESOLUTION

Team communication is geared toward keeping the team informed and motivated. But what about the customer, who is the sponsor of the project and hence a major stakeholder? Many problems are the result of misunderstandings between the customer and the developers. Regular communication between the development team and the customer can help avoid these kinds of problems.

Status reports (discussed in Chapter 11), one such means of communication, are designed to give the customer a clear idea of the state of the project on an ongoing basis. However, these reports, no matter how elaborate, are not enough. Project managers should plan other means of communication, including weekly teleconferencing or videoconferencing and regular e-mails. In a weekly virtual meeting, the project leader walks through the status report with the customer and explains the project constraints. A key point of discussion is resolution of pending issues. The customer, on the other hand, seeks clarifications and explains her perspective in these meetings. Overall, through regular communication that goes beyond sending reports, both the customer and the development team remain in sync. This prevents many potential problems rooted in misunderstandings.

Despite the use of regular communication channels, issues crop up that the representatives at the two ends cannot resolve. Such issues can potentially delay the project and must be escalated. To facilitate resolution of such issues, a project plan specifies the escalation channels at both the customer end and at the Infosys end. The plan also clearly states the policies regarding when these channels are to be deployed. In addition to providing a mechanism for issue resolution, the specification of this escalation channel and policies creates pressure on the two parties to resolve issues quickly and when necessary to take them to the higher-ups.

8.3 THE STRUCTURE OF THE PROJECT MANAGEMENT PLAN

The project management plan template provided at Infosys has four major sections. The *project summary* section gives a high-level overview of the project. It includes information on the start and end dates, the project leader, contacts at the customer end, project objectives, major commitments made to the customer on milestones and deliverables, and assumptions made. The assumptions made are explicitly listed because they frequently serve as a source of risks. Details of billing may also be described (so that the business manager can track them). The objectives of the project—from the customer's perspective as well as from Infosys's perspective—are mentioned so that it is clear to everyone why the project is being executed.

The *project planning* section lists the outputs of executing the various project planning procedures. It includes the development process being used, tailoring notes, the requirement change management process, requirement traceability plans, effort and schedule estimates along with their basis, and the people requirement by skill, role, monthwise, or a combination of these. It also specifies the development environment needed, the tools employed, and any project-specific training plans. The quality plan and the risk management plan are also given in this section.

The *project tracking* section defines the measurements to be taken and the systems to be used for recording data, various project tracking activities to be undertaken, the frequency and nature of the progress reporting, and escalation procedures.

The *project team* section defines the project team and its structure, as well as the roles and responsibilities of the various people.

8.4 THE ACIC PROJECT PLAN

This section presents the project plan for our case study, the ACIC project. The first section of the PMP gives the main players, milestones, and an overview of the project. (Chapter 4 explains how the schedule and milestones were determined.)

Section 2 contains details about planning. First, it lists the output of process planning. The plan states that the "development process" will be used and gives the tailoring that has been done for the project. In this project the Rational Rose Unified Process (RUP) will be used because it is a commitment to the customer. In RUP, the main phases are inception, elaboration, construction, and transition. Elaboration and construction are usually done in iterations. In the elaboration phase, analysis and design are the primary tasks, whereas in the construction phase, coding and unit testing are the primary activities. The project will employ two elaboration iterations and three construction iterations. To accommodate this approach requires that the standard development process of Infosys be tailored. The tailoring notes specify the tailoring done to the standard process.

For requirements change management, the plan specifies where the change requests will be logged and the process of handling them. It also specifies that if any change request takes more than 2% of the total effort, it will be reestimated. For requirements traceability, it states that a tool will be used.

The subsection on effort estimation gives the effort estimates and the basis for estimation. (Chapter 4 discusses the estimation of the ACIC project.) Along with the effort estimate, it specifies the project schedule (which is the same as the milestones committed to the customer) and the people it needs to meet the schedule commitments. The people requirement is also specified by skill. The training plan for the team is also given, along with the criteria that will be used for someone to waive the training.

The subsection on the quality plan gives the quality goals and intermediate goals for defects. (Chapter 5 discusses the development of this plan.) Because the project has set higher goals for itself, the strategy for meeting those goals is also given, along with the reviews that the project aims to do.

The planning section also specifies the hardware and software resources that are needed and the risk management plan (discussed in Chapter 6).

The project tracking section (section 3) mentions that Microsoft Project (MSP) will be used for task scheduling, assignment, and status monitoring. Bugs-Bunny, a tool developed in-house, will be used to track issues local to the project. The project manager is responsible for reviewing and ensuring resolution of these problems, except for the issues relating to the business manager. BugsBunny will also be used for tracking customer complaints and feedback. Status reports will be sent every two weeks, and the customer will receive a report at each milestone. Detailed analysis is planned at milestones. Escalation channels at both ends are established.

Section 4 specifies the team structure. The team is headed by the project leader (PL) (referred to elsewhere in this book as the project manager), who manages a defect prevention (DP) team, a module leader, and the configuration controller. The DP team is responsible for analyzing the defects and proposing solutions to prevent them. (Chapter 5 discusses DP planning, and Chapter 11 explains the execution of the DP activities. The role of the CC is discussed further in Chapter 9.) The team structure specifies that a software quality adviser is associated with the team but does not report to the PL. The plan also specifies the roles and responsibilities of each person on the team.

Project Management Plan for the ACIC Project

1. PROJECT SUMMARY

1.1 Project Overview

ACIC is a U.S.-based investment firm. This application has two components: first, a Brokerage Account Opening application on ACIC's Web site that will allow any Internet user to open a brokerage account with ACIC; second, an account opening and maintenance application, which is primarily for ACIC's representatives to open accounts for the applications received in paper format. This is an Intranet application. The application will provide features such as account history viewing and account balance, status, and activity information. This will allow ACIC to effectively evolve to a client/account servicing application in addition to being an account opening engine. This is an enhancement of an existing application; the earlier development was also done by Infosys.

Project Code	Project Name	Customer
xxxxxxxxx	ACIC Project	ACIC Corporation

Project Leader (PL)	Configuration Controller (CC)	Business Manager (BM)	Backup PL	Backup CC
BB	SB	HR	BJ	HP

Project Type	Platform	Number of Phases
Development	Java, Win NT, DB2	Four

Project Start Date (including onsite, offshore)		Project End Date	Total Estimated Revenue
Onsite	**Offshore**		
April 3, 2000	May 15, 2000	Nov. 3, 2000	US $ xxx,xxx

Project and Customer Contact Personnel

Name and Designation	Phone Number	Fax Number	E-mail ID

Project Scope

- To provide an effective, efficient means of account maintenance activities
- To allow reps to access information
- To provide a complete picture to the client rep for account status, valuation, order status, and trade activity
- To increase the intelligence of the update process
- To provide an interface that can display required account history elements
- To provide the capability to close and reactivate an account

Project's Value-add to the Customer

- This project will allow ACIC to effectively evolve to a client account servicing application in addition to being the account opening engine.

Infosys Objectives

- Strengthen relationship with ACIC by delivering high-quality software on time.
- Become preferred vendor by developing expertise on ACIC products and systems.

1.2 Commitments Made to the Customer

Sequence Number	Milestone Date	Milestones	Deliverables
1	26 May 2000	Inception: Requirements sign-off	Business analysis and requirements specifications, use case catalog, screens, iteration plan
2	15 May–23 June 2000	Elaboration: Iteration 1	Sequence diagrams, class diagram, source code, plan for the next cycle
3	26 June–7 July 2000	Elaboration: Iteration 2	Supplementary specifications, sequence diagrams, class diagram, architecture document, source code, iteration plan for the next cycle
4	10 July–21 July 2000	Construction: Iteration 1	Source code, review reports, test reports, iteration plan for the next cycle
5	20 July–28 July 2000	Construction: Iteration 2	Source code, review reports, test reports, iteration plan for the next cycle
6	31 July–8 Aug 2000	Construction: Iteration 3	Source code, review reports, test reports, iteration plan for the next cycle, deployment plan for the product
7	9 Aug–1 Sep 2000	Integration testing phase	Test plans, test reports
8	4 Sep–15 Sep 2000	Onsite code delivery and setup	Code
9	18 Sep–22 Sep 2000	Acceptance test and production migration	Test reports
10	18 Sep–29 Sep 2000	Onsite reconciliation and regression test	Code
11	2 Oct–26 Oct 2000	Acceptance test	Test results
12	27 Oct–3 Nov 2000	Rollout and support	Project sign-off

Other Commitments

Sequence Number	Commitments
1	This project will follow the Rational Unified Methodology (RUP).

1.3 Assumptions

Assumptions Made while Planning

- Migration to Visual Age for Java 3.0 will not be done by this team.
- Intelligent update to business partners will be incorporated in only the maintenance part of the application and not in the "Account opening" engine.
- Qualified people will approve Rational Unified Process methodology for implementing this project.
- Changes in functional and technical requirements during the life cycle of the project may have an impact on the schedule. Any impact on cost or schedule due to these changes will be intimated to ACIC.
- ACIC reviewers will get seven days to approve a milestone document. If no comments are received within this time period, it will be considered as approved.

2. PROJECT PLANNING

2.1 Project Processes

Standard Process Followed

The standard development process of Infosys will be followed. However, it will be enhanced with Rational Unified Process methodology (RUP), as it is a commitment. The development process will be tailored to match the RUP.

Tailoring Notes

Deviations from Standard Process	Added/ Modified/ Deleted	Reasons for Deviations
Only those use cases that are going to be taken up in a particular iteration will be elaborated at that point in time.	Modified	Iteration-based development is being done.
Development of logical object model will be done incrementally in the first few iterations.	Modified	Conformance to RUP methodology.

Deviations from Standard Process	Added/ Modified/ Deleted	Reasons for Deviations
Development of physical object model will be done incrementally in the first few iterations.	Modified	Conformance to RUP methodology.
Physical database design may be refined in later iterations.	Modified	Conformance to RUP methodology.
Development of unit test plan will be done in each iteration.	Modified	Iterative approach is being used.
Logging of defects will be iteration-wise.	Modified	Iterative approach is being used.
Requirement traceability will be done through the Requisite Pro tool.	Modified	Conformance to RUP methodology.
No vision document and business case as we started with the Scope document, which serves the same purpose.	Modified	Deviation from RUP.

Requirements Change Management Process

Change Requests Tracking

- Changes requested by customer will be logged in ChangeRequest.xls and analyzed for impact on the project. A change request form will be submitted to customer for approval. Change requests that are approved will be attached to the project contract as addenda.
- Major changes usually have an effort/delivery-on-time impact on the project. The customer needs to formally approve these.
- Because this is a short-duration project, if any one or a group of change requests takes more than 2% of the total estimated effort for the project, reestimation of the project schedule and effort will be done.

Requirements Traceability

Requisite Pro tool will be used.

2.2 Estimated Size and Effort

Estimation Criteria

Program/Function (Use Case)	Criteria
Simple use case	3 or fewer transactions
Medium use case	4 to 7 transactions
Complex use case	> 7 transactions

Use Case Number	Description	Complexity
Use Case 1	Navigate screen	Complex
Use Case 2	Update personal details	Medium
Use Case 3	Add address	Medium
Use Case 4	Update address	Complex
Use Case 5	Delete address	Complex
Use Case 6	Add telephone number	Medium
Use Case 7	Update telephone number	Complex
Use Case 8	Delete telephone number	Complex
Use Case 9	Add e-mail	Medium
Use Case 10	Update e-mail	Medium
Use Case 11	Delete e-mail	Medium
Use Case 12	Update employment details of a party	Medium
Use Case 13	Update financial details of a party	Medium
Use Case 14	Update details of an account	Medium
Use Case 15	Maintain activities of an account	Complex
Use Case 16	Maintain memos of an account	Simple
Use Case 17	View history of party details	Complex
Use Case 18	View history of account details	Complex
Use Case 19	View history of option level and service options	Simple
Use Case 20	View history of activities and memos	Simple
Use Case 21	View history of roles	Complex
Use Case 22	View account details	Simple
Use Case 23	View holdings of an account	Complex
Use Case 24	View pending orders of an account	Complex
Use Case 25	Close/reactivate account	Simple
Use Case 26	Make intelligent update to business partner of ACIC	Complex

Estimated Build Effort

Program/Function	Effort (Based on Data from Earlier Project)	Number of Units	Total Build Effort (in person-days)
Simple use cases	1 Person-days	5	5
Medium use cases	5 Person-days	9	45
Complex use cases	8 Person-days	12	96
Total			146

Phase-wise Effort Estimate

Activity/Phase	Person-days	% of total effort
Requirements	50	10
Design	60	12
Build	146	29
Integration testing	35	7
Regression testing	10	2
Acceptance testing	30	6
Project management	75	15
Configuration management	16	3
Training	50	10
Others	40	6
Estimated effort	501	100%

Effort Estimate by Iterations	Person-days	% of Total Effort
Project initiation	25	5
Inception phase	24	5
Elaboration phase: Iteration 1	45	9
Elaboration phase: Iteration 2	34	7
Construction phase: Iteration 1	27	5
Construction phase: Iteration 2	24	5

Effort Estimate by Iterations	Person-days	% of Total Effort
Construction phase: Iteration 3	21	4
Transition phase	110	22
Project closure	10	2
Project management	75	15
Configuration management	16	3
Training	50	10
Others	40	8
Total estimated effort	501 Person-days	100%

2.3 Schedule

Specified as milestones in the section on Commitments to the Customer.

2.4 People

People by Role

Role	Required Number	Date
PL	1	4 May 2000
Onsite coordinator	1 (50% time)	4 May 2000
Module leader	1	15 May 2000
Developers	3	15 May 2000
Developers	1	17 July 2000
Developers	1	1 August 2000
Developers	1	14 August 2000
Total	9 (actually 8.5)	

People by Skill and Experience

Area	Total #	0–12 months' experience	> 12 months' experience
Java	7	7	0
DB2	2	0	2
Total	9	7	2

People Requirement Plan

Month	Offshore	Onsite	Total
May 2000	4	1 (50%)	5
June 2000	5	1	6
July 2000	5	1	6
Aug 2000	8	1	9
Sep 2000	7	2	9
Oct 2000	3	2	5

2.5 Development Environment

Hardware	Software
NT Server	Win NT
MainFrame	DB2
Intel PC	VisualAge for Java, Java, Win NT

2.6 Hardware and Software Resources Required

Item Description	Required #	Date
PCs with 128 RAM	6	1 May 2000
1GB space on server	1	1 May 2000
VisualAge for Java	6	4 May 2000
DB2	6	4 May 2000
Rational Rose	5	15 May 2000
Requisite Pro	1	15 May 2000

2.7 Tools

Tools List

Tools to be developed in the project	None
In-house tools to be used in the project	BugsBunny, WAR

2.8 Training Plan

Training Area	Duration	Waiver Criteria
Technical		
Java Language	7 days	If already trained
VisualAge for Java	3days	Exposed as part of initial training
Java Applets	4 hrs	If already trained
Java Swing	4 hrs	If already trained
Persistence Builder	4 hrs	If already trained
Rational Rose and Requisite Pro	8 hrs	Mandatory
OOAD	1day	If already trained
Business Domain		
System appreciation	7 days	If already trained
Process-Related		
Quality system	3 hrs	If already trained
Configuration management	2 hrs	If already trained for CC. For others, on-the-job training
Group review	4 hrs	If already trained
Defect prevention	4.5 hrs	Mandatory
SPC tool	4.5 hrs	If already trained
RUP methodology	2 hrs	Mandatory

2.9 Quality Plan

Quality Goals

Project Quality Goals

Goals	Value	Basis for Setting Goals	Org.-wide Norms
Total number of defects injected	145	0.033 defects/person-hour. This is 10% better than Synergy, which is 0.036 defects/person-hour.	0.052 defects/person-hour
Quality (acceptance defect density)	5	3% or less of total estimated number of defects.	6% of estimated number of defects

Goals	Value	Basis for Setting Goals	Org.-wide Norms
Productivity	57	3.4% productivity improvement over Synergy.	50
Schedule	Delivery on time		10%
Cost of quality (in %)	32%	31.5%	32%

Estimates of Defects to Be Detected

Review/Testing Stage	Estimated Number of Defects to Be Detected	% of Defects to Be Detected	Basis for Estimation
Requirements and design review	29	20%	Referenced similar project estimations (Synergy) and PCB
Code review	29	20%	Referenced similar project estimations (Synergy) and PCB
Unit testing	57	40%	Referenced similar project estimations (Synergy) and PCB
Integration and regression testing	25	17%	Referenced similar project estimations (Synergy) and PCB
Acceptance testing	5	3%	Referenced similar project estimations (Synergy) and PCB
Total estimated number of defects to be detected	143	100%	

Strategy for Meeting Quality Goals

Strategy	Expected Benefits
Do defect prevention using the standard defect prevention guidelines and process; use standards developed in Synergy for coding.	10–20% reduction in defect injection rate and about 2% improvement in productivity
Group review of program specs for first few/ logically complex use cases. Group review of design docs/first time-generated code by project leader, developer, and one consultant.	Improvement in quality as overall defect removal efficiency will improve; some benefits in productivity as defects will be detected early
Introduction of RUP methodology and implementing the project in iterations. Milestone analysis and defect prevention exercise will be done after each Iteration.	Approximately 5% reduction in defect injection rate and 1% improvement in overall productivity

Reviews

Review Point	Review Item	Type of Review
End of project planning	Project plan DCS set up Project schedule	Group review SQA review SQA review
End of project planning	CM Plan	Group review
End of 90% of requirements (This should be at the end of first elaboration iteration)	Business analysis and requirements specification document, Use Case catalog	Group review
End of 90% design (This should be at the end of second elaboration iteration)	Design document, object model	Group review
Beginning of each iteration	Iteration plans	One-person review
End of detailed design	Complex/first time generated program specs incl. test cases, interactive diagrams	Group review
After coding for first few programs	Code	Group review
After self-testing of a process	Code	One-person review
End of unit test plan	Unit test plan	One-person review
Beginning of integration test	Integration test plan	Group review

2.10 Risk Management Plan

Sequence Number	Risks	Probability	Impact	Risk Exposure	Mitigation Plan
1	Support from database architect and the database administrator of the customer.	0.5	8	4	Plan carefully for the time required from each of these groups and give enough prior notice. Onsite coordinator to work closely with these groups.
2	As RUP is being used for the first time, the understanding of the team may not be complete.	0.9	3	2.7	Work closely with experts in the R&D lab of Infosys. Keep the customer in the loop throughout the project and escalate for any schedule/effort deviations. Train the team on RUP methodology.
3	Personnel attrition: Team members might leave on short notice.	0.3	7	2.1	Assign tasks so that more than one person is aware of the units/use cases in the project.
4	Working with customer's mainframe DB2 over the link; link may not be as efficient as it is expected.	0.1	8	0.8	Do extra code reviews, desk checking, etc. to minimize the reliance on link. Escalate as soon as the link goes down.

3. PROJECT TRACKING

3.1 Measurement Plan

Metric to Be Collected	Unit of Measurement	Tools Used
Size	LOC, FP, S/M/C count	Line counters
Effort	Person-days	WAR
Defects	Number of defects	BugsBunny
Schedule	Elapsed time	MSP

3.2 Task Tracking

Activity	Procedure
Task scheduling	The PL schedules tasks using MS Project. Refinement and rescheduling will be done when necessary.
Task assignment	The latest schedule is made available to the team members. Once the schedule is uploaded to WAR-MSP system, the tasks will show in their respective WARs.
Task status tracking	Task tracking is done daily.
Project meeting	Once a week.
Causal analysis meeting	After every iteration.

3.3 Issues Tracking

Issue Types	Where Logged	Who Can Log	Who Reviews, When	When Escalated
Onsite issues	IssueTracker.xls	Any member of the project	PL, daily	2 days
Customer issues	Issues Log.xls	Onsite team, PL	PL, daily	2 days
Business manager issues	Weekly Status report	BM	BM, PL weekly	5 days
Issues with support services	Request Tracker	Any team member	Support services, daily	2 days

3.4 Customer Feedback

Item	Logging and Tracking Process
Customer feedback	The AM/PL gets the customer feedback. The BM files it.
Customer complaints	Customer complaints received will be entered and tracked using CustomerComplaints.xls.

3.5 Quality Tracking

Quality Activity	Action
Defect tracking	Use DCS for logging defects and tracking them to closure.
Reviews (requirements, high-level design, detailed design)	Check against project goals in quality plan.
Code review	Check against limits for each program through SPC tool.
Independent unit testing	Check against limits for each program through SPC tool.
Integration testing/System testing	Check against project goals in quality plan.

3.6 Review by Senior Management (BM)

Sequence Number	Item for Review	Frequency of Review
1	Schedule	Every version change
2	Project plan	When significant changes are made
3	Milestone report	End of milestones

3.7 Status Reporting

Report To	Frequency
Business manager	Weekly on Monday by e-mail
Customer	Weekly on Monday

3.8 Deviation Limits at Milestones

Actual vs Estimated of:	For the First Five Milestones	For the Rest of the Milestones
Effort	10%	5%
Schedule	10%	5%
Defects	20%	20%

3.9 Report to the Customer

- Milestones reports and weekly status reports
- Issues requiring clarifications
- Escalation, if any

3.10 Report to the BM

- Customer feedback
- Milestones and weekly status reports
- Issues requiring clarifications/attention
- Escalation, if any
- Number of requirement changes and estimated effort for them
- Major changes in plan

3.11 Escalation Procedures

Escalate Where	Threshold Period	Name of the Person	Designation of the Person
At ACIC	3 days	Xxxx	Project manager
At Infosys	3 days	Xxxx	Account manager
At Infosys	3 days	Xxxx	Business manager

4. PROJECT TEAM

4.1 Project Organization

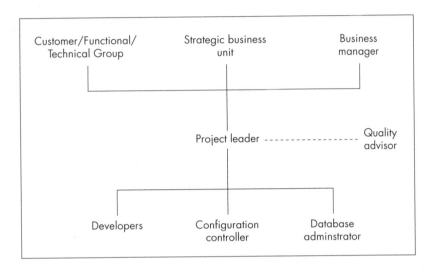

4.2 Project Team

Sequence Number	Initials	Responsibility	Start Date	Expected End Date
1	BB	Project manager	4 April 2000	3 November 2000
2	KP	Onsite coordinator	4 April 2000	3 November 2000
3	BJ	Module leader, backup project lead	15 May 2000	3 November 2000
4	SP	Configuration controller	22 May 2000	13 October 2000
5	DD	Developer	22 May 2000	29 September 2000
6	HP	Developer, backup configuration controller	22 May 2000	29 September 2000
7	NA	Developer	17 July 2000	3 November 2000

Sequence Number	Initials	Responsibility	Start Date	Expected End Date
8	SH	Developer	1 August 2000	15 September 2000
9	AL	Developer	14 August 2000	31 August 2000
10	JP	Developer	1 September 2000	22 September 2000
11	SDS	Account manager	4 April 2000	3 November 2000
12	SB	SQA	15 May 2000	3 November 2000

4.3 Roles and Responsibilities

Role	Responsibilities
Business manager (BM)	• Resolve escalated issues • Review project status • Participate in critical technical reviews
Customer	• Review design • Resolve escalated issues • Acceptance test planning and testing
Account manager (AM)	• Customer satisfaction • Business growth • Project financial plan • Interface with sales and marketing • Training-related issues • Employee-related issues
Project manager (PM)	• Project planning and scheduling • Design • Customer interaction • Reviews • Testing • Reporting • Task assignment and tracking • Interact with software quality adviser from SEPG • Ensure delivery as per contract • Interface with other departments as per need • Ensure open issues/customer complaints are closed properly • Ensure project members are adequately trained

Role	Responsibilities
Module leader (ML)	• Design • Development • Testing • Reporting
Defect prevention (DP) team	• Spread awareness in the team on defects and their prevention • Analyze defect data • Identify methods to reduce defect injection
Developer (DV)	• Detail design for use cases • Development • Unit testing and integration testing
Configuration controller (CC)	• Prepare the CM plan • Manage the configuration as per the CM plan
Software quality adviser (SQA) from the SEPG	• Process consultancy • Quality assurance (audits) • Install measurement tools and train project personnel • Participate in reviews of project plan and processes as necessary
Onsite coordinator	• Resolve any issues from customer/offshore • Support during development

5. REFERENCES

Omitted.

6. ABBREVIATIONS USED

Omitted.

8.5 SUMMARY

It's important for project managers to plan for team and communication management and to prepare a comprehensive final project management plan document.
The following are the important takeaways from this chapter:

- Software project is a team effort. In managing the team, you must take into account the project goals as well as team members' goals.

- Have regular communication within the team and with the customer. Explicitly plan for escalation channels at both ends to resolve issues that are hard to resolve otherwise.

- Document the outcome of various planning tasks in a comprehensive plan. Have this document reviewed to identify potential planning defects and to exploit the experience of senior managers to improve it.

- The documented plan must contain information on the project, the process to be used, the change management method, the effort estimates, the milestones, the risk management plans, the quality plans, the project tracking and reporting plans, the escalation channels for resolving issues that go beyond the project, and the team organization.

With respect to the CMM, a documented project management plan is a requirement of the Project Planning and Project Tracking and Oversight KPAs of level 2. The approaches discussed in this chapter and the contents of the project management plan also satisfy many requirements of the Integrated Software Management and Intergroup Coordination KPAs at level 3, the two KPAs of level 4, and some aspects of the Training KPA at level 3.

Chapter 9

Configuration Management

Changes—those due to the evolution of work products and those due to requirement changes—take place continuously in a software project. All these changes eventually get reflected as changes in the files containing source, data, or documentation. When multiple people create and change the huge number of files in a software project, it can lead to complications unless the changes are properly controlled. Consider these situations, taken from various projects.

- Two different change requests came from the customer. The project manager assigned one request to Rao for implementation, and the other to Meera. Both had to modify code for module X. When Meera finished her modification, she saved the file for X, inadvertently overwriting the changes Rao had made a day earlier.

- Friday was the deadline for release of a module for which three team members were developing the code. Integration of unit-tested code was planned for the final two days. On Tuesday night, Subbu, the developer of several key functions, left town to attend to an emergency. The next day the module leader and the team members spent many hours looking through Subbu's files. They managed to identify some files containing the various functions Subbu was developing, but they found umpteen versions of these files. One of the team members had to work on the problem over the weekend. Starting with some version of Subbu's programs, he developed and tested the unit, redoing the work that Subbu had almost finished before leaving. The module was finally delivered three days late.

- Srinath's team was in good spirits. They had finished the development on time, and the final testing had shown no bugs. The software was released to the customer for implementation. The next day Srinath received angry e-mails from the users and the customer, reporting problems in the software. After frantic effort by the team, the cause was found: The release version of the software contained an older version of a key component.

Stories like this can be found in most organizations. *Configuration management* (CM)—also known as software configuration management (SCM)—is the aspect of project management that focuses exclusively on systematically controlling the changes so that such problems do not occur.

This chapter first discusses some general concepts relating to CM and then describes the CM process followed at Infosys. It also gives the CM plan for the case study.

9.1 CONCEPTS IN CONFIGURATION MANAGEMENT

CM is essential to satisfy one of the basic objectives of a project: delivery of a high-quality software product to the client. What is this "software" that is delivered? At the least, it contains the various source or object files that make up the source or object code, scripts to build the working system from these files, and associated documentation. During the project, the files change, leading to the creation of different versions. In this situation, how does a program manager ensure that the appropriate versions of source code files are combined without missing any source, and that the correct versions of the documents, consistent with the final source, are sent? All this is ensured through proper CM.

A primary objective of CM is to manage the evolving configuration of the software system.[1,2] In a project, a program's evolution takes it through many states. At the beginning, when a programmer develops it, the program is under development (or "private"). Once the programmer is satisfied with the program, it moves into the "ready for unit testing" state. Only when the program reaches this state can it be unit tested. After it has been unit tested, the programmer must fix any defects found. If the unit testing succeeds, however, then the program's state changes to "ready for system testing." Only when all programs reach this state can system testing commence. Again, if defects are found during system testing, the state of a program reverts to "private"; otherwise, it moves to "ready for acceptance testing." If the acceptance testing succeeds, the state of all programs changes to "ready for release," implying that they can now be released for "production use." Once a program is released and is in production use, all the programs (and associated documentation) move to the "baselined" state, which represents the state of the production system.

In addition to the changes that take place during the normal course of software development, requirement change requests may be submitted, and their implementation may alter programs. When a project has a large number of items that can be changed, developers may be called on to take many actions; these actions can be performed only if proper support is available from the CM process.

To better understand CM, let's consider the kinds of CM functionality projects require. Although these requirements can depend on the nature of the project and the exact situation, some general functions can be specified. Following is a list of some of these functions along with scenarios where they might be needed. These functions are more detailed than the CM functions defined in Humphrey.[3]

- Give the states of the programs. You need this information to decide when to start testing or when to release the software.

- Give the latest version of a program. Suppose that a program must be modified. Clearly, the modification must be carried out in the latest version; otherwise, earlier changes may be lost.

- Handle concurrent update requests. Two programmers, in response to two different change requests, might change the same program concurrently. One of the changes could potentially overwrite the other change. Avoiding such a situation requires access control so that only one person can make changes to a program at a time. If multiple parallel changes are allowed, reconciliation procedures should be implemented to ensure that all changes are reflected in the final version.

- Undo a program change. A change is made to a program (to implement a change request), but later a need arises to reverse this change request.

- Prevent unauthorized changes or deletions. A programmer may decide to change some programs, only to discover that the change has adverse side effects. Access control mechanisms are needed to disallow unapproved changes.

- Provide traceability between requirement change requests and program changes. Suppose a requirement change request dictates that three programs be modified, and these modifications have been assigned to three team members. How does a project manager ensure that this change request has been properly implemented—that is, that all programs have been changed and that the changed programs have gone through their life cycle and are in a "ready for release" state? Answering this question requires a mechanism to track change requests that can specify all programs to be changed as well as the state of each program.

- Undo a requirement change. A requirement change request that was implemented (by changing many programs) may later need to be undone (perhaps because the users do not like the new features).

- Show associated changes. Suppose a bug is found in a program, and it is suspected that this bug came from the implementation of a change request. It is desirable to review all changes made as a result of that change request.

- Gather all sources, documents, and other information for the current system. As a result of file corruption or a system crash, it might be necessary to recover all files. Similarly, a change to an existing system (one that is in operation) might be needed, making it essential to obtain all source files and documents that represent the current system.

These are some of the more frequently occurring scenarios in a project that require support from the CM process. Furthermore, if multiple versions of a single software product coexist, each using a different version of the programs, other situations related to changes might come up that require the CM to have additional functionality (for example, handling variance[4]). Still, the main purpose of CM is to provide mechanisms that handle the type of scenarios in the preceding list. These mechanisms include the following:

- Conventions for naming and organization of files
- Version control
- Change request traceability
- Access control
- Reconciliation procedures
- Modification login programs

Naming program files (and document files) according to a standard convention and keeping the files in specific directories help in finding a desired file quickly. Proper naming (for example, by using standard extensions) also helps developers to readily understand the nature of file contents without looking at the files. In addition, segregating programs by their states into separate directories helps developers to identify the program state easily.

Version control is a key issue for CM,[1,2,4] and many tools are available to help manage this task. Version control helps preserve older versions of the programs whenever they are changed. Without such a mechanism, the system cannot support many of the required CM functions.

A change request traceability mechanism provides mapping from a requirement change request to subsequent changes in the programs, and that helps in managing requirement changes. To trace a change back to the change request, the modification log is useful.

Access control mechanisms ensure that only authorized people can modify certain files and that only one person can modify a file at any given time. Reconciliation procedures specify how two changes made independently to a program can be merged to create a new version that reflects both.

If these mechanisms are provided, the scenarios given earlier can be handled satisfactorily. Some of these scenarios necessitate the use of more than one mechanism. For example, undoing a requirement change involves a mechanism to show the traceability of a requirement change to subsequent changes in programs, as well as a version control mechanism to actually undo the changes.

Some CM mechanisms may be supported by a tool, whereas others may require that the users perform them explicitly. For example, version control may be carried out by a tool, but capturing the state of a program may require the programmer to explicitly maintain this information. The CM process defines all steps needed to implement such mechanisms and explains how these mechanisms are to be used in a project.

The discussion so far has focused on programs. The documents that are produced in a project (such as requirements documents, design documents, and plans) also need configuration management. During the normal course of a project, a document passes through three states: "under development," "under review," and "baselined." The state transition is straightforward and similar to the one proposed in Whitgift.[4] The CM process must also implement the state diagram for documents.

9.2 THE CONFIGURATION MANAGEMENT PROCESS

The CM process defines the sequence of activities that must be performed in support of the CM mechanisms. As with most activities in project management, the first stage in the CM process at Infosys is planning—identifying those items that need to be under CM (known as *configuration items*), locations to store them, procedures for change control, and so on. The project manager or the configuration controller (CC) of the project prepares this plan. Then the process must be executed, perhaps by deploying a tool (the use of which also must be planned). Finally, because any CM plan requires discipline on the part of the project personnel in terms of maintaining versions, storing items in proper locations, and making changes properly, monitoring the status of the configuration items and performing CM audits are therefore other activities in the CM process. This chapter discusses these three activities of the CM process at Infosys.

9.2.1 Planning and Setting Up Configuration Management

Planning for configuration management involves identifying the configuration items and specifying the procedures to be used for controlling and implementing changes to them. Identifying configuration items is a fundamental activity in any type of CM.[2,3,4] Typical examples of configuration items include requirements specifications, design documents, source code, test plans, test scripts, test procedures, test data, standards used in the project (such as coding standards and design standards), the acceptance plan, documents such as the CM plan and the project plan, user documentation such as the user manual, and documents such as the training material, contract documents (including support tools such as a compiler or in-house tools), quality records (review records, test records), and CM records (release records, status tracking records). Any customer-supplied products or purchased items that will be part of the delivery (called "included software product") are also configuration items.

During planning, the types of items that come under the aegis of CM are identified, but a detailed list of items is not prepared. This omission reflects the fact that some items may not be known during CM planning (which occurs at the beginning of the project). To facilitate proper naming of configuration items, the naming conventions for CM items are established during the CM planning stages. In addition to naming standards, project managers must plan version numbering. When a configuration item is changed, the old item is not replaced with the new copy; instead, the old copy is maintained and a new one is created. This approach results in multiple versions of an item, so policies for version number assignment are needed. If a CM tool is being used, sometimes the tool handles the version numbering. Otherwise, it must be explicitly handled in the project.

During planning, the project manager must decide how to maintain the state of a program. One way of collecting items in different states is to create separate directories for them. All items in a certain state reside in the directory for that state. When the state of a program changes, that program is moved from the directory for the old state to the directory for the new state. This approach is a general one and does not require the use of any tool to maintain the state information. If a CM tool is available, however, the directory structure needed for managing the states of programs depends on the tool. During the planning phase, project managers must set the directory structure employed for managing the states, keeping in mind the requirements of the CM tool, if any.

The configuration controller or the project manager does the CM planning. It is begun only when the project has been initiated and the operating environment and requirements specifications are clearly documented. The activities in this stage include the following:

- Identify configuration items, including customer-supplied and purchased items.
- Define a naming and numbering scheme for the configuration items.
- Define the directory structure needed for CM.
- Define access restrictions.
- Define change control procedures.
- Identify and define the responsibility and authority of the CC or Configuration Control Board (CCB).
- Define a method for tracking the status of configuration items.
- Define a backup procedure.
- Define a reconciliation procedure, if needed.
- Define a release procedure.
- Define an archival procedure.
- Identify points at which the configuration items will be moved to the baseline.

The output of this phase is the CM plan. The CC is responsible for the implementation of the CM plan. Depending on the size of the system under development, the CC's role may be a part-time or a full-time job. The CC can also be responsible for managing the release, archiving the release, retrieving and releasing appropriate versions when required, and more.

In certain cases—when there are large teams or when two or more teams or groups are involved in the development of the same or different portions of the software or interfacing systems—it may be necessary to have a CCB. This board includes representatives from each of the teams. A CCB (or a CC) is considered essential for CM,[3] and the CM plan must clearly define the roles and responsibilities of the CC or CCB. These duties also depend on the type of file system and tools being used.

As noted earlier, CM requires that access to some items in some states remain restricted. For example, the programmers' access and right to modify a program in the baseline must be limited. Planning activities must therefore specify the access rights of the CC, the project manager, and the developers.

Policies and procedures for change control are also established during planning. This includes controlling normal changes that take place during the life cycle as well as changes that are driven by requirement changes. Normal changes are generally managed through a library mechanism and directory structure. Changes due to requirement change requests, which may necessitate that many programs be changed, are frequently tracked through a spreadsheet that lists all items that must be changed as well as the directory for each item (thereby giving its state).

If project managers allow concurrent updates to programs, they must specify reconciliation procedures. Concurrent updates are sometimes necessary. For example, suppose a high-priority change request comes in at the same time that another change request is being implemented. Clearly, the new change request cannot be put on hold until the first one is finished. Similarly, if problems occur in the working system while a change request is being implemented, then changes must be made immediately to ensure that the system can continue to function. For such situations, reconciliation procedures are needed.

One possible procedure is to state that the differences between the original version and the new versions will be examined, and the changes in the version having fewer changes will be merged in the other version. If the changes affect different parts of the program, merging is straightforward; some CM tools readily support this capability. Otherwise, the programmer must review the overlap and then accommodate both changes.

All elements of the plan are documented in the CM plan. Later in this chapter we give the CM plan for the ACIC project.

9.2.2 Perform Configuration Control

Although configuration control activities are undertaken during the execution phase of the project, we discuss them here along with other aspects of CM. Two main configuration control activities are performed: one that deals with managing the state transitions of programs (and documents), and one that deals with managing the change requests that must be implemented.

State transition management involves moving the items from one directory to another when the state changes and then creating versions when changes are made.

Frequently, tools are used to manage the states and versions of items and access to them. Many CM tools employ the check-in/check-out procedure for controlling access and handling version control. The basic idea behind this approach is as follows. A program is considered to be in a *controlled environment* when it is in any state in which others can use it. Once a program is in the controlled environment, it cannot be modified, even by the original author, without proper *authorization*, because others may be using it. To make an approved change, the developer must check the program out of the controlled environment. Checking out essentially implies making a copy of the item without destroying the earlier version, and making a note that the item has been checked out.

An item is modified after it has been checked out. The modifications must then be reflected in the controlled environment so that others have the benefit of the new version and so that the change request (which may have forced the changes) can be truly implemented. Because other team members may be using the items, some checks are done to ensure that the changed item is suitable before it is checked back in. When an item is checked back into the controlled environment, the older copy is not destroyed; instead, a new version is created. Often, only the CC or the project leader can check items in. This limitation makes it possible to roll back the changes if the need arises.

To provide information about changes that have been made, project managers can opt to keep a modification log in the program source itself. This log essentially identifies the start and end of a change and includes a reference to the change request that prompted it.

All these tasks—checking in, checking out, version maintenance, and creation of a modification log—can be handled through the use of proper CM tools. Various tools are available that perform many aspects of this CM library function.

To implement requirement changes, which in turn trigger changes to configuration items, a change request is first analyzed by performing an impact analysis (discussed in Chapter 3). This analysis determines the programs and documents that need to be changed and the cost and schedule implications of making the change. Once the change is approved by the project leader and the CC, all programs and documents identified in the impact analysis must be changed appropriately. The following activities are part of implementing a change request:

- Accept the change request (with impact analysis).
- Set up a tracking mechanism.
- Check out configuration items that need to be changed.
- Perform the changes.
- Check in the configuration items.
- Take the item through its life cycle.

A spreadsheet-based mechanism is frequently used for tracking the status of change requests. For each change request, a spreadsheet is created that lists all programs being changed and their status. To implement a change, the CC or CCB assigns modifications to different items as tasks to members of the team, who check the items out so as to make these changes. After a team member makes a change, the changed program (or document) can be viewed as a new program that must go through different states (representing the life cycle of the program) before it can become part of the final in-operation system. Once all altered programs and their associated documents reach the baseline (after following their life cycle), the change request is considered to be fully implemented.

9.2.3 Status Monitoring and Audits

A configuration item can exist in one of several states. The set of possible states varies according to whether the item is a program or a document and the type of CM tools being used. It is important to accurately represent the state of each item because state-related mistakes can lead to problems. For example, if a program has not been unit tested but is moved to the state "ready for release," it can cause problems. Similarly, if the system fails to reflect the fact that a program has been checked out from the baseline to implement a change, the software might be delivered without the change. Thus, when a requirement change request is implemented, it is also important that the mechanisms used to capture the state accurately represent the state.

If projects use a mechanism based on a directory structure to represent the state of a program, mistakes are possible. This type of mechanism requires that the programs be moved properly from one directory to another when their state changes and that the change of state be reflected in the master table that maintains the states of the various items. To minimize mistakes and catch any errors early, projects must perform regular status checking of the configuration items. A report can be produced about the discrepancies, and all such discrepancies must be resolved.

In addition to checking the status of the items, projects must check the status of change requests. To accomplish this goal, change requests that have been received since the last CM status monitoring operation are examined. For each change request, the state of the item as mentioned in the change request records is compared to the actual state. Checks can also be done to ensure that all modified items go through their full life cycle (that is, the state diagram) before they are incorporated in the baseline.

Finally, projects can perform a configuration audit. As in other audits, the main focus here is to ensure that the CM process of the project is indeed being followed. The baseline for the system can also be audited to ensure that its integrity is not being violated and that items are moved to and from the baseline in a manner consistent with the CM plans.

The project's configuration controller generally conducts the CM audits. After a CM audit, a report is usually issued that lists what needs to be done to keep the CM activities consistent with the CM plan. Table 9.1 shows an example of the CM audit report for the ACIC project (whose CM plan is given later in this chapter). As you can see, in addition to looking at the process, the CM audit focuses on the status and location of the configuration items.

Table 9.1 CM Audit Report for the ACIC Project

Sequence Number	Observation	Responsible	Complete By
1	Mails to be logged in to the Messages/User folder	PL, DVs	06 Aug 2000
2	Reviewed sequence diagrams to be moved under VSS	PL	06 Aug 2000
3	CM plan to be updated with the changed directory structure	CC	05 Aug 2000
4	Completed sequence diagrams to be moved from users' area to the review area	PL	06 Aug 2000
5	Update VSS to reflect the modifications in the storage structure	CC	06 Aug 2000
6	ProjectDocs subfolder in Users folder to be cleaned up	All	06 Aug 2000

9.3 THE ACIC CONFIGURATION MANAGEMENT PLAN

The CM plan presented here specifies the CM environment and the directory structure to be followed in the ACIC project. (The CM plan for a different case study is given in my earlier book.[5]) The ACIC CM plan clarifies that under the project area is a directory structure, controlled through the Visual Source Safe (VSS) tool, where all documents that need to be controlled are kept. Source code files are controlled through the Visual Age for Java (VAJ) tool. Within the VSS directory, the various directories are specified; the names clearly indicate what goes in these directories. The user area, which is uncontrolled, is also specified; there is a directory for each user, and each team member is supposed to follow the directory guidelines in his area. Similarly, the area for reviews is specified; this is the directory where items to be reviewed are kept.

Then the plan lists the configuration items, their names, and their storage locations. Only the controlled configuration items are mentioned here. Items that are not controlled—for example, testing results, review results, messages, templates, standards, and so on—are omitted; they are stored in their respective directories in the uncontrolled area. For each item, the area where it should be kept when it is being developed is given in the work area. If the item is to be reviewed, the plan states where it should be moved to for review, as well as the baseline area under VSS where it goes after it is approved. In other words, the plan outlines the storage areas for these items as they evolve.

Next, the plan describes how a document moves through these different areas—that is, the configuration control process for documents. It is quite straightforward: The user works on the document in the work area. When the document is ready for review, it is moved to its specified review area. If the review does not require any further rework, the document is baselined. The plan does not specify a similar process for code because the methods of VAJ are used.

Access rights for the various areas and VSS are then specified. Because this project had a small team, a relatively liberal access scheme is followed, with all the team members having check-in and check-out access to the controlled area.

Next, the change control process is specified. First, the plan specifies who is responsible for logging change requests, who reviews, and so on. It then gives the change implementation process.

Reconciliation is a major issue in many projects. As mentioned earlier, the need for reconciliation arises when multiple people make changes to a configuration item in parallel. For documents, there is no such need for reconciliation because parallel changes are not envisaged, and VSS has formal check-in and check-out procedures that disallow parallel changes. Reconciliation of source code, however, may be needed. At a class level, the responsibility for reconciliation rests with the owner of the class, who uses VAJ features for this. (If multiple people have made changes to a class, VAJ highlights the differences in the class and methods in the different versions.) At each milestone, or whenever needed, all reconciliation is done for all sources.

Reconciliation may also be needed if some changes are made in parallel at the development site (offshore) as well as the deployment site (onsite). If this happens, again VAJ is used; the differences are identified, and then the changes are merged.

If multiple projects are using some common source code, reconciliation across projects might also be needed. Typically, all projects send their VAJ files to a central coordinator, who reconciles the files and returns them. These reconciled files then become the baseline for each project.

Next, the CM plan specifies the release area and the backup procedures. The release area for source code is the VAJ repository, and source is released at the end of construction milestones. ("Release" here means that reconciliation is finished and that a baseline, which may also be released to the customer, is created.) The high-level design (HLD) is released from the VSS area at the end of the relevant milestone. For backup, the area and frequency are specified. Then the nature and frequency of configuration audits are mentioned, along with the roles and responsibilities of the configuration controller. In this project, the CC is responsible for maintaining the tool, making backups, conducting audits, and helping the team to follow the CM procedures. (The complete CM plan has some additional elements that are omitted here.)

The Configuration Management Plan of the ACIC Project

1. INTRODUCTION

Omitted

2. CM ENVIRONMENT

- **Operating system**: Windows NT on servers, Windows 98 on PCs
- **Other software/tools**: MS Project 4.0, Rational Rose, Requisite Pro
- **CM Tools**: Visual Source Safe (VSS) for documents, and Visual Age for Java (VAJ) for source files

3. DIRECTORY STRUCTURE

Project area: Itlkec02/ACIC. All directories will be under this.

Controlled Storage Area for Documents: Itlkec02/ACIC/vss. In this controlled area, there are directories such as HLD, ProgSpecs, ProjectDocs, ProjectMgmt, Requirements, Scope, TestPlans, etc.

Source Code: InfosysKEC/C://ivj.dat (file where VAJ keeps the source files).

Uncontrolled Project Area: In addition to the controlled directory for VSS, there are separate directories such as ChangeRequest, ImpacAnalysis, Issues, MilestoneReports, ReviewReports, StandardsAndChecklists, StatusReports, Templates, etc. These directories are uncontrolled.

User Area: Areas for different users will be ACIC/Users/<UserId>. Each user will follow the structure of the controlled area.

Review Area: ACIC/Review. Under this are separate directories such as ProjectDocs, ChangeRequest, TestPlans, etc.

4. CONFIGURATION ITEMS, NAMING, AND STORAGE

Only the items that are in controlled areas are mentioned. Standard Infosys naming conventions will be used for naming all document and source files.

Configuration Item	Name	Work Area	Review/ Test Area	Baseline/ Release Area
Project scope document	ScopeDocument.doc			/vss/Scope
Use case catalog	UseCaseCatalog			/vss/Requirements

Configuration Item	Name	Work Area	Review/ Test Area	Baseline/ Release Area
Screens	Screens			/vss/Requirements
BAR document	BAR			/vss/Requirements
Project plan	ProjectPlan.doc	/Users/ <UserName> /ProjectDocs	/Reviews/ ProjectDocs	/vss/ProjectMgmt
CM plan	CM Plan.doc	/Users/ <UserName> /ProjectDocs/	/Reviews/ ProjectDocs	/vss/ProjectDocs
Project schedule	ProjectSchedule.mpp	/Users/ <UserName> /ProjectDocs	/Reviews/ ProjectDocs	/vss/ProjectMgmt
High-level design document	TAD3.0 .doc	/Users/ <UserName> /ProjectDocs	/Reviews/ ProjectDocs	/vss/HLD
Program specifications	ProgSpec#<n>	/Users/ <UserName> /ProgSpecs/	/Reviews/ ProgSpecs	/vss/ProgSpecs
Unit test plans	UnitTestPlan#<n>.doc	/Users/ <UserName> /TestPlans/	/Reviews/ TestPlans/	/vss/TestPlans
Sequence diagrams	<Description>SeqDiag	/Users/ <UserName> /ProjectDocs/	/Reviews/ ProjectDocs	/VSS/ RoseElements/ SequenceDiagrams
Class diagrams	<Description>ClassDiag	/Users/ <UserName> /ProjectDocs/	/Reviews/ ProjectDocs	/VSS/ RoseElements/ ClassDiagrams
Activity diagrams	<Description>ActDiag	/users/ <UserName> /ProjectDocs/	/Reviews/ ProjectDocs	/VSS/ RoseElements/ ActivityDiagrams
Source code	PackageName.Classname	VAJ Repository	VAJ Repository	VAJ Repository
Integration test plan	IntegrationTestPlan	/Users/ ProjectDocs/ TestPlans	/Reviews/ TestPlans	/vss/TestPlans
Test plans	/UseCase#.tst	/Users/ <UserName> /TestPlans/	/Reviews/ TestPlans	/vss/TestPlans
Closure report	ClosureReport.doc	/Users/ UserName/ ProjectDocs/	/Reviews/ ProjectDocs	/vss/ProjectDocs

5. VERSION/REVISION NUMBERING

For Software Source Files: The program source files have an automated versioning mechanism. The scratch edition will be 1.0. Any major change in source will be assigned version 1.1, 1.2, etc., and minor changes will have versioning 1.1.1, 1.1.2, etc.

For Documents: The original version will be numbered 0.0a. Subsequent revisions will be numbered 0.0b, 0.0c, etc. The baseline version will be 1.0. Documents may be changed as a result of redesign or customer change requests. New versions created are numbered 1.1, 1.2, etc.

6. MOVEMENT OF CONFIGURATION ITEMS THROUGH THEIR STORAGE AREAS

Configuration control process for documents:

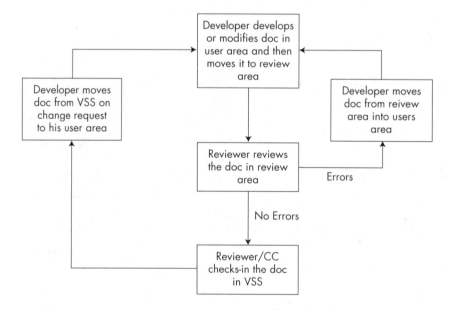

Configuration control process for source code: The code is reviewed in VAJ. If any changes are to be made, they are made in the open edition in which the user is working.

Access Rights

User Area: Each user has R/W access to his or her area. The project leader has R/W access to all.

Review Area: All have R/W access.

VSS Area: All have check-in and check-out rights.

Change Control

Where is the change request logged?	ChangeRequest.xls
Who logs the change request?	Any team members
Who reviews the change request?	Project leader
Who approves the change request?	Project leader or business manager

Workflow for Change Request

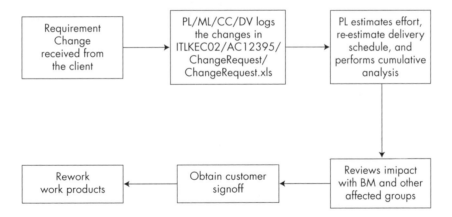

Reconciliation Documents

All documents are stored in VSS. Only one check-out at a time is allowed.

Source Code

Onsite/Offshore Reconciliation: Refer to the approach paper on VAJ Setup & Reconciliation.

Interproject Reconciliation: Interproject reconciliation will be undertaken as soon as there is a release.

Intraproject Reconciliation: The class-level reconciliation will be the responsibility of the class owner. Reconciliation dates will be decided in weekly project meetings. VAJ guidelines for reconciliation will be used.

Release

Configuration Item	Release Area	Responsibility for Building the Release and Releasing	When Released
Source Code	VAJ Repository	Workspace Owner	At the end of the milestone analysis
HLD	vss/HLD	PL	At the end of high-level design phase

Backup

Storage Area to Be Backed Up	Backup Media	Numbering Scheme	Backup	
			Frequency	Responsibility
Itlkec15 /	Tape	As per Infosys stds.	Weekly	System administrator
VAJ repository (ivj.dat of server)	ITLKEC02\\\\ ProjectBackup	mmmddyyyy.dat	Twice a week	CC
VAJ .icx and .ide files	ITLKEC02\\\\Users \\<Username> \\General	mmmddyyyy.ide and mmmddyyyy.ic x	Daily	Users

Archival Procedure

Archiving will be done by Infosys systems manager using standard procedures.

Configuration Audit

Type of Audit	Frequency
CC audit	Every two weeks
Baseline audit	Once a month
Work product completion	At the end of a milestone
Release	Before release
Surprise audit	Any time

Responsibilities of Configuration Controller

- CM orientation for project team
- CM tool deployment if applicable
- Configuration item status tracking
- Ensuring backups and archival
- Conducting CM audits as planned
- Generating CM audit reports
- Tracking CM audit discrepancies to closure

9.4 SUMMARY

A software product typically consists of many programs and documents, and these items change and evolve before they are ready for the final system. For this reason, software configuration management is an important issue.

Following are some of the lessons from the CM process followed at Infosys:

- Define the CM process so that it lets projects handle concurrent updates, undo a change, obtain the latest version of a program, determine the status of a program, and prevent unauthorized changes. Use version control, change request tracking, and library management mechanisms to support these capabilities.

- Develop a CM plan separately from the project management plan. The CM plan must specify the environment, configuration items and their naming convention, storage areas for the items in different states, and the method of managing changes to the items, including version numbering and reconciliation, access control, and release and backup policies.

- Perform CM audits and status checking to ensure that the CM plan is being followed.

With respect to the CMM, the activities discussed in this chapter satisfy many of the requirements of the Software Configuration Management KPA of level 2. Implementation methods for requirement changes satisfy some aspects of the Requirements Management KPA. The baselining and control of work products other than code also satisfy the baselining requirements of KPAs such as Requirements Management and Software Project Planning.

9.5 REFERENCES

1. E.H. Bersoff, V.D. Henderson, and S.G. Siegel. Software configuration management: A tutorial. *IEEE Computer,* Jan. 1979.

2. E.H. Bersoff. Elements of software configuration management. *IEEE Transactions on Software Engineering,* Jan. 1984.

3. W. Humphrey. *Managing the Software Process.* Addison-Wesley, 1989.

4. D. Whitgift. *Methods and Tools for Software Configuration Management.* John Wiley and Sons, 1991.

5. P. Jalote. *CMM in Practice: Processes for Executing Software Projects at Infosys.* Addison-Wesley, 2000.

Part II

PROJECT EXECUTION AND CLOSURE

Chapter 10

Reviews

You can check a program for quality by testing. But how do you check that the test plan being used for testing has the right test cases? And how do you check the design for design errors or check the requirement specifications for defects? Reviews are the most effective and commonly used method for identifying defects, not only in nonexecutable documents such as the test plan and design document but also in code. Reviews also give managers visibility into the progress of the project, something that can help them to take timely corrective actions. For a project manager, reviews offer some other advantages as well:

- Through reviews, the best talent in the organization can be utilized in a project even if they are not assigned to it.
- Reviews help preserve team motivation by giving people a sense of achievement, participation, and recognition.
- Through reviews, team members can develop their skills and senior people can mentor less-experienced colleagues.
- Reviews help prevent defects by creating more awareness about them.

This chapter discusses the review process employed at Infosys and explains how data is collected and used to monitor and control these reviews. We also briefly consider how experimentation was used to convince project managers of the value of group reviews.

10.1 THE REVIEW PROCESS

Reviews can be done in many different ways. A formal *group review*, also called an *inspection*, is perhaps the best of these options for identifying defects. Software inspections were first proposed by Fagan.[1,2] Earlier inspections focused on code, but over the years this technique has spread to other work products. Today, software inspections are a recognized industry best practice, with considerable data to prove that they improve quality and productivity (for example, see the reports in Gilb and Graham,[3] Grady and Slack,[4] and Weller[5]). Several books on the topic describe in great detail how inspections should be conducted.[3,6,7]

The basic review process at Infosys is the group review, which is similar to an inspection. A group review is an analysis of a software work product by a group of peers following a clearly defined process. The goals of such reviews are to improve quality by finding defects and to improve productivity by finding defects in a cost-effective manner. In addition, reviews provide inputs and visibility for project management into the quality of the work products. A group review is conducted by technical people for technical people, and the focus is on identifying problems, not resolving them.

The group review process includes several stages: planning, preparation and overview, a group review meeting, and rework and follow-up. As shown in Figure 10.1, these stages are usually executed in a linear order.

In some situations, a group review may be overkill; a more limited form of group review may be more cost-effective. At Infosys, a one-person review, discussed later in this section, is also done.

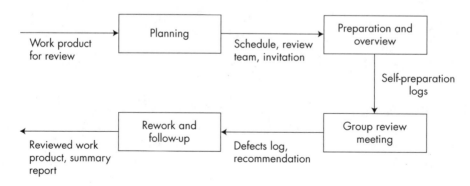

Figure 10.1 The group review process

10.1.1 Planning

The objective of the planning phase is to prepare for the group review by selecting the group review team and scheduling the review. The author of the work product ensures that the work product is ready for group review and that all pertinent standards have been met. The project manager, with the author's agreement, first selects the moderator; then, with the moderator's agreement, the project manager selects the other reviewers. The *moderator* has the overall responsibility of ensuring that the review is done properly and that all steps in the review process are followed. The *reviewers* (also called inspectors) have the responsibility of identifying defects in the work product. Generally, the author is also one of the reviewers; the moderator may be a reviewer as well.

As far as possible, no superiors should be included because their presence might discourage the reviewers from raising issues or errors. If the author desires, however, the project leader can also take part.

Once the review team is selected, the author prepares a package that is distributed for group review. This package includes the work product to be reviewed, its specifications, and relevant checklists and standards. Often, the specifications for the work product are the output of the preceding phase and are needed to check the correctness of the current work product.

10.1.2 Overview and Preparation

The purpose of the overview and preparation phase is to deliver the package for review to the reviewers and to explain the work product, if necessary. The material can be distributed and explained in an initial meeting. The moderator opens this meeting with a brief statement on the work product, the group review objectives, and, if needed, an overview of the group review process. The author may provide a brief tutorial on the work product, including a summary of any special considerations or areas that might be particularly difficult to understand. During this overview, anything unique about the project or the work product is highlighted. This step is optional and can be omitted. In that case, the moderator simply provides a copy of the group review package to the reviewers.

To prepare for the group review meeting, the reviewers then individually review (*self-review*) the work product. Wherever the work product appears to have a defect, reviewers make notes with explanations in a self-preparation log (described in detail in section 10.2.1). They also record the time spent in individual review. During this review, they use any relevant checklists, guidelines, and standards.

Ideally, this preparation step should be done in one sitting. The recommended time for preparation is one hour for every hour of group review meeting scheduled.

10.1.3 Group Review Meeting

The basic purpose of the group review meeting is to come up with the final defect list; this list is based on the initial list of defects and issues reported by the reviewers and any new ones found during the meeting discussion.

Before the meeting is scheduled, the moderator first checks whether all reviewers are prepared. This verification involves a brief examination of the effort and defect data in the self-preparation logs to confirm that sufficient time and attention have gone into the preparation. If preparation is not adequate, the group review is deferred until all participants are fully prepared.

When everything is ready, the group review meeting is held. One reviewer is designated as the scribe and another the reader. The meeting is conducted as follows. The reader goes over the work product line by line (or any other convenient small unit), paraphrasing each line to the team. (Some meetings do not include paraphrasing, in which case the reader role may not be present.) At any line, if any reviewer has previously identified any issues or finds new issues in the meeting while listening to others, he raises the point. There may be a discussion on the issue raised, and other reviewers may agree or disagree with it. In any event, the author reviews the issue under discussion and either clarifies why it is not an issue or accepts it as a defect or open issue. The scribe records the issues and defects identified.

At the end of the meeting, the scribe presents the list of open issues and defects identified during the meeting, and it undergoes a final review by the team members. Note that defects and issues are merely identified during the review process. It is not the purpose of the group to identify solutions; that action is taken later by the author.

If few modifications are required, the group review status is "accepted." If many modifications are required, a follow-up meeting or a re-review might be necessary to verify whether the changes have been incorporated correctly. The moderator recommends what is to be done. Unlike a defect, which the author is responsible for fixing, the moderator may assign issues to different persons for resolution. The assignment is made before the meeting is closed. Sometimes, recommendations regarding reviews in the next stages are also made. For example, in a detailed design review, the group may recommend which code modules should undergo group reviews in the build phase.

The moderator is in charge of the meeting and ensures that the meeting stays focused on its basic purpose—defect identification—and does not degenerate into a general brainstorming session or personal attacks on the author. The moderator should undergo formal training on how to conduct reviews or should have experience as a participant in a few reviews. During the meeting, the moderator must make sure that all participants contribute effectively, that everyone is heard, that agreement is reached on the findings of the review, and that the interest level does not drop. A key responsibility is to ensure that the focus remains on problem identification and does not drift into problem resolution. Overall, orderly and amicable conduct of the meeting is largely the responsibility of the moderator. After the meeting, the moderator must make sure that all participants are satisfied, the review report is filled and communicated, and follow-up actions are taken.

In a review meeting, a person can be assigned several of these logical roles, with the restrictions that the author cannot be the moderator or the reader, and the moderator cannot be the reader. This limitation implies that the minimum size of the group review team is three: the author, the moderator, and the reader. These three people are also reviewers, and one of them can act as the scribe.

10.1.4 Rework and Follow-up

The author performs rework to correct all defects raised during the group review meeting. The author may also have to redo the work product if the moderator recommends it. In addition, if the reviewers have been assigned open issues, they must investigate those problems and give the investigation results to the author and the moderator.

The author reviews the corrections with the moderator or, if the moderator has decided one is necessary, in a re-review. The scribe ensures that the group review report and minutes of the meetings are communicated to the group review team. After all the issues and defects are closed, the moderator ensures that the group review results and data are recorded and that the group review summary form (see section 10.2.3) is submitted to the SEPG and the project leader.

10.1.5 One-Person Review

Group review is a highly effective way of identifying defects. Unfortunately, its cost is also high: Many people spend time in preparation as well as in the review meeting. In addition, arranging group review meetings is a complex logistical problem, with associated overhead. If the work product has many defects or is a critical one, this cost is justified. Indeed, group reviews may turn out to be a cost-effective way of uncovering those defects. But what if the work product is relatively straightforward, is not likely to have many defects, and is not very critical? In this case, the group review effort may not be justified. Nevertheless, some review of such work products may be useful—not only to detect defects but also to gain the psychological benefits that accrue when the author knows that someone else will be reviewing the product.

For such situations, a one-person review may be more appropriate. That is, for work products of medium criticality or complexity, a one-person review may be substituted for a group review. *One-person reviews* are formal reviews but are less costly than group reviews because they do not involve a review team.

The process for one-person reviews is similar to the group review process. The author, in consultation with the project leader, identifies the reviewer. The review is scheduled, and the reviewer receives the review package in advance. The reviewer reviews the work product individually and prepares for the meeting with the author. The review meeting has only two participants: the author and the reviewer. During the meeting, an issues log and a defects log are generated. The reviewer informs the project leader when the review is finished. The project leader is responsible for tracking defects to closure.

10.1.6 Guidelines for Reviews in Projects

Not all work products in a project undergo group review because it may be prohibitively expensive and may not give commensurate returns. Following are some general guidelines for the selection of work products for reviews.

For a specific project, the actual criteria and the decision regarding the work products to be reviewed are left to the project manager and the team reviewing the work products of the early phases. Armed with the outcome of the reviews, the team can make better decisions regarding what to review in the rest of the project and which method to use. Because the work products of the early part of the life cycle are critical and because defects in them have a multiplier effect in the later stages, it is recommended that the following work products be group reviewed:

- The project management plan
- The requirement specification
- The system test plan
- The high-level design
- The integration test plan

At the end of high-level design review, the group review team makes a recommendation for review of the detailed design. Similar recommendations are made for the code at the end of the review of the detailed design.

Although the review process is the same for any work product, some differences arise in terms of the focus of the review, the entry criteria, and the makeup of the review team based on the nature of the work product. The checklists used also depend on the nature of the work product. Table 10.1 summarizes the guidelines for a few of the work products. Guidelines for other work products are similar.

Table 10.1 Guidelines for Review of Work Products

Work Product	Focus	Entry Criteria	Participants
Requirement specification	• Requirements meet customer needs. • Requirements are implementable. • Omissions, inconsistencies, and ambiguities in the requirements.	• The document conforms to the standards.	• Customer • Designers • Tester (system testing) • Installation team member • User documentation author
High-level design	• High-level design implements the requirements. • The design is implementable. • Omissions and other defects in the design.	• The document conforms to standards. • The requirements have been reviewed and finalized.	• Requirements author • Detailed designer • Developer
Code	• Code implements the design. • Code is complete and correct. • Defects in code.	• The code compiles and passes style and other norms.	• Designer • Tester • Developer
System test cases	• The set of test cases checks all conditions in the requirements. • System test cases are correct. • Test cases are executable.	• Requirements have been baselined. • System test plan is consistent with the standards.	• Requirements author • Tester • Project leader
Project management plan	• Project management plan meets project management and control needs. • Completeness. • Project management plan is implementable. • Omissions and ambiguities.	• The project management plan follows the standard template.	• Project leader • SEPG member • Another project leader

10.2 DATA COLLECTION

Data collection during reviews is crucial. You have already seen that at various stages in the process, data are recorded. Because reviews are largely human processes, if data are not properly recorded, the information can easily be lost. In addition to logging the defects identified by the review process, effort data must also be captured. Detailed defect data are needed for tracking defects in the project. The overall defect and effort data are needed for analyzing the effectiveness of the review and for constructing the review capability baseline. Hence, the summary data for each review are maintained in a review database. This section describes the key forms used for data collection during reviews at Infosys.

10.2.1 Self-Preparation Log

Reviewers use the *self-preparation log* to record all defects or issues found during their independent reviews. The effort spent during the reviews is also recorded. Each reviewer prepares this log. In addition to identifying the project, the work product, the reviewer, and other facts, entries in the log specify the location of the issue or defect and the reviewer's assessment regarding its seriousness or criticality. The form shown in Figure 10.2 can be used as is or implemented via a spreadsheet.

10.2.2 Group Review Meeting Log

The scribe prepares a log of the group review meeting that lists the defects and issues that were identified during the meeting. Hence, it includes all defects found

Project code:

Work product ID:

Reviewer name:

Effort spent for preparation (hours):

Issue list:

Sl #	Location	Description	Criticality/Seriousness

Figure 10.2 Self-preparation log

by individual reviewers in their self-reviews that were validated as defects or issues during the meeting, as well as the additional defects found during the meeting. Unlike the self-preparation log, which lists defects as perceived by a reviewer, the group review meeting log lists only those defects that have been agreed to by the author. In other words, it lists actual defects found, and it is the official defects list of the review.

In addition to each defect's location and description, its severity is recorded in this log. The severity reflects the consensus of the group review team. As discussed in Chapter 7, the severity of a defect can be either critical, major, minor, or cosmetic. If it can be determined at which stage the defect was injected, this information can also be recorded, as can the type of the defect.

The issues raised are listed in a separate log. For each issue, a person is assigned to resolve it. This log also contains the total effort spent (in person-hours) in the meeting.

Figure 10.3 shows the format of the group review meeting log. It can be implemented via a spreadsheet or some other mechanism.

Project code: Meeting type:
Moderator: Scribe:
Author: Reviewer(s):
SEPG member: Observer(s):
Date: Work product ID:
Effort spent on review meeting (person-hours):
Defects to be closed by (date):
Defect List:

SI #	Defect Location	Type	Severity	Stage injected	Description

Open Issues Log:

SI #	Issue Description	Assigned to	Targeted date	Closed date

Figure 10.3 Group review meeting log

10.2.3 Group Review Summary Report

The defects log is used to track all defects to closure. To analyze the effectiveness of a review, however, only summary-level information is needed. This information is also needed for updating the review baseline. For process improvement and understanding of the review process, the group review summary report is the most important element. Hence, this information is maintained in a separate review database that is available for analysis.

The summary report describes the work product; the total effort spent and the amounts spent in each of the review process activities; the total number of defects found for each category; and the size of the work product being reviewed. If the types of defects were recorded, the number of defects in each category can be recorded in the summary. In addition to the data on effort and defects, the summary contains suggestions for the next phase. Finally, the summary indicates whether a re-review is needed. A completed summary report is shown later in this chapter.

10.3 MONITORING AND CONTROL

The effectiveness of the review process depends on how well the process has been deployed. For example, if only two defects were found during the review of a 500-line program or a 20-page design document, clearly the review was not effective. The most common reason for a poor review is that it was not done with the proper focus and seriousness. Unless reviews are taken seriously, they will likely be a huge waste of time that does not give any due return, or they may be seen as a step to be checked off by performing it perfunctorily.

How does a project manager or a moderator evaluate whether a review has been effective so that she can decide the future course of action? One effective way of monitoring and controlling reviews is to use statistical process control (SPC) concepts implemented through control charts. Because the number of data points for reviews—particularly for code reviews—can be large, statistical techniques can be applied with confidence and rigor. This section discusses how Infosys monitors and controls reviews using statistical techniques.

10.3.1 The Review Capability Baseline

How can SPC be applied to monitoring reviews? To apply SPC, project managers must identify critical performance parameters, determine control limits for them, and then monitor the actual performance. They can build control charts by plotting the performance parameters of reviews and then use the plots to evaluate the effectiveness of a review. Another approach is to set the control limits for the various parameters and then use that range to determine the effectiveness. Although this latter approach has limitations because the run chart is not available, it is easy to apply. At Infosys, this latter approach is followed.

At Infosys, control limits have been determined for the following performance parameters: the coverage rate during preparation, the coverage rate during the group review meeting, the defect density for minor or cosmetic defects, and the defect density for serious or major defects (the overall defect density is simply the sum of the two preceding defect densities). These limits are determined from past data and from the review capability baseline. Creating and maintaining this baseline are important reasons for collecting summary data on reviews. Table 10.2 shows the group review capability baseline.

The group review baseline in Table 10.2 gives, for the various types of work products, the coverage rate during preparation, the coverage rate during review, and the defect density for minor and critical defects (the overall defect density is the sum of the two). The defect density is normalized with respect to size, where size is measured in the number of pages for all noncode work products and in lines of code for code work products. (For a design, size can also be measured in terms of the number of specification statements.) The coverage rate is stated in terms of size per unit effort, where effort is measured in person-hours. As you can see, for documents the coverage rates and defect densities are quite similar, but they are different for code (where the unit of size is also different).

The rates for one-person reviews can be expected to differ. Detailed design documents, test plans, and code undergo this form of review regularly. Hence, a one-person review baseline has been developed for these work products. In the baseline for one-person review of documents, the coverage rate per hour is about twice the corresponding coverage rate of group reviews; the defect detection rate per page is about half of that found with group reviews. For code, the coverage rate per hour is about the same, but the defect detection rate per LOC is about 30% less.

This baseline is the foundation for monitoring a review conducted in a project.

10.3.2 Analysis and Control Guidelines

The ranges given in the baseline are used to determine whether the performance of the review falls within acceptable limits. This check is specified as an exit criterion

Table 10.2 Infosys Review Capability Baseline

Review Item	Preparation Coverage Rate (If Different from Coverage Rate)	Group Review Coverage Rate	Defect Density Cosmetic/ Minor	Serious/ Major Defect Density
Requirements	5–7 pages/hour	0.5–1.5 defects/page	0.1–0.3 defects/page	
High-level design	4–5 pages/hour (or 200–250 specification statements/hour)	0.5–1.5 defects/page	0.1–0.3 defects/page	
Detailed design	3–4 pages/hour (or 70–100 specification statements/hour)	0.5–1.5 defects/page	0.2–0.6 defects/page	
Code	160–200 LOC/hour	110–150 LOC/hour	0.01–0.06 defects/LOC	0.01–0.06 defects/LOC
Integration test plan	5–7 pages/hour	0.5–1.5 defects/page	0.1–0.3 defects/page	
Integration test cases	3–4 pages/hour			
System test plan	5–7 pages/hour	0.5–1.5 defects/page	0.1–0.3 defects/page	
System test cases	3–4 pages/hour			
Project management and configuration management plan	4–6 pages/hour	2–4 pages/ hour	0.6–1.8 defects/page	0.1–0.3 defects/page

for the review process. Project managers can define the exit criteria as in-range checking of all the various parameters, but because detecting defects is the central purpose of reviews, the exit criterion is that the overall defect density should lie within the specified limits. (Another option is to check that the defect densities for the two types of defects are within the appropriate ranges.) If the number of defects found during the review is within the range given in the baseline, the review is considered effective, the exit criteria are satisfied, and no further action is needed for this review.

Instead of using the review capability baseline, a project manager can monitor reviews using an SPC tool developed in-house. This tool is essentially a spreadsheet that has the capability baseline data built into it. It also has data about the defect injection rate, defect removal efficiencies, organization-wide quality capability, and so on. From these data, the tool determines the performance specifications for a review—that is, the range in which its outcome is expected to fall if the quality goal is to be met. The SPC tool gives warnings when a piece of review data falls outside either the control limits or the expected limits (defined shortly).

If the density of defects found in a review is not within the range given in the capability baseline, it does not automatically mean failure of the review. The project manager or the moderator critically evaluates the situation and decides on the next steps. The preparation rate and review rate become very useful here; if the review rate is "too fast" compared with that given in the baseline, the reason for the ineffectiveness of the review is relatively clear. The defect densities for minor and critical defects can also be useful in this analysis. Although the moderator or the project manager can use any technique to determine the cause of performance deviation and the corrective and preventive actions that should be taken, a set of guidelines, shown in Table 10.3, helps in this endeavor.

Table 10.3 includes two groups of guidelines: one set that is applicable when the defect density is below the range, and another set that is applicable when the defect density is above the range. Both cases suggest that something abnormal may have taken place, and the situation must be examined carefully. Table 10.3 lists some possible causes; the project leader or moderator can use this information to identify the cause and then decide on the corrective actions for this review and preventive actions for future reviews.

Static control limits work well when the process is operating in a steady state. However, if changes are consciously made to the process, control charts must be used with care because the process performance is expected to change. If changes in the process are likely to be regular, it is best to have dynamic control limits. One way to do this is to reset the control limits to new values based on the past n performance data points (n must be selected; it can be some number greater than about 10 to 15). With this approach, if the process is changed, its performance will change, and after a few data points, the control limits will reflect the performance capability of the changed process.

Another approach is to adjust the performance data or control limits based on the expected impact of the process changes. For example, if the review process is changed and if it is expected that the reviews will detect 10% more defects, then when a point falls outside the control limits, this fact should be taken into account during the analysis.

This latter approach is used at Infosys when defect prevention is employed during reviews. With DP, the defect injection rate is expected to decline. Consequently, the defect density detected in reviews is also likely to fall. If a project is using

Table 10.3 Analysis Guidelines for Review

Possible Reason	Actions to Consider
If Defects Found Are Less Than Norms	
Work product was very simple.	• Convert group reviews of similar work products to one-person reviews. • Combine reviews.
Reviews may not be thorough.	• Check coverage rate; if too low, reschedule a review, perhaps with a different team.
Reviewers do not have sufficient training on group reviews or experience with the reviewed material.	• Schedule or conduct group review training. • Re-review with a different team.
Work product is of very good quality.	• Confirm this fact by coverage rate, experience of the author, reviewers, and so on; see if this quality can be duplicated in other parts of the project. • Revise defect prediction in downstream activities; see if there are general process improvement lessons.
If Defects Found Are More Than Norms	
Work product is of low quality.	• Examine training needs for author. • Have the work product redone. • Consider reassigning future tasks (e.g., assign easier tasks only to the author).
Work product is very complex.	• Ensure good review or testing downstream. • Increase estimates for system testing. • Break the work product into smaller components.
There are too many minor defects (and too few major defects).	• Identify causes of minor defects; correct in the future by suitably enhancing checklists and making authors aware of the common causes. • Reviewer may have insufficient understanding of the work product. If so, hold an overview meeting or have another review with different reviewers.
Reference document against which review was done is not precise and clear.	• Get the reference document reviewed and approved.
Reviewed modules are the first ones in the project.	• Analyze the defects, update the review checklist, and inform developers. Schedule training.

DP, then during project planning the expected impact of DP is also recorded. Using the defect injection rate, the expected reduction from using DP, and the defect detection rate, the *expected limits* for performance are established. If a review performance falls outside these limits, it is carefully examined for causes.

10.3.3 An Example

Consider the summary report for the group review of a project management plan given in Table 10.4. This summary covers a group review of a 14-page project management plan. The total number of minor and cosmetic defects found was 16, and the total number of major defects found was 3. Thus, the defect density found is 16/14 = 1.2 minor defects per page, and 3/14 = 0.2 major defects per page. Both rates are within the range given in the capability baseline, so the exit criteria are satisfied and it can be assumed that the review was conducted properly.

Table 10.4 Summary Report of a Review

Project	
Work product type	Project plan, v. 1.0
Size of product	14 pages
Moderator	Meera
Reviewer(s)	Biju, Meera
Author	JC
Effort (Person-Hours)	
a. Overview meeting	0
b. Preparation	10 person-hours
c. Group review meeting	10 person-hours
Total Effort	20 person-hours
Defects	
Number of critical defects	0
Number of major defects	3
Number of minor defects	12
Number of cosmetic defects	4
Number of defects detected during preparation	—
Number of defects detected during group review meeting	—
Number of open issues raised	1
Total number of defects	19
Result	Moderator reexamination
Recommendations for Next Phase	
Units to undergo group review	N/A
Units to undergo one-person review	N/A
Comments (Moderator)	The plan has been well documented and presented.

Prepared by: Meera; **Date:** xx-xx-xxxx

Although not needed for this review because the exit criteria are satisfied, other rates can also be checked. The review team had 4 members, each of whom spent 2.5 hours in individual review; the review meeting lasted 2.5 hours. Thus, the coverage rate during preparation and review was 14/2.5 = 5.6 pages per hour, which is within the range for preparation but somewhat higher for review.

When summary data is given to the SPC tool, it graphically displays the performance of this review, along with the control limits and expected limits.

10.4 INTRODUCTION OF REVIEWS AND THE NAH SYNDROME

Reviews are, in many ways, counterintuitive. A programmer cannot understand how a review by a group of people can be more effective than testing. When human effort is the most critical resource in a project, it is not easy to accept the position that the highly manpower-intensive review process can make the overall process more productive and improve quality. As a result, convincing people to use reviews is one of the most difficult process deployment tasks. One SEI report indicates that only 22% of software organizations employ some form of inspections.[8]

Clearly, hard data are invaluable for proving the case. A fair amount of published data supports the claim that reviews can be cost-effective and can improve quality substantially. Nevertheless, such published data from organizations around the world often fail to convince engineers that reviews can be good for their organization. One reason for this skepticism is the Not Applicable Here (NAH) syndrome: People believe that reviews are good for other organizations but that the situation in their company is different and thus the reviews are not applicable.[9]

If inspections are to be deployed in a project, the NAH syndrome must be overcome. Managers as well as developers must be shown that inspections can provide real benefits. By definition, data from other organizations cannot be used to overcome the NAH syndrome. Instead, data from within the organization itself must be used to build a case for inspections. An experimental setup is therefore needed that can be quickly deployed in real-life scenarios to evaluate the suitability of inspections in the organization.

In an attempt to overcome the NAH syndrome, Infosys used a simple experiment, described in the next section. The experiment is general and simple and can be conducted easily by any organization. Further details of this endeavor appear in a paper I co-authored.[9]

10.4.1 The Infosys Experiment

Infosys's experiment focused on code inspections because developers relate to coding and it is usually the source of the greatest number of errors. Historically, inspections started with code and only later were extended to design, requirements, test plans, and other items. Once you build a strong case for code inspections and they are deployed, the advantages of these inspections will become obvious and will build a case for inspection of other work products.

For Infosys's experiment, six system enhancement requests (SERs) on a banking product were selected. Six developers were assigned one SER each. These developers were first trained in the inspection process; for practice, they were asked to inspect the implementation of an earlier SER that had been seeded with defects.

The personnel were divided into two groups of three developers. Each group formed an inspection team. Before submitting the SER, each developer was asked to implement the SER, compile his code, and do some self-testing. Once submitted, the SER went through two independent paths: inspections and unit testing. During the experiment, an inspection team inspected the code of the three SERs developed by the members of the group. In each inspection, the author, rather than the moderator or the reader, acted as an inspector. In parallel, the SERs were unit tested independently by the module leader for the domain to which the SER belonged. The flow diagram in Figure 10.4 shows the basic experiment steps.

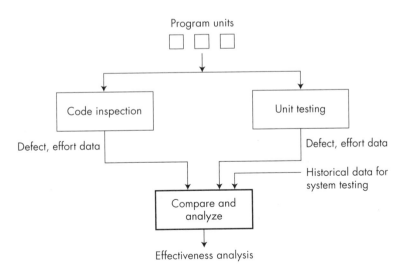

Figure 10.4 Steps in the Infosys experiment

For each of the two paths, the effort spent and defects found were recorded. These data were then used to evaluate the cost-effectiveness and quality of the reviews. If the sets of defects found by these two approaches were not the same and if one set was not a subset of the other, then the claim could be made that inspections do find a different set of defects than unit testing and that adding inspections will be beneficial. Understanding the cost implications is more difficult (and is where most doubts arise). This cost was estimated based on past data for system testing.

10.4.2 Data from the Experiment

Table 10.5 gives the sizes of the SERs, the total effort, and the number of defects found in the two paths. Clearly, the inspection route identified more defects than did the unit testing route. This finding was consistently observed for all the SERs. Overall, inspections caught about 2.5 times as many defects as unit testing did, although inspections consumed more effort than testing did. The number of defects detected per person-hour, however, are similar for inspection and unit testing; both detected about 1.9 defects per person-hour.

Now let's look at the nature of the defects found by the two approaches, shown in Table 10.6. In almost all categories, inspections caught more defects than did unit testing, particularly for categories related to quality attributes such as maintainability, portability, and so on (as might be expected given that testing generally focuses on errors in functionality). The data also show that even in logic and interface defects (the focus of testing), inspections do better than unit testing.

Table 10.5 Effort and Defect Data

Size SER	Inspections			Unit Testing	
	Total Effort (LOC)	**(Hours)**	**Total Number of Defects**	**Total Effort (Hours)**	**Total Number of Defects**
1	968	8.0	8	2.0	4
2	432	5.0	8	1.5	3
3	85	4.0	4	1.5	1
4	667	6.5	26	1.5	7
5	50	12.5	3	1.5	0
6	408	2.5	5	2.5	5
Total	2,610	27.5	54	10.5	20

Table 10.6 Defect Distribution

Defect Type	Inspections	Unit Testing	Common Defects
Data	3	1	0
Function	4	2	0
Interface	14	11	7
Logic	12	5	4
Maintainability	11	0	0
Portability	5	0	0
Other	5	1	1
Total	54	20	12

From these data, the case for adding inspections to improve the error detection capability is clear and convincing.

With these data, the cost per defect is about the same. However, reviews offer cost benefits. From past experience and data, it is known that it takes about 4 person-hours to identify and remove a defect during system testing. If a defect escapes system testing, it takes about 2 person-days (17 person-hours) to identify and remove it.

Testing rarely catches maintainability and portability–type defects. We assume that all logic, interface, function, and data defects that are not caught by unit testing are found later. The number of such defects in Table 10.6 is 3, 4, 14, and 12, respectively. After eliminating common defects, which are also caught by unit testing, the number is 3, 4, 7, and 8. If all these defects are caught in system testing, then the system testing cost will increase by 22 * 4 = 88 hours, or about 11 person-days. If 75% of these errors are caught in system testing and 25% are caught later, the additional cost in system testing is 0.75 * 22 * 4 = 66 hours (9.5 person-days); the additional cost of fixing defects found later is 0.25 * 22 * 2.5 = 11 person-days. That is, if no inspections are done, an additional 20.5 person-days will be spent in fixing the extra defects.

Thus, the cost saving due to inspections is 11 person-days if all defects are caught in system testing and 20.5 person-days if 25% of the defects are not caught in system testing. The cost of the inspections, which yielded these savings, is about 3.5 person-days. The case is clear: If we spend one additional day in code inspection, for this product we can expect to save three to six days in defect fixing later in the development cycle!

The experiment lasted only about two weeks, but it had a substantial effect. The results convinced developers and managers alike that inspections should be tried. The data from the experiment also indicated that the inspections would offer fewer benefits if the code was simple or small (in smaller SERs, the benefit was unimpressive). The banking product team therefore made the policy decision to classify the SERs in three categories (simple, medium, and complex) and to consider formal inspections for all complex modules.

10.5 SUMMARY

The purpose of a review is to identify defects and issues in a work product through a process of formal and structured review by a group of peers. Reviews are cost-effective and can be applied even to work products that cannot be executed. Reviews are an important technique for improving both quality and productivity as well as for providing visibility into the state of the project.

Following are some of the lessons learned from reviews at Infosys:

- Include external experts in the review team to augment the talent of the project team.

- Use a well-defined and structured review process with clear guidelines and formal data collection. The process should include planning, self-review, and a group meeting.

- During the review, focus exclusively on finding defects and issues. Defects and issues are resolved later.

- When it is more practical, use a one-person review for work products. For the one-person review, follow the same process and data collection guidelines as for group reviews.

- Monitor each review for effectiveness. Create performance expectations from past data, and use them to evaluate a review's effectiveness.

- If a review's performance is not as expected, analyze the causes and take corrective and preventive actions.

- To understand the impact of reviews, conduct simple experiments within the project. Data from within their own organization convinces people in ways that no amount of outside data can.

With respect to the CMM, the review practices described here satisfy the Peer Review KPA at level 3. The monitoring and control method satisfies some requirements of the Quantitative Project Management and the Software Quality Management KPAs of level 4. Reviewing of various work products satisfies the review requirements of many KPAs.

10.6 REFERENCES

1. M.E. Fagan. Design and code inspections to reduce errors in program development. *IBM System Journal*, (3), 1976.

2. M.E. Fagan. Advances in software inspections. *IEEE Transactions on Software Engineering*, SE-12(7), 1986.

3. T. Gilb and D. Graham. *Software Inspection.* Addison-Wesley, 1993.

4. 4. R.B. Grady and T.V. Slack. Key lessons learned in achieving widespread inspection use. *IEEE Software*, July 1994.

5. E.F. Weller. Lessons learned from three years of inspection data. *IEEE Software*, Sept. 1993.

6. R.G. Ebenau and S.H. Strauss. *Software Inspection Process.* McGraw Hill, 1993.

7. D.P. Freedman and G.M. Weinberg. *Handbook of Walkthroughs, Inspections, and Technical Reviews: Evaluating Programs, Projects, and Products.* Dorset House, 1990.

8. D.H. Kitson and S.M. Masters. An analysis of SEI software process assessment results: 1987–1991. *Proceedings of the 15th International Conference on Software Engineering*, 1993.

9. P. Jalote and M. Haragopal. Overcoming the NAH syndrome for inspection deployment. *Proceedings of the 20th International Conference on Software Engineering*, 1998.

Chapter 11

Project Monitoring and Control

A project plan, no matter how carefully prepared, is still only a piece of paper. During project execution, Dr. Project Manager must carefully monitor the health of his project-patient and give the right doses of corrective-action medicines when necessary. If the right doses are given at the right times, the patient survives. But failing to read the symptoms properly and failing to give the bitter pills on time can lead to further complications and possibly the death of the patient. The following two mini-cases illustrate this point.

Case A: Shiva was the project manager in charge of developing a secure transaction system for a large mutual fund company. His team, consisting of many dedicated but junior people, had little experience in computer security. The unit testing for the first few modules found a large number of defects—much more than expected. Upon analysis, Shiva concluded that because of the difficulty of the programs and the inexperience of the programmers, the code being produced had more defects. Consequently, he felt, more defects would reach the integration and system testing stage, and unless something was done, more defects would be delivered. The corrective and preventive action Shiva took was to create a separate test team headed by a person who had a knack for detail and the right temperament for testing. Through discussion with the customer, he was able to expand the system testing phase by 15 days. Finally, even though there was a delay of 15 days, the delivered system exceeded its quality goal by showing fewer than expected defects during acceptance testing.

Case B: After the detailed design phase, the milestone analysis in Bala's project showed that even though there was no schedule slippage, there was an effort overrun of 40%. Because the schedule had not slipped, no action was taken. At the next milestone a month later, however, the project showed a delay of one week, which Bala explained as the result of special circumstances. Eventually, the development was finished one month late. To top it off, the number of defects found in acceptance testing was many times Bala's quality goal. In the end, his project failed on all three dimensions: effort, schedule, and quality. Later analysis showed that he had misunderstood the scope of the system and consequently had grossly underestimated the effort. If the scope or the schedule had been renegotiated when problems first appeared after the design milestone, the final outcome would have been entirely different.

These mini-cases bring out the two key aspects of project monitoring. First, project managers must have visibility into the true status of the project, for which the best approach is to quantitatively measure the key parameters.[1,2] For project managers, the main use of software metrics is to provide this visibility.[3] Second, the visibility by itself does not solve any problem. Project managers must properly interpret the data, and if they find that the project is not moving along the planned path, they must apply proper corrective actions to bring it back on track. This collection of data to provide feedback about the current state and any needed corrective actions forms a fundamental paradigm of project management. Figure 11.1 illustrates this control cycle.[4]

This chapter describes how the monitoring and control cycle is applied at Infosys. This is the longest chapter in the book and covers a range of monitoring activities, including status reporting, milestone analysis, event-level control through SPC, process audits, and analysis for defect prevention.

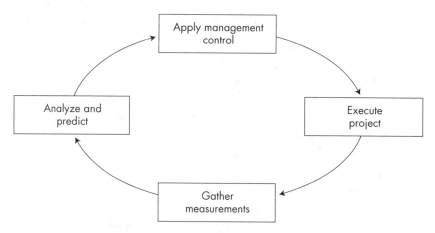

Figure 11.1 The project monitoring and control cycle

11.1 PROJECT TRACKING

Let's first examine basic project tracking at Infosys. Once a detailed project plan is made—in which all schedulable tasks are listed along with their start and end dates and the people assigned to them—at the very least the project manager must track the execution of these tasks. That endeavor constitutes activities tracking. In addition, a project manager must track the unresolved issues that crop up and the defects that are detected. The outcome of this tracking is captured in the status report of the project. This status report is also distributed to senior management and the customer, thus ensuring that they have visibility into the project.

11.1.1 Activities Tracking

One of the first tasks in project tracking is to ensure that planned activities are done on time. As mentioned earlier, at Infosys activities are usually scheduled using Microsoft Project (MSP). Hence, MSP is also used for activities tracking.

Every day (or more or less frequently), the project manager checks the status of the scheduled tasks and updates the status in MSP. Although MSP allows users to specify an activity as partially completed, for tracking purposes an activity is typically specified as 0% done until it is completed. When the activity is finished, it is marked as 100% done. This level of tracking suffices because tasks are decomposed so that the lowest-level, schedulable tasks take less than one or two days. Using MSP features, a project manager can then determine which higher-level tasks are lagging behind, what percentage of a task has been done, what effects slippage will have on the execution of the overall project, and so on. For the current phase (the next milestone), based on the activities completed and the actual time they took, the project manager reschedules the remaining tasks as needed to ensure that the milestone is met.

11.1.2 Defect Tracking

Tracking of defects is another key point in tracking. As mentioned in Chapter 7, Infosys uses a defect control system for tracking defects. Once information about a defect is entered in this system, it remains open until it has been fixed. The defect is marked as "closed" when its removal has been verified. In this way, each defect is logged and tracked to closure. Sometimes, project managers track the state of a defect by recording the date of submission and the date of closure for each defect. At the end of the project, ideally no open defects should remain (or a deliberate decision has been made to leave them uncorrected). At any time, the project manager can check the overall rate of defect injection and defect closure, information that is useful in seeing whether the gap between the number of defects submitted and the number of defects closed is in control.

Table 11.1 shows parts of the defect data for the case study, the ACIC project. In addition, other columns (not shown here) captured the submitter ID, the submit date, the owner ID (the ID of the person assigned to fix the defect), and the closing date. As you can see, standard information, such as stage injected, stage detected, severity level, and so on, is recorded for each defect.

11.1.3 Issues Tracking

Inevitably, many small jobs or clarifications come up during a project. These problems are called *issues*. Managing issues is an important task for any project manager because they can be numerous and can potentially delay a project. For example, a clarification sought regarding a requirement from the customer (an issue) can delay many activities unless it is resolved. Many such issues have the potential to stop some activities. Hence, it is important for a project manager to track and manage issues properly.

One method is to simply write the issues down and check them off in due course. But because any team member can raise an issue, the list of issues can become large. Formal methods are therefore useful for tracking them. For this purpose, projects usually open an *issues log*.

In the issues log, issues are recorded as they arise, along with related information. When issues are closed, they are marked as closed. For the issues log, project managers can use a spreadsheet, maintain a document, use an issue tracker utility, or use the defect tracking system. If an automated tool is used, simple queries become feasible. Table 11.2 provides part of the issue log for the ACIC project to give you an idea of the type of items that go into it (the actual log contains the submit and close dates and other information for tracking).

Project managers must regularly monitor the status of issues, particularly if all team members can enter them. As mentioned in Chapter 8, unresolved issues pose a risk to the project. If issues remain open for too long, escalation channels need to be used to resolve them, as specified in the project management plan.

11.1.4 Status Reports

Status reports are the main mechanism for regularly communicating the state of the project to senior management and the customer. The parties who receive the

Table 11.1 Defect Data for the ACIC Project

ID	Title	Description	Stage Injected	Stage Detected	Defect Type	Severity
7	Redundant import statement.	In ActivitiesMaintenanceJPanel, AccountSearchResult class is imported twice.	Coding	Code review	Redundant code	Minor
10	Naming convention not followed.	The panel has been named ActivityMaintJPanel, and it should be ActivitiesMaintenanceJPanel.	Coding	Code review	Standards	Cosmetic
15	Transaction handling.	Transaction started for reading need not be committed as other methods can make use of it. It is done in addTask and updateTask.	Coding	Code review	Logic	Minor
16	Panel structure not proper.	In Options/Services panel of View History, Regy block panel and Options/ Services panel were put on a parent panel. However, the correct method would have been to place it on the Option Services Panel.	Detailed design	Detailed design review	UI	Minor
21	Layering not followed.	Business model Party is imported in ViewPartyHistoryPanel.	Coding	Code review	Architecture	Major
22	UI standards not followed.	The labels in the screens are not in black.	Coding	Code review	Standards	Cosmetic
26	TypeCasting is incorrect.	TypeCasting to IIndividualName and IOrganizationName in methods getIndividualNames and getOrganizationNames should be changed to IName.	Coding	Code review	Logic	Major

Table continued on next page.

Table 11.1 Defect Data for the ACIC Project (continued)

ID	Title	Description	Stage Injected	Stage Detected	Defect Type	Severity
27	Incorrect assigning	Author wanted to assign the value of existing vector to another vector. The assigning is not done correctly. It creates a new vector of the existing vector size.	Coding	Code review	Logic	Critical
30	Null Value acceptance	Need to check whether null values are allowed.	Coding	Unit testing	Logic	Major
35	Financial info	Clicking on other panels should not clear the fields on the screen for financial info.	Coding	Unit testing	UI	Major
39	Financial info	Exception handling in refresh panel from ApplicationContext not done.	Coding	Unit testing	UI	Major
152	Tab setting	Tab movement is not set in the panel.	Coding	Integration testing	Performance	Cosmetic
153	Disabled Add button	Add button is disabled in Address after a role is selected in the Account Roles Table.	Coding	Integration testing	Performance	Major
154	Clear button not clearing AssociatedAccounts table	Clear button in address maintenance panel is not clearing the Associated Accounts table.	Coding	Integration testing	Performance	Minor
155	Phone dissociation not working	In phoneMaintenance panel, dissociating the phone is not working.	Coding	Integration testing	Performance	Major
156	Updating phone not working	When you update a phone number, the changes are not saved.	Coding	Integration testing	Performance	Major

Table 11.1 Defect Data for the ACIC Project (continued)

ID	Title	Description	Stage Injected	Stage Detected	Defect Type	Severity
157	E-mail updating not working	Following a certain sequence of actions—updating an e-mail without clicking the button Update, selecting another role, clicking Yes on the confirmation dialog—and then selecting the previous role, only the updated e-mail is shown; other e-mails are missing.	Coding	Integration testing	Performance	Major
158	Account type not updated	When you change the account type and click Update, the account type is not saved.	Coding	Integration testing	Performance	Major

status reports are specified in the project management plan. Typically, status reports are generated weekly and contain these items:

- Customer complaints
- Milestones achieved this week
- Milestones missed this week and the reasons for them
- Milestones planned for the next week
- Issues requiring clarification or attention
- Escalation, if any
- Estimated work versus available time by milestone

Clearly, the focus is on ensuring that the project continues to progress according to the plan and on resolving pending issues. Project managers can also check the project's "comfort level" by seeing whether the available time matches the required effort. A project manager may add more items, such as the number of requirement changes, and may delete some of those shown.

Figure 11.2 gives a sample status report for the ACIC project. This weekly status report focuses on what was done last week, what needs to be done, what open issues remain, and so on.

Table 11.2 A Sample Issues Log for the ACIC Project

Issue Description	Comments/Closure Comments	Status
For what fields will the record be sent to the business partner of ACIC?	Use case updated.	Closed
Alternate scenario 1 in UC 3 is not clear. Why does 9 mean manual update?	Added alternate scenario in use case 4.	Closed
Wizard allows only one value for both Stmts and Confirms. Why should it be different for the Maintenance screens?	Included the explanation in the use case.	Closed
Clarify all the conditions when the Address Change should be sent to the business partner of ACIC.		Open
Primary indicator was removed in Synergy. If it must be put back, it must be mentioned as a requirement in the use case.	Refer to the PPT sent yesterday. It has the field on the screen.	Closed
In Update, the alternate scenarios are not discussed. What if the updated e-mail is associated with other accounts?	Clarification added to the use cases.	Closed
In the table in which history of service options is displayed, there is one timestamp for all three service options types. Will this not cause problems in dealing with the options separately?		Open
Regarding populating the tables, they should be populated with some meaningful data.		Open
If any change is made on tax liable role or interested party, should it affect other accounts?	This is mentioned in the use case. Please look at "Flow of Events" in the main scenario.	Closed
Does Country Combo Box need to be prefilled with country code values, or does it have to be changed to a text field?		Open
Can the text field ForeignAddressLine4 be deleted?		Open
Foreign Address and Foreign Phone number from the Maintenance team may not be ready for integration.		Open
VAJ 3.0 conversion is going to impact this project.	This conversion will be done only after this project is completed.	Closed

STATUS SUMMARY

Project	Life-Cycle Stage	Next Milestone Date	% Complete	Number of Resources	Remarks
Release 2.0	Build	7 July 2000	90%	4	
Release 3.0	Elaboration 1, Elaboration 2	28 June 2000	Elaboration 1: 95% Elaboration 2: 20%	5.5	There are two elaboration phases and three construction phases.

TASKS COMPLETED AND MISSED

	Tasks Completed	Tasks Missed
Release 2.0	• Construction of iteration 2 complete. • Code review done. • Test plans for iteration 2 and 3 done. • Independent test environment set up.	None
Release 3.0	• As part of elaboration 1, 10 use cases were taken up for design and 4 critical use cases for implementation. This is 95% complete. • Elaboration 2 started.	Review of the requirements will be taken up next week.

TASKS PLANNED FOR THE WEEK 4 JULY 2000 TO 9 JULY 2000

Release 2.0	• Construction for iteration 3 to be complete. • Independent testing of iteration 1 to continue. • Code review of iterations 2 and 3 to be performed. • Test plans for iterations 2 and 3 to be done.
Release 3.0	• Elaboration 2 • Complete architecture document. • Review BARs. • Schedule PMR review.

ISSUES/MISCELLANEOUS ITEMS

Open Issues	None
Misc. Items	None

Figure 11.2 ACIC project status report for week ending July 3

11.2 MILESTONE ANALYSIS

A status report provides the mechanism for regular monitoring of the project. It focuses primarily on whether the schedule is being met. A key advantage of status reports is that they do not require very much metrics data or analysis. This section discusses how metrics are used at Infosys to evaluate the state of a project at milestones.

If the project plan has been carefully derived and evaluated, the project will succeed if the plan is followed. Therefore, a milestone analysis should use the project plan and schedule as its baseline and compare the plan to the actual progress. This strategy is employed in the two common approaches for metrics-based tracking: the cost-schedule-milestone chart and the earned value method.[5] Analyzing planned versus actual progress is considered a best practice for project management.[3] At Infosys, planned versus actual is also tracked at milestones.

Because the main objective of metrics analysis for monitoring and control is to take corrective and preventive actions in a timely manner, such analysis should be done at regular intervals. For this reason, a project manager may define project milestones over and above the customer-driven milestones so that successive milestones are only a few weeks apart.

11.2.1 Actual Versus Estimated Analysis of Effort and Schedule

For schedule and effort, a project is likely to show deviation from planned in its actual progress. Small deviations on the effort or schedule front, however, can be considered "normal" and do not merit special attention. On the other hand, "significant" deviations may mean that the project may be heading for failure and hence call for further analysis and control actions.

To differentiate the normal from the significant, acceptable deviation limits are set in the project plan, as discussed in Chapter 7. Many projects at Infosys have a limit of about 20% for effort deviation and 10% for schedule deviation. The actual limits for a project are specified in its management plan.

If the deviation at a milestone exceeds these limits, it may imply that the project will run into trouble and might not meet its objectives; under time pressure, the project members might therefore start taking undesirable shortcuts. This situation demands that the project manager understand the reasons for the variation and apply corrective and preventive actions if necessary. Table 11.3 lists guidelines for analysis and possible control actions that a project manager may consider.

Table 11.3 includes suggestions for both types of variation: estimated effort too low or estimated effort too high. Some reasons are given, along with possible control actions. For example, if the estimate is too low, the possible reasons are that the estimate was too aggressive, resource utilization is low (that is, there is wastage in the project), a critical resource is not available, or team members have a low expertise level. For each reason, some control actions have been suggested. For example, if the estimates were too aggressive, the project manager might revise the

Table 11.3 Guidelines for Effort/Schedule Performance

Possible Reason	Actions to Consider
If Actual Is Less Than Estimate by More Than the Allowable Limit	
Estimates for programs were too high or project team has more domain knowledge or experience than expected.	• Reestimate for future modules. • Release resources.
The tasks so far have not been thoroughly performed.	• Review tasks done so far and schedule reviews for work products not reviewed. • Examine issues log.
If Actual Is More Than Estimate by More Than the Allowable Limit	
Low domain knowledge.	• Schedule training.
Low software/coding experience of author.	• Reassign to leverage existing experience.
New technology area.	• Reestimate or request resources. • Negotiate delivery dates.
Estimates were too aggressive.	• Identify main components for extra effort, and revise estimate for future activities. • Request resources. • Negotiate to scale down project objectives.
Resource optimization is low.	• Reschedule and reprioritize tasks, and identify and eliminate "waiting times."
Nonavailability of a critical resource.	• Escalate the issue. • Get a backup resource. • Reschedule, keeping critical resource(s) in mind.
Too much rework due to poor-quality of output of earlier phases.	• Identify sources of problems and rectify them. • Change project schedule.

estimates, request resources, or try to scale down the project. Most of the items in Table 11.3 are self-explanatory.

The pattern of effort deviation can also be useful for analysis. If the effort deviation has been consistently increasing from milestone to milestone, then even if it remains below the threshold, some action might be warranted. Similarly, if control actions are taken and the deviation percentage is reduced at the next milestone, it suggests that the actions are having the desired effect. On the other hand, if the effort deviation increases even more after the actions are taken, it implies that the previous actions are not working well and more drastic actions might be needed.

In addition to past performance, at a milestone the project manager may examine the prognosis for the rest of the project. For effort, in the milestone analysis, the number of resources available and needed is also reported. If the amount of effort available (based on the number of resources) is significantly lower than what is needed, clearly some action is required. Achieving this kind of visibility so that timely action can be taken is the purpose of this analysis.

11.2.2 Monitoring Quality

To monitor the third dimension—quality—the main metric is the number of defects found. In addition, the number and status of reviews done and the status and effect of defect prevention activities are also monitored. Because the number of defects was also estimated during planning, defects are assessed in the same way as schedule and effort. That is, using the defect levels predicted in the project plan for the various stages and the actual number of defects found, the project manager prepares an actual versus estimated analysis. If the deviation exceeds the threshold set for the project, she must analyze the causes for the deviation based on the decision she made on the actions to bring the project back under control. Table 11.4 gives guidelines relating to possible reasons and possible control actions. (Chapter 10 describes guidelines for evaluating reviews.)

For the quality control tasks of testing and reviews, in addition to the number of defects found, project managers also analyze the actual versus estimated for the effort spent in these tasks. These data are useful for analyzing the situation when the actual number of defects found differs substantially from the estimated. For example, if too few defects are found after system testing and if the amount of time spent in system testing is also too low, the reason for the testing performance becomes clearer.

Table 11.4 Guidelines If the Number of Defects Found Differs from the Estimate

Possible Reason	Actions to Consider
If Fewer than Estimate	
Work product is of high quality.	• Identify reason and see whether there are possible lessons for the project or for the process.
Inadequate testing.	• Check the effort spent on testing; review the test plan and enhance it. • Schedule further testing.
Very thorough execution of earlier quality control activities.	• Examine all review and testing records for the project. • Check whether there are possible lessons for the project or the process.
Defect estimates are too high.	• Identify cause and correct estimates.
If More than Estimate	
Inadequate execution of quality control activities so far.	• Examine all testing and review records. • Schedule reviews of critical modules before continuing with testing.
Insufficient reviews and unit tests planned.	• Enhance test plan and schedule further testing. • Review estimates and plans for acceptance.
Defect estimates are too low.	• Identify cause and correct estimates.

The second metric monitored is the number of reviews conducted. As time pressures mount, there can be a tendency to skip the planned reviews. Because these reviews are an important part of the quality plan developed to achieve the project's quality goal, their satisfactory execution is essential. The milestone report therefore indicates which reviews were planned and which were actually executed. The actual performance of reviews is monitored at the completion of each review, as discussed in Chapter 10.

11.2.3 Risk-Related Monitoring

Risks and related activities are also monitored at milestones. As discussed in Chapter 7, risks for a project are not static; risk perceptions change over time and as risk mitigation steps are executed. Thus, it is important to take stock of risks and note the effects of the risk mitigation steps taken so far. For this reason, the current risk perception, along with the status of current risk mitigation steps, is reported in the milestone analysis report. Clearly, if risk exposure due to some risk has not been reduced, it implies that the risk mitigation steps are not having the desired effect. The risk and its mitigation steps must therefore be evaluated.

An important risk mitigation step is training, which is suggested to counter many types of risks. Training is also an important component in any project involving new technology or new people and if not done properly can introduce new risks. To prevent monitoring of training from slipping through the cracks, the milestone report describes the project-related training planned and actually executed.

Requirement changes also pose a risk to the project because they have an adverse impact on cost, schedule, and quality. Chapter 3 explains the process for managing requirement changes. In milestone analysis, a summary is reported of the changes that have been requested and their impact on effort and schedule.

Issues, if left unresolved for long, also frequently become risks. Hence, the status of issues is also reported in the milestone analysis. In addition, customer complaints, which clearly represent serious risks to the project, are also reported. In particular, the number of new customer complaints received, the number of customer complaints addressed, and the number of pending customer complaints are all reported.

11.2.4 Milestone Analysis for the ACIC Project

Let's look at a milestone analysis report of the ACIC project (other examples can be found in my earlier book[6]). This analysis, shown in Figure 11.3, was performed when the first construction iteration of the ACIC project was completed. It revealed almost no slippage in schedule and effort, and the available effort was close to the effort required until completion. Hence, the project was under control in these dimensions, and no action needed to be taken. On the quality front, however, the report indicated that the defect levels were higher than expected because of a higher number of defects injected. Hence, a defect prevention activity was to be undertaken. Furthermore, the defect injection rate for the rest of the project was revised.

The project manager reevaluated the risks and found that although the risks the project was currently facing were different from the risks at the start of the project, there was no change in the risks and their prioritization since the last milestone. The analysis report also indicated that the training activity that was planned had taken place.

MILESTONE NAME: Construction: Iteration-1   **DATE:** Aug 18, 2000

Schedule (for the milestone)

Planned date	Actual date	Slippage
July 21, 2000	July 21, 2000	0

Reasons for deviation: N/A
Actions taken to bring schedule back in control: Nil
Overall impact on project: Nil

Effort (person-hours)

Estimated Effort Before This Milestone	Actual Effort Before This Milestone	Deviation	Estimated Effort from Milestone to Project End	Effort Available Until Project End
2019	2191	9	2231	2059

Reasons for Deviation: N/A
Actions Taken: Nil
Overall impact on project: Nil

Defects

No.	QC Activity	Size of Work Product	Estimated Effort from MSP (Person-Hours)	Actual Effort (Person-Hours)	Estimated Defects	Actual Defects	Defect Deviation
1	Code review and unit testing	Appx. 4000	31	25.5	25	57	125%

Reasons for Deviation: One of the use cases had too many defects.

Action Taken: A number of steps have been taken to prevent these defects from occurring. More details are given in the causal analysis report.

Impact on Quality Goals: The defect injection rate in the project may be higher than projected. It has been revised by 20%, and the quality plan has been suitably modified. Project goals remain unchanged, however. To minimize the future impact, DP activities will be done more vigorously.

Figure 11.3 Milestone analysis report of the ACIC project (continued on next page)

Defect prevention activities

One causal analysis was done followed by a root cause analysis, based on which some preventive actions were recommended. These are being implemented. The potential impact of these, and the analysis, is given in the causal analysis report.

Requirements Change Tracking

Total number of major requirement changes to date	0
Total number of minor requirements changes to date	0

Risks

Sl. No.	Previous State			Risk Item	Status of Mitigation Action	Current Status		
	Proba-bility	Im-pact	Expo-sure			Proba-bility	Im-pact	Expo-sure
1	0.9	9	8.1	VAJ 3.0 conversion time line not known and could impact this project if planned prior to Release 3.0 delivery.	Escalated to customer and they are aware.	0.9	9	8.1
2	0.9	9	8.1	Time line for screen resizing not known.	Effort sized and given to the customer. No response yet.	0.9	9	8.1
3	0.8	8	6.4	Dependency on certain components by the onsite maintenance team for Rel 3.0.	Issue raised with the maintenance team. They may not have the bandwidth to work on this.	0.9	8	7.2
4	0.3	7	2.1	Dependency on Rel 2.0 for certain components used by Rel 3.0.	2.0 looks to be on time.	0.2	7	1.4
5	0.9	1	0.9	There is some mainframe work that must be taken up, and this has not been planned.	Customer has approved a mainframe resource. Not a risk anymore.	0	0	0

Figure 11.3 Milestone analysis report of the ACIC project (continued)

Customer Complaints

Number of customer complaints raised	0
Number of customer complaints closed	0
Number of customer complaints open	0

Training

Planned	Architecting Distributed Applications in J2EE for Bhaskar and Balajee
Actual	The same was completed

Group Reviews

Planned	None
Actual held	None

Issues

Risks 1, 2, and 3 are still issues. Follow up with the stakeholders for a resolution to these.

Figure 11.3 Milestone analysis report of the ACIC project (continued)

11.3 ACTIVITY-LEVEL ANALYSIS USING SPC

Milestone analysis uses metrics to monitor the state of the project at defined milestones and to suggest corrective actions if needed. However, with milestone-based analysis, it is hard to determine which of the many activities performed since the last milestone may be the cause of performance degradation. This situation is similar to performing system testing; debugging is much harder when the system comprises many units. It is far easier to debug during unit testing. This difficulty in pinning down the cause of poor performance limits the corrective actions that can be taken.

To provide finer control, activity-level analysis is also done at Infosys. In activity-level analysis, some metrics are analyzed immediately after a task is performed. The analysis is used to evaluate the effectiveness of the task performance. If the task has not been performed satisfactorily, immediate action can be taken to correct it and to prevent a repetition.

Activity-level analysis is usually done using statistical process control (SPC). At Infosys, reviews and unit testing have been identified as the two tasks for which SPC is applied. Using control charts, the project manager immediately evaluates the effectiveness of a review or a unit test. If the performance is not satisfactory, necessary action can be taken.

Note that the broad activities of design, detailed design, system testing, and so on are already evaluated individually through milestone analysis because they typically start and finish at milestones. Hence, the focus of activity-level monitoring is on the coding-related activities of reviews and unit testing.

Chapter 7 discusses the basics of statistical process control, and Chapter 10 explains the monitoring and control of reviews using SPC. Here we discuss activity-level monitoring and control of unit testing—the other activity for which SPC is applied. The approach for unit testing is similar to that used for monitoring reviews. The main performance characteristic that is monitored is the density of defects detected in unit testing. From the past data on unit testing, the control limits (that is, the range of acceptable density) are obtained. At the end of each unit test, the defect density is checked against the range. If it falls outside the limits, corrective or preventive actions may have to be taken. The guidelines given earlier for testing can be used to decide which actions are needed (for analysis, project managers can use supporting information about effort spent on the task, effort expended on previous tasks, and defects found). Figure 11.4 shows the control chart for defect density for unit testing of one programming language. The defect den-

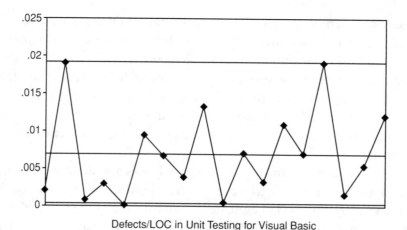

Defects/LOC in Unit Testing for Visual Basic

Figure 11.4 Control chart for unit testing of Visual Basic programs

Table 11.5 Unit Testing Defect Rates for Some Languages

Language	Defect Rate Range (Average)
PB	0.0003–0.0266 defects/LOC (Avg: 0.008)
C	0.0004–0.0206 defects/LOC (Avg: 0.0052)
C++	0.00009–0.0067 defects/LOC (Avg: 0.0017)
RPG	0.0006–0.0075 defects/LOC (Avg: 0.0025)

sity can be plotted in terms of the number of defects per LOC or the number of defects per person-hour. Table 11.5 shows the capability baseline for unit testing, giving defect rates for a few languages.

As with reviews, project managers can use the SPC tool to implement activity-level control of unit testing. This tool contains relevant past performance data such as the defect injection rate, the defect removal percentage, and so on. Using this data, it determines the control limits as well as expected limits. When the performance data of a unit test is entered, the tool immediately tells whether or not the performance is outside the limits. If it is outside the limits, further analysis must be done to determine what action, if any, should be taken.

11.4 DEFECT ANALYSIS AND PREVENTION

Defect prevention aims to learn from defects found so far on the project and to prevent defects in the rest of the project. As discussed in Chapter 5, defect prevention activities are usually done twice in a project: once when about 20% of the modules have been coded and unit tested, and again when 50% of the modules have been coded and unit tested. The main tasks of defect prevention are to perform Pareto analysis to identify the main defect types, perform causal analysis to identify the causes of defects, and identify solutions to attack the causes. Here we discuss how these tasks are performed in a project.

11.4.1 Performing Pareto Analysis

A common statistical technique used for analyzing causes, *Pareto analysis* is one of the primary tools for quality management.[7,8] It is also sometimes called the *80-20 rule*: 80% of the problems come from 20% of the possible sources. In software it can mean that 80% of the defects stem from 20% of the root causes or that 80% of the defects are found in 20% of the code.

The first step in defect prevention is to draw a Pareto chart from the defect data. The number of defects found of different types is computed from the defect data and is plotted as a bar chart in decreasing order. Along with the bar chart, another chart is plotted on the same graph showing the cumulative number of defects as we move from types of defects on the left of the x-axis to the right of the x-axis. The Pareto chart makes it immediately clear in visual as well as quantitative terms which are the main types of defects, and also which types of defects together form 80%–85% of the total defects. Instead of plotting the number of defects, you can plot a weighted sum by assigning different weights to different types of defects.

The overall procedure for doing the Pareto analysis is as follows:

1. List all the defects identified so far.

2. Calculate the total number of defects by type.

3. Sort defects by type in descending order of number of defects.

4. Calculate the percentage of each defect type with respect to the total number of defects detected.

5. Identify the defect type that is the cause for about 80% of the total defects.

For example, consider the Pareto chart of the defect data for the ACE project shown in Figure 11.5. In this project, features are being added to an existing system. The defects data for all previous enhancements was used for this analysis. As you can see, the highest number of defects are logic defects, followed by user interface defects and standards defects. Defects in these three categories together account for more than 88% of the total defects, and the defects in the top two categories account for more than 75%. Clearly, the target for defect prevention should be the top two or three categories.

11.4.2 Performing Causal Analysis

The Pareto chart helps to identify the main types of defects that have been found in the project so far and are likely to be found in the rest of the project unless action is taken. These defects can be treated as "effects" that you want to minimize in the future. To reduce these defects, you must find their main causes and then try to eliminate them. A *cause-effect* (CE) diagram can be used to determine the causes of the observed effects.[7,8] For example, the cause-effect diagram can be used to de-

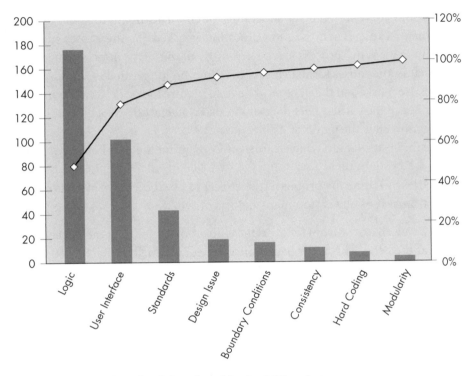

Figure 11.5 Pareto chart for defects found in the ACE project

termine the main causes for the high number of GUI defects (or logic defects) in the ACE project. The main purpose of the CE diagram is to graphically represent the relationship between an effect and its various possible causes. Understanding the causes helps to identify solutions to eliminate them.

The first step in building a cause-effect diagram is to identify the effect to be analyzed. In the ACE example, the effect could be "too many GUI errors." To identify the causes, you first establish some major categories of causes. For manufacturing, these major causes often are manpower, machines, methods, materials, measurement, and environment. For causal analysis at Infosys, the standard set of major causes of defects is process, people, technology, and training (training is separated from people because it shows up very often). The main structure of the diagram shows the effect as a box on the right; a straight horizontal line extends from the box, and an angular line for each major cause connects to the main line.

To analyze the causes, the key is to ask, "Why does this cause produce this effect?" for each of the major causes. The answers to these questions become the subcauses and are represented as short horizontal lines joining the line representing the major cause. Then the same question is asked for the causes identified. This "Why-Why-Why" process is repeated until all the *root causes* have been identified—that is, the causes for which asking "Why" no longer makes sense. When all the causes are marked in the diagram, the final picture looks like a fish-bone structure, and hence the cause-effect diagram is also called a *fish-bone* diagram, or Ishikawa diagram after the name of its inventor.

The main steps in drawing a cause-effect diagram are as follows[8]:

1. Clearly define the problem (the effect) to be studied. For defect prevention, it typically is "too many defects of type X."

2. Draw an arrow from left to right with a box containing the effect drawn at the head. This is the backbone of the diagram.

3. Determine the major categories of causes. These could be the standard categories or some variation to suit the problem.

4. Write these major categories in boxes and connect them with diagonal arrows to the backbone. These form the major bones of the diagram.

5. Brainstorm for the subcauses of the major causes by asking repeatedly, for each major cause, "Why does this major cause produce the effect?"

6. Add the subcauses to the diagram clustered around the bone of the major cause. If necessary, further subdivide these causes. Stop when no worthwhile answer to the question can be found.

When the fishbone diagram is finished, you have identified all the causes of the effect under study. However, most likely the initial fishbone diagram will have too many causes. Clearly, some of the causes have a greater impact than others. Hence, before completing the root cause analysis, you identify the top few causes, largely through discussion. For defect prevention, you can conduct this entire exercise for the top one or two categories of defects found in the Pareto analysis.

Figure 11.6 shows the fish-bone diagram for the ACE project. In this analysis, causes of the three major types of defects were discussed in one brainstorming session. Hence, our effect was "too many logic/GUI/standards defects." When we asked the question, "Why do people cause too many logic or GUI or standards defects?" we identified some of the (almost obvious) reasons: lack of training, oversight (that is, incomplete attention), lack of technical skills. Similarly, when we

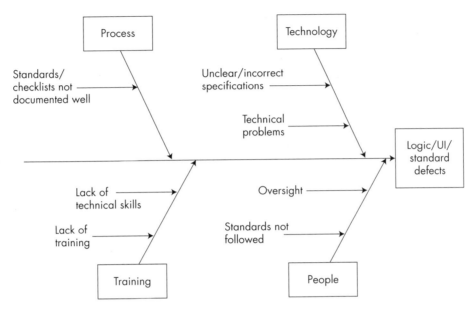

Figure 11.6 Cause-effect diagram for the ACE project

asked, "Why do processes cause too many logic/GUI/standards defects?" the answers were "standards not comprehensively documented" and "people not aware of standards." For technology the causes were "unclear specifications" and "technical problems of tools." The brainstorming sessions for the causal analysis generated many more causes. After listing all the suggestions made during the meeting, the defect prevention team prioritized them by considering each of the defects and identifying its causes. The causes that show up most frequently are the ones that are high priority. They are shown in Figure 11.6.

11.4.3 Developing and Implementing Solutions

So far we have discussed how to identify the types of frequently occurring defects and their root causes. The next phase is to take action to reduce the occurrence of defects.

The basic paradigm is the adage "An ounce of prevention is worth a pound of cure." With defect prevention, you are not trying to "cure" the software of defects; instead, you are taking preventive actions so that the software does not "fall sick" from defects. Common prevention actions are creating or improving checklists, holding training programs and reviews, and using a specific tool.

Sometimes, of course, you must take drastic actions such as changing the process or the technology.

The solutions, like the cause-effect analysis, are developed through a brainstorming session. Hence, these two steps are often done in the same session. This is how it is done at Infosys.

The preventive solutions are designated as action items that someone must perform. Hence, the implementation of the solutions is the key. Unless the solutions are implemented, they are of no use. At Infosys, along with the solution, the person responsible for implementing it is also specified. These action items are then added to the detailed schedule of tasks for the project, and their implementation is tracked like other tasks. Table 11.6 shows the root causes and the preventive actions developed for the ACE project. The proposed preventive actions are self-explanatory. They were scheduled in the MSP schedule of the project.

An important part of implementing these solutions is to see whether they are having the desired effect of reducing the injection of defects and thereby reducing the rework effort. Further analysis of defects found after the solutions have been implemented can give insight into this question. Generally, the next analysis for defect prevention can be used for this purpose. In addition to tracking the impact, such follow-up analysis has a tremendous reinforcing effect. Seeing the benefits convinces people as nothing else does. Hence, in addition to implementation, the impact of implementation should also be analyzed.

11.4.4 DP in the ACIC Project

Now let's look at the DP process for the ACIC case study. Defect data after the first construction iteration were analyzed, and the frequency of the various types of defects is shown in Table 11.7. Figure 11.7 shows the Pareto chart for the defect data.

The main purpose of defect prevention activities is to reduce the defect injection rate. In the first iteration, the ACIC project manager knew that at least 57 defects were injected. From the effort data, he calculated the defect injection rate for the build phase as 0.33 defects per hour. As per the plan, it was expected that about 70% of the defects would be injected in the build activity, whose estimated effort was about 110 days (excluding the estimate for the rework effort). That is, as per the quality and effort plan, the defect injection rate during coding was expected to be around 0.1 defects per person-hour. But after the first iteration, the defect injection rate was three times that much! Clearly, defect prevention activities were needed to achieve the target.

Table 11.6 Root Causes and Proposed Solutions for the ACE Project

Root Cause	Preventive Actions	Assigned to	Implementation Date
Standards not followed	• Do a group reading of the standards (after they have been updated). • Ensure that standards are followed in the mock projects done.	All	15/12/00
Standards/checklists not documented well	• Do a group review of the standards with expert from outside and then update the standards.	Xxxx	Next week
Oversight (incomplete attention)	• Effective self-review • Rigorous code reviews	All	Immediate effect Immediate effect
Unclear/incorrect specifications	• Specification reviews	All	Immediate effect
Lack of training	• Every new entrant will do a mock project, whose code will be reviewed and tested thoroughly. • A detailed specification and test plan will be made for the same.	xxxx	29/12/00
Technical problems	• Create awareness in people about the problems with the tools and how to avoid them. • Write a BOK on this and make it available.		
Lack of technical skills	• Document a BOK on topics like Sheridan grids, recordsets, Active Reports.	xxxx	31/01/01

To reduce the defect injection rate significantly, the project manager decided to tackle the top three categories of defects: logic, standards, and redundant code. A brainstorming session was held to identify the root causes and possible preventive actions. The regular procedure for brainstorming was followed. First, all the possible causes that anyone suggested were listed, and then the ones that were identified as the main culprits were separated out. For these causes, possible preventive actions were discussed and finally agreed on. Table 11.8 shows the final result of the causal analysis meeting—namely, the main root causes and preventive actions to be implemented. Many of these preventive actions became schedulable

Table 11.7 Summary of Defect Data after First Iteration, ACIC Project

Defect Type	Number of Defects
Logic	19
Standards	17
Redundant code	11
UI	8
Architecture	2
Total	57

activities and were added to the project schedule and then later executed (those as-signed to "self" were monitored informally).

The preventive actions given in the table are proposals by the team members; the project manager had to ascertain that they gave the desired result. Whether or not these measures were successful in reducing the defect injection rate could be checked only through the defect data.

The defect prevention activities were performed after the first construction iteration was done. Because the ACIC project had three such iterations, the defect injection rate after the next two iterations was also computed. Figure 11.8 shows the result of the analysis done after the other two iterations. This chart clearly shows the impact of implementing the preventive actions on the defect injection rate: It fell from more than 0.33 to less than 0.1!

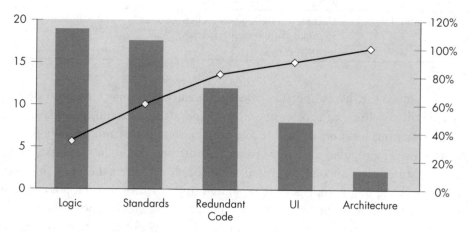

Figure 11.7 Pareto chart for defects

Table 11.8 Root Causes and Preventive Actions for the ACIC Project

Defect Type (Number of Defects)	Root Cause	Preventive Action	Assigned To
Standards (17)	Lack of programming experience	Training.	Self
	Oversight	Developers should read the coding standards carefully and adhere to them strictly.	Self
	Lack of understanding of program specs use and need	(i) Come up with a method to generate program specs from Rational Rose. (ii) Prepare a checklist for reviewing program specs. (iii) Prepare guidelines for writing program specs.	xxxx
	Coding standards not updated	Update coding standards and prepare a document listing the applicable project-specific UI standards.	xxxx
Redundant Code (11)	Lack of understanding of language	Training.	xxxx
	Lack of understanding of object model and database	(i) Training on database structure. (ii) Developer should go through the object model thoroughly.	Session on DB to be taken by xxxxx
	Lack of understanding of existing code	Group to discuss in a meeting and finalize the set of general method calls and identify where they should be called from.	Team
	Lack of understanding of table model	Understand the functionality of table model and dependency on Table Selection and inform the team about it.	xxxx
Logic (19)	Lack of understanding of existing code	Arrange code reading sessions.	Self
	Lack of programming experience	Training.	xxxx
	Lack of understanding of sequence diagrams representations	Give training in Rational Rose.	xxxx

Table continued on next page.

Table 11.8 Root Causes and Preventive Actions for the ACIC Project (continued)

Defect Type (Number of Defects)	Root Cause	Preventive Action	Assigned To
Logic (19)	Lack of understanding of database and associated processes.	Same as earlier.	xxxx
	Lack of understanding of object model	Same as earlier.	Self
	Oversight	Self-testing by programmer should be made more thorough. A session on how to test a small part of code to be taken.	Training by xxxx
	Lack of understanding of use cases	Developers will do a requirement walkthrough.	Self
	Lack of understanding of business rules	(i) Developer to refer to the matrix available that deals with various rules. (ii) Developer to review use cases of earlier application for better understanding of business rules.	Self
	Lack of understanding of defect	Follow-up with the reviewer should be taken by the owner of the defect. An attempt shall be made to reduce any existing communication gaps by more frequent follow-ups of the issues with the team/member concerned.	Team

Reduction in defect injection implies that there are fewer defects to be detected and fixed. Hence, a successful defect prevention activity should lead to reduction in the rework effort that follows testing. Figure 11.9 shows the rework effort in the three iterations. (This rework effort is obtained from the WAR because there is a different code for rework, and the program and module are also specified.) The rework effort after the first construction iteration was about 16% of the total effort for that iteration. This effort fell to about 5% and 3% in the next two construction cycles. The effort spent in the causal analysis was a few hours for data analysis, along with a brainstorming meeting of about in defect prevention.

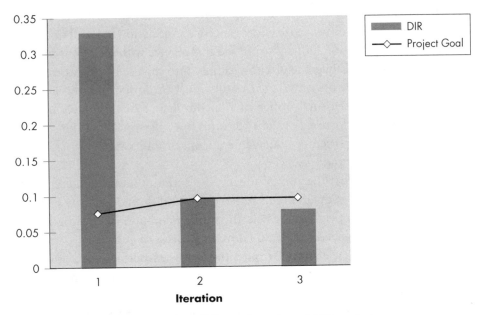

Figure 11.8 Defect injection rate in different iterations, ACIC project

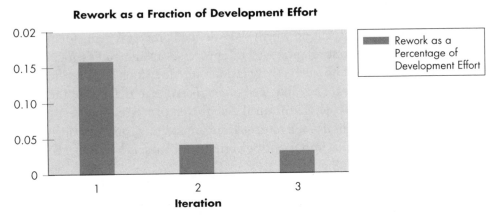

Figure 11.9 Rework reduction in ACIC due to defect prevention

11.5 PROCESS MONITORING AND AUDIT

To gain the benefits of plans and processes, projects must follow them properly. People can make mistakes, and under deadline pressures they tend to take shortcuts or expedient measures, often failing to follow processes correctly. To ensure compliance with the defined processes, an active effort is needed. Audits aim to fulfill this need.

The basic objective of audits is to ensure compliance with the defined process and to provide senior management with visibility into the use of processes. To ensure a reasonable degree of compliance, audits must be done regularly. They also must be formal, with a formal notice of noncompliance being issued and later tracked to satisfactory closure. Formality ensures that "personal equations" do not play a major role and that senior management gains visibility into process compliance through summary audit reports.

Who should conduct the audits? Ideally, the auditors should understand the processes of the organization and their importance, and should have the necessary maturity and stature to be able to assess the implementation on a project objectively. The auditors also need to be trained in the process of auditing.

At Infosys, project personnel from other projects perform the audit of a project, with SEPG providing the training. Every month, the audit coordinator announces an audit schedule that specifies which project is to be audited by whom and the focus area for the audit (which aspect of the process the audit should focus on). A team of two people normally conducts the audit.

11.5.1 Conducting the Audit

In the audit, the auditors focus on whether the defined process is being followed in the project, paying greatest attention to the processes in the audit's focus area. They ask questions about how an activity is done, and they look at the evidence or outputs of these activities. They may use *audit checklists* to determine the questions. These checklists are derived from the approved processes and past experience, and they try to maximize the returns from an audit by concentrating on the key aspects rather than less important or peripheral issues. Here are parts of the checklist for project planning:

- Is the project plan documented in the standard project plan template?
- Has the project plan been group reviewed?
- Has the project plan been approved and baselined, and is it under configuration management?
- Is there a signed contract?
- Have the commitments to the customer or other groups been reviewed?
- Is there an estimated effort for the project that is based on historical data?

- Have the effort estimates and the schedule been reviewed?
- Is the quality plan complete, and has it been reviewed?
- Is the life cycle used in the project identified and documented?
- Are personnel identified and the responsibility for each work element defined and tracked?
- Are reestimation triggers, such as scope changes and required corrective actions, defined?
- Are deliverables to the customer, including user documentation, clearly identified?
- Are risks and risk mitigation plans identified and properly documented?
- Are reviews, progress reporting, tracking, and approval mechanisms identified?

The audit is considered complete when the audit team has asked all questions and looked at any desired artifacts. A noncompliance report (NCR) is issued if the evidence suggests that the approved processes are not being followed, or that some weaknesses exist in the process that might lead to loss of control or to suboptimality.

A key aspect of auditing (and one that is stressed in training) is that the procedure seeks to audit the compliance to the process and not to audit people. This idea is fundamental to the entire process-oriented approach; the focus should always remain on the process and process improvement, and problems found in a project should be attributed to process factors and not to people. The NCR clearly indicates the type of deviation found.

Identifying noncompliance is the goal of audits (and the analysis of audit results is used to evaluate the effectiveness of processes), but when two software professionals evaluate a project, they are likely to develop some ideas regarding the project's technical or management aspects that might be useful in improving the project. These issues often do not constitute noncompliance, but one would not like to lose this insight. Such observations are therefore recorded on a separate form as the auditors' suggestions. The audit reports, including NCRs and suggestions, are sent to the coordinator of audits.

11.5.2 Follow-up Actions

The submission of the NCR is not the end of the auditing activity. Because the audit's basic purpose is to ensure that projects deploy the organization's approved processes, these reports should be used to make the necessary changes in the project so that any issue raised in the NCR is satisfactorily addressed. This step is called a *corrective action*. For each NCR, some corrective action must be taken. Once taken, it is recorded on the NCR form itself.

To ensure that the issue raised in the NCR is satisfactorily resolved, the audit coordinator ensures that the action is approved by the auditors. If these personnel are not available, the quality adviser for the project or the audit coordinator may approve the action. Once the action is approved, the NCR is considered closed.

Figure 11.10 gives an example of an NCR and its corrective action. This NCR specifies the project, the date, and the severity of the noncompliance. The severity indicates both the seriousness of the issue and its consequences (major or minor). Project personnel usually take the corrective action. In this case, the issue raised

---

INFOSYS   **NON-CONFORMITY REPORT**

Project/ Dept.: Projyyy   **Date:**   21 Oct 97

QSD Ref.:   Req. chg. Process   **Severity:**   **Serious/**Minor

Non-Conformity

Requirement changes in the development project are not being tracked/recorded. E.g., 5 programs sent for modification. The mails pertaining to those changes were not logged.

Corrective action: **Action by:** PL

                                               Action date: 10 Dec 97

A spreadsheet will be created in which all changes, along with their impact analysis, will be recorded.

Preventive action: **Action by:**

                                               Action date:

Auditor

Auditee

(Signature)

(Signature)

Follow-up action

Done.

Closed by   **Recommendation:**   Closed

(Signature)

Figure 11.10 A noncompliance report with corrective action

concerned requirements changes, which are handled generally by the project manager, who therefore instituted the corrective action. The date of the corrective action is also mentioned.

Sometimes, the issue is likely to recur, either in the same project or in other projects. In that case, in addition taking a corrective action, the project may need to take a preventive action to ensure that a similar problem does not crop up again. Hence, preventive actions might need to be taken in some situations. The NCR includes a section in which to record the preventive actions taken and who took them. Figure 11.11 shows an example of an NCR that required both corrective and preventive action. The preventive action for this NCR is to upgrade a checklist to ensure that a similar problem does not happen in the future.

INFOSYS	**NON-CONFORMITY REPORT**
Project/ Dept.: Projxxx	**Date:** 15 Dec 97
ISO 9001 clause :	**Severity:** **Serious**/<u>Minor</u>
QSD Ref.:	

Non-Conformity

When a review finds no defects, no evidence exists to show that the review was done.

Corrective action:	**Action by:** PL
	Action date: 28 Dec 97

Reviewed documents will be marked as **'reviewed'** with reviewer's signature.

Preventive action:	**Action by:** Manager – SEPG
	Action date: 31 Jan 98

The review checklist will be enhanced to ensure that some review record is created even if no defects are found during the review.

Auditor
Auditee
(Signature)
(Signature)

Follow-up action
Done.

Closed by	
(Signature)	**Recommendation:** <u>Closed</u>

Figure 11.11 A noncompliance report with preventive action

At Infosys, an NCR must be closed within 60 days of the audit. Typically, the audit coordinator sends a reminder at the end of one month and another one a week before the time limit expires. NCRs older than 60 days are reported to the senior management for the project. This kind of formal follow-up ensures that audit reports are taken seriously and that the issues raised are addressed properly.

11.6 SUMMARY

When a plan is executed, regardless of how carefully the planning was done, things frequently do not work out as planned. With proper monitoring, a project manager can check whether or not the project is progressing as planned. If it is not progressing along the desired path, control must be applied to ensure that the project still meets its objectives.

At Infosys, project monitoring occurs at several different levels. Following are the lessons from this approach:

- Track the completion of scheduled activities, the defects found, and the issues that come up. Use a weekly status report for regular tracking and reporting.

- At project milestones, compare the actual values for schedule, effort, and defects with the estimated values. If the deviation exceeds the predetermined threshold, take corrective and preventive actions if the situation warrants. Also, revisit the risks and situations that affect risks.

- Evaluate some tasks immediately after they have been executed and take corrective actions if the performance is not within the expected range, as determined from past data. Reviews and unit testing are best suited for this level of tracking.

- Analyze the defect data from the first few modules in the project to understand the root causes of the defects. Then take actions to eliminate the root causes. Later, repeat this analysis to understand the impact of defect prevention.

- Audit the project formally for compliance with the defined processes. Based on the noncompliance reports, take corrective and preventive actions.

From the CMM perspective, the techniques discussed in this chapter satisfy some of the requirements of the Project Tracking and Oversight KPA at level 2, the

Integrated Project Management KPA at level 3, and the Quantitative Process Management KPA at level 4. The process monitoring and audit activities satisfy some requirements of the Software Quality Assurance KPA at level 2 and the audit requirements of some other KPAs. The defect analysis and prevention activities satisfy some of the requirements of the Defect Prevention KPA at level 5.

11.7 REFERENCES

1. P. Hsia. Making software development visible. *IEEE Software,* May 1996.

2. D.P. Youll. *Making Software Development Visible: Effective Project Control.* John Wiley and Sons, 1990.

3. N. Brown. Industrial-strength management strategies. *IEEE Software,* July 1996.

4. D.B. Simmons, N.C. Ellis, H. Fujihara, and W. Kuo. *Software Measurement: A Visualization Toolkit.* Prentice Hall PTR, 1998.

5. B. Boehm. *Software Engineering Economics.* Prentice Hall, 1981.

6. P. Jalote. *CMM in Practice: Processes for Executing Software Projects at Infosys.* Addison-Wesley, 2000.

7. D.C. Montgomery. *Introduction to Statistical Quality Control, third edition.* John Wiley and Sons, 1996.

8. J.A. Swift. *Introduction to Modern Statistical Quality Control and Management.* St. Lucie Press, Delray Beach, Florida, 1995.

Chapter 12

Project Closure

The software has been delivered and installed successfully. After working long hours and weekends for many months on this project, the project manager and his team heave a sigh of relief that this not very successful project is finished. But did the project manager learn any lessons? Will he and the team members be able to avoid repeating the problems they got into in this project? If the project ends now, it is likely that the story will be repeated in another project, perhaps with minor improvements.

For the project manager, the team, and the organization, the project does not end until a postmortem has been done to uncover what went wrong and why, and what worked and why. This analysis will enable the project manager and the team members to cull out key lessons on project execution. In addition to helping the team members in their future projects, these lessons will also help other projects to improve their execution.

A project closure analysis, or postmortem analysis, is a golden opportunity for process improvement that should not be missed.[1,2,3,4] Indeed, this exercise is considered a best practice of software engineering.[5] One step in the quality improvement paradigm of the experience factory[6] is to analyze the data at the end of each project to evaluate current practices, determine problems, and so on. But despite its benefits, a postmortem analysis is not a "standard" activity.[7]

This chapter describes the contents of a project closure analysis report at Infosys and gives the closure report of the ACIC case study.

12.1 PROJECT CLOSURE ANALYSIS

Project closure analysis is the key to learning from the past so as to provide future improvements. To achieve this goal, it must be done carefully in an atmosphere of safety so that lessons can be captured and used to improve the process and future projects. Before we describe the details of the closure analysis report, we briefly discuss the role of closure analysis and its implementation.

12.1.1 The Role of Closure Analysis

The objective of a postmortem or closure analysis is "to determine what went right, what went wrong, what worked, what did not, and how it could be made better the next time."[2] Relevant information must be collected from the project, primarily for use by future projects. That is, the purpose of having an identified completion analysis activity, rather than simply saying, "The project is done," is not to help this project but rather to improve the organization by leveraging the lessons learned. This type of learning can be supported effectively by analysis of data from completed projects. This analysis is also needed to understand the performance of the process on this project, which in turn is needed to determine the process capability.

As noted earlier, the data obtained during the closure analysis are used to populate the process database (PDB). The data from the PDB can be used directly by subsequent projects for planning purposes. This information is also used in computing the process capability, which is used by projects in planning and for analyzing trends. Figure 12.1 illustrates the role of closure analysis.

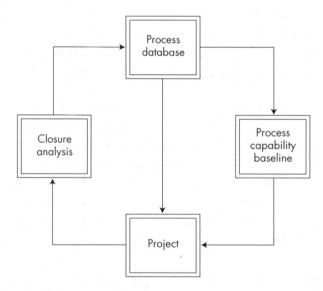

Figure 12.1 The role of closure analysis

Earlier chapters discuss the types of data generally collected in a project and describe the collection methods. The amount of raw data collected in a project can be quite large. For example, a project involving five people and lasting for 25 weeks will have 125 entries for weekly effort, data for about 250 defects (assuming about 0.05 defects injected per person-hour), data on many change requests, various outputs, and so on. Clearly, these data will be of limited use unless they are analyzed and presented within a proper framework and at a suitable level of abstraction. Closure analysis aims to accomplish this goal.

After data analysis and extraction of all lessons learned from the analyses, the results should be packaged so that they can be used by others (packaging is the last step in the quality improvement paradigm[6]). Furthermore, to leverage this information, project processes must be constructed so that their execution requires the effective use of data. It can be argued, however, that even if others do not learn from the packaged information, the project personnel will have consolidated their experience and will carry the lessons learned from the analysis into future projects.[2] In other words, a closure analysis is useful even if others do not directly gain from it.

12.1.2 Performing Closure Analysis

At Infosys, the project manager carries out the closure analysis with help from the SEPG quality adviser associated with the project. A template for the analysis report has been defined. The person carrying out the closure analysis must fill out this template properly, using mostly the metrics data, thereby keeping the focus on objective information.

As discussed earlier, the effort data are available from the weekly activity report database. The defect data can be gathered from the defect control system. Size data are obtained from the project. Planning data appear in the project management plan. These data constitute the main information needed for metrics analysis.

The data are first analyzed by the quality adviser, who develops an initial interpretation of the results. A meeting is then held among the quality adviser, the project leader, and other project members. The initial report serves as the basis of discussion, and further points and observations from the meeting are also noted. This meeting yields the basis of the final closure analysis report.

The final report is submitted to the SEPG and the business manager of the project and is shared among the project team members. The report is also entered in the PDB, making it available for future projects and analyses.

12.1.3 Closure Analysis Report

This section briefly discusses the major elements in an Infosys project closure analysis report; later, we present the closure report of the ACIC project. The contents of this analysis report form a superset of the data that are put in the PDB. The PDB contains only those metrics data that are needed often by projects and whose use is required by the current processes. The analysis report, however, may capture other data that might shed light on process performance or help to better explain the process.

General and Process-Related Information   The closure report first gives general information about the project, the overall productivity achieved and quality delivered, the process used and process deviations, the estimated and actual start and end dates, the tools used, and so on. This section might also include a brief description of the project's experience with tools (detailed "experience reports" are put into the BOK system). The information about tools can be used by other projects to decide whether use of the tool is warranted. It can also be examined to identify tools that have good advantages and to propagate their use throughout the rest of the organization.

Risk Management   The risk management section gives the risks initially anticipated for the project along with the risk mitigation steps planned. In addition, this section lists the top risks as viewed in the post-project analysis (they are the real risks for the project). This information can be used by later projects and can be used to update risk management guidelines. Notes may also be provided on the effectiveness of the mitigation steps employed.

Size   As discussed in Chapter 6, many projects use the bottom-up method for estimation. In this method, the size of the software is estimated in terms of the number of simple, medium, or complex modules. Hence, this size is captured along with the criteria used for classification (different projects may use different criteria). Data on both the estimated size and the actual size are included.

For normalization purposes, the productivity of a project is measured in terms of function points (FP) per person-month. Although FP can be counted by studying the functionality of the system, at closure time it is computed from the measured size in lines of code (LOC). If multiple languages are used, we simply add the sizes (in FP) of the modules in different languages. Strictly speaking, function points (unlike lines of code) are not an additive measure. Because we are measuring only the size of the complete system in FP, however, this approach is equivalent to converting all LOC counts into an LOC count of some "universal" language and then converting that size into FP. Furthermore, because of the inherent limitations of software metrics and their use, some inaccuracies are acceptable, provided that the methods are used consistently. The size in FP is also captured in the closure analysis report.

Effort The closure analysis report also contains the total estimated effort and the actual effort in person-hours. The total estimated effort is obtained from the project management plan. The total actual effort is the sum of the total effort reported in all WARs submitted by the project members, including the project leader. If the deviation between the actual and the estimated values is large, reasons for this variation are recorded.

For each of the major steps in the process, the total actual effort and estimated effort for the stage are captured, too. This information can be useful in planning, and it is a key input in forming the PCB. For each stage, where possible, the effort is separated into the effort for the task, for the review, and for the rework. The WAR codes described earlier in the book permit this separation. The distribution of effort in the various phases can then be computed and recorded. The separation of effort between task, review, and rework aids in identifying the scope of productivity improvement.

The cost of quality for the project is also computed. It measures the cost of all activities that directly contributed to achieving quality. The cost of quality can be defined in many ways; here it is defined as the percentage of the total effort spent in review, testing, rework to remove defects, and project-specific training.

Defects The defects section of the closure analysis report contains a summary of the defects found during the project. The defects can be analyzed with respect to severity (percentage of defects that were major, minor, or cosmetic), stage detected (percentage of total detected defects detected by which activity), stage injected (which activity introduced what percentage of total defects), and so on. Injection rate and defect distribution are also determined.

The defect removal efficiency of a defect removal task is defined as the percentage of total defects that existed at the time of execution of the task that are detected by the execution of the task. This metric is useful for determining which quality activities need improvement. The closure report gives the defect removal efficiency of the major quality control tasks, as well as the overall defect removal efficiency of the process. Other analyses of defect data may also be included. Sometimes, a separate analysis of the review data may be performed. The estimated versus actual defect levels are also analyzed.

Causal Analysis   When the project is finished, the performance of the overall process on this project is known. If the performance is outside the range given in the capability baseline, there is a good chance that the variability has an assignable cause. Causal analysis involves looking at large variations and then identifying their causes, generally through discussion and brainstorming.

Process Assets   In addition to the metrics data, other project artifacts are potentially useful for future projects. Chapter 2 discusses the use of process assets. These process assets are collected at project closure. The potential entries to the BOK are also identified during closure, although they are submitted later.

12.2 THE ACIC CLOSURE ANALYSIS REPORT

This section presents the closure analysis report of the ACIC project. First, the report gives some general information about the project. The performance summary that follows shows that the project had an effort overrun of about 19% caused by two major change requests. It also gives the planned versus actual data for team size, start and end dates, quality, productivity, cost of quality, defect injection rate, and defect removal efficiency. In almost all these parameters, the actual performance was very close to the estimated. The actual defect injection rate is about 26% lower than estimated, largely because of the defect prevention activities.

The report gives an overview of the process tailoring done in the project and specifies the internal and external tools that were used. For risk management, the report discusses the risks that were originally identified as well as the real risks that the project leader and SEPG feel existed for the project. As you can see, these are not the same; a new risk—conversion to VAJ 3.0—arose during the project. The notes on risk mitigation state that this risk was effectively managed by showing the impact of the change to the customer and then agreeing to postpone this conversion to a future version. For other risks, the notes assess the effectiveness of the risk mitigation strategies.

The report records the estimated and actual size in terms of the number of programs of different complexity. The size of the final output system is also given in LOC, along with the language. For this project, the size was about 33 KLOC of Java code, which translates to about 1612 FP, and about 1K of COBOL code, which translates to about 12FP. This size figure was used to compute the project's productivity and quality.

Next, the estimated and actual schedules for various phases are given. Where the deviation is large (for example, in acceptance testing), the report gives a reason for the slippage.

Next are shown the data on effort. First, the report gives the distribution of actual effort over the various project phases, along with the task, review, and rework effort for each phase. Using this breakdown, the cost of quality has been computed at 31.4% for this project. Then the estimated and actual effort for the various stages of the project are given, along with the reason for deviation, where the deviation is large. As you can see, in this project the overall deviation is not very large, although for a few phases the deviation is substantial and is sometimes negative.

Next, the report contains an analysis of the defects. The distribution of defects among the various defect detection stages is given, along with the estimates for those stages. As with other parameters, the percent deviation is also shown. Here, too, the overall the deviation is –20%, although there is significant deviation for some phases. The report states the reason for the overall reduction and for the significant deviation in the distribution of actual defects. Then the defect data are given by stage detected and stage injected. Using these data, defect removal efficiencies for each defect removal stage are computed. In this project, the removal efficiency was 100% for requirements and design review, only 55% for code review, only 32% for unit testing, 91% for system testing, and 100% for acceptance testing (as only those defects removed before the end of acceptance testing are known). The overall defect removal efficiency is 97.5%, which is satisfactory; the goal was 97%. The defects distribution with respect to severity and defect type has also been computed.

Finally, a causal analysis provides the possible process reasons for the situations in which the planned goals were not met. In this project, the reasons for performance deviation are discussed, along with the performance data. The lessons learned from this project are summarized here. The process assets that have been submitted are also recorded.

Closure Report of the ACIC Project

1. GENERAL INFORMATION

Project Code	Xxxxx
Life Cycle	Development, Full life cycle
Business Domain	Finance. Web-based application for managing accounts.
Project leader/Module Leader	Xxxxxx
Business Manager	
Software Quality Adviser	Xxxxx

2. PERFORMANCE SUMMARY

Performance Parameter	Actual	Estimated	Deviation	Reasons for Deviation (If Large)
Total Effort (person-days)	597	501	19%	Two major change requests that came.
Peak Team Size	9	9	0	N/A
Start Date	03 Apr 2000	03 Apr 2000	0	N/A
End Date	03 Nov 2000	30 Nov 2000	27 Days	Two major change requests consumed more than 5% of the effort.
Quality (number of defects delivered per FP)	0.002	0.0125		Quality improved because of defect prevention and use of incremental process.
Productivity	58	57	2%	N/A
Cost of quality	31.4%	33%	5%	N/A
Defect injection rate	0.022	0.03	−26%	Improved because of defect prevention.
Defect removal efficiency	97.4	97	Small	N/A

3. PROCESS DETAILS

Process Tailoring	• Rational Unified Process was employed. • Development and analysis were done iteratively—3 iterations for development and 2 for design and analysis. • Requirement traceability was done through Requisite Pro tool.

4. TOOLS USED

Notes on Tools Used	• External Tools: VSS, VJA, Requisite Pro, MSP • Internal Tools: BugsBunny, WAR

5. RISK MANAGEMENT

Risks identified at the start of the project

Risk 1	Lack of support from database architect and database administrator of the customer
Risk 2	Improper use of RUP, as it is being used for the first time
Risk 3	Personnel attrition
Risk 4	Problems with working on customer's database over the link

Risks encountered during the project

Risk 1	Impact of conversion to VAJ 3.0
Risk 2	Lack of support from database architect and database administrator of the customer
Risk 3	Improper use of RUP, as it is being used for the first time
Risk 4	Personnel attrition

Notes on Risk Mitigation

Risk1: Clearly articulating the risk helped in customer agreeing to postpone the conversion with proper budgeting of its impact.

Risk2: Mitigation strategies of careful and advance planning and employing the on-site coordinator were effective.

Risk3: Training the team in RUP was effective. So was keeping the customer informed.

Risk 4: Remained as a risk, although it did not materialize. Impact would have been minimal because multiple people were kept informed of each critical activity.

6. SIZE

	Estimated	Actual
Number of simple use cases	5	5
Number of medium use cases	9	9
Number of complex use cases	12	12

Notes on Estimation

Classification Criteria. The standard definition of simple, medium, and complex was used for classifying the use cases. This worked fine.

Final System Size in FP

The size of the final source is measured in LOC. It is normalized to FP by using the published conversion tables. For Java, the published tables suggest that 21 LOC equals 1 FP and for COBOL, 107 LOC equal 1 FP.

Output Language	Size in LOC	Size in FP
Java	33,865	1612
COBOL	1241	12

7. SCHEDULE

Phase	Actual Elapsed Time (days)	Estimated Time (days)	% Slippage	Reasons for Slippage
Requirements	28.67	31	−6.5	
High-level design	0	0	0.0	
Detailed design	38.8	42	−6.7	
Coding	132	135	−1.6	

Phase	Actual Elapsed Time (days)	Estimated Time (days)	% Slippage	Reasons for Slippage
Unit testing	9	10	−9.3	
Total - Build	141	144	−2.1	
Integration test	40	40	0	
System testing	15	0	0.0	
Acceptance testing	30	10	200.0	AT completion was extended on customer's request.

8. EFFORT

Distribution over Life-Cycle Stages

Stage	Task	Review	Rework	Total
Requirements	210.0	10.0	60.0	280.0
High-level design	0.0	0.0	0.0	0.0
Detailed design	652.0	14.0	29.5	695.5
Coding	1188.0	39.5	76.5	1304.0
Unit testing	129.5	0.0	17.0	146.5
Integration testing	567.5	6.0	160.5	734.0
System testing	90.0	0.0	0.0	90.0
Acceptance testing	336.5	0.0	0.0	336.5
Total - LC stages	3173.5	69.5	343.5	3586.5
Project management	733.1	0.0	0.0	733.1
Training	104.5	0.0	0.0	104.5
CM	317.0	0.0	0.0	317.0
Misc.	488.5	0.0	0.0	488.5
Total – mgmt, training, and misc.	1643.0	0.0	0.0	1643.0
Total Effort (Person-hours)	4816.50	69.50	343.50	5229.50
Total Effort (Person-months)	25.76	0.37	1.84	27.97

Cost of Quality

$$COQ = \frac{\text{Review effort} + \text{rework effort} + \text{test effort} + \text{training effort}}{\text{total effort}} = 100$$

$$= (69.5 + 343.5 + 129.5 + 567.5 + 90 + 336.5 + 104.5)/5229.5 \times 100$$

$$= 31.4\%$$

Effort Distribution and Actual Versus Estimated

Stage	Actual		Estimated		% Deviation	Reasons or Deviation
	Effort (person-hours)	%	Effort (person-hours)	%		
Requirements	280	5.35	475.0	10	−30	Overestimated this effort (data from earlier project did not help because it did not have this phase).
Design (HLD and detailed)	695.5	13.30	569.0	12	22	Design took more time because team was inexperienced with Rational Rose and OOAD.
Coding	1304.0	24.94	1235.3	26	6	
Unit testing	146.5	2.80	142.5	3	3	
Integration testing	734.0	14.04	331.0	7	120	Much effort spent on fixing bugs introduced during reconciliation with Synergy and Window Resized code.
System testing	90.0	1.72	95.0	2	−5	
Acceptance testing	336.5	6.43	285.0	6	18	Acceptance testing was not completed on Nov 3 and was extended until Nov 23 due to delays from the customer.
Total—LC stages	3586.5	68.58	3132.8	66	14.5	

Effort Distribution and Actual Versus Estimated (continued)

| Stage | Actual | | Estimated | | | |
	Effort (person-hours)	%	Effort (person-hours)	%	% Deviation	Reasons or Deviation
Project management	733.1	14.02	713.0	15	3	
Training	104.5	2.00	455.0	10	−77	
CM	317.0	6.06	142.0	3	123	Deviation due to reconciliation issues.
Misc.	488.5	9.34	285.0	6	71	More because of training.
Total—mgmt, training, and misc.	1643.0	31.42	1595.0	34	3.01	
Total	5229.5	100	4727.8	100	10.6	

9. DEFECTS

Defect Distribution

Stage Detected	Actual Number of Defects	% of Total Defects Found	Estimated Number of Defects	% of Total Estimated Defects	% Deviation
Req. and design review	11	10	29	20	−62
Code review	58	50	29	20	100
Unit testing	15	13	57	40	−73
Integration and system testing	29	25	25	17	16
Acceptance testing	3	2	5	3	−40
Total	116	100	145	100	−20

Reasons for Deviation

1. Defect prevention reduced the defect injection rate in later stages, resulting in overall reduction in the defect injection rate.
2. In the earlier project from which the estimates were derived, fewer code reviews were done and there was a heavier reliance on UT. In this project, because code reviews were done more rigorously and widely, more defects were found in reviews, leading to a substantial decrease in the defects found in unit testing.

Defect Removal Efficiencies

Defects Detection Stage	Defects Injection Stage			Defect Removal Efficiency
	Req.	**Build**	**Design**	
Req. review	5			100%
Design review	0	6		100%
Code review	0	0	58	55% (58 / 58 + 15 + 29 + 3)
Unit testing	0	0	15	32% (15 / 15 + 29 + 3)
Integration/system testing	0	0	29	91% (29 / 29 + 3)
Acceptance testing	0	0	3	100%

Overall Defect Removal Efficiency = 113 / 116 = 97.4 %

Distribution by Severity

Sequence Number	Severity	Number of Defects	% of Total Defects
1	Cosmetic	26	22.4
2	Minor	51	44
3	Major	36	31
4	Critical	3	2.6
5	Others	—	—
	Total	116	

Distribution by Defect Type

Sequence Number	Defect Type	Number of Defects	% of Total Defects
1.	Logic	33	28.4
2.	Standards	29	25
3.	Performance	24	20.7
4.	Redundant code	14	12
5.	User interface	9	7.7
6.	Architecture	4	3.5
7.	Consistency	2	1.7
8.	Reusability	1	0.9

Total	365

10. CAUSAL ANALYSIS AND LESSONS LEARNED

There were very few large deviations in the process performance; the actual performance was close to what was expected. The reasons for the deviations, where they are large, are given along with the deviation. Some key lessons learned are:

1. Incremental or phased development is extremely helpful in achieving higher quality and productivity because data from the first phase can be used to improve the remaining phases through defect prevention.
2. Defect prevention can substantially reduce the defect injection rate. In terms of effort also, defect prevention pays off handsomely; by putting in a few hours of effort, up to 5 to 10 times effort savings can be achieved in the form of reduced rework effort.
3. If a change request has a major impact, discussion with the customer using a detailed impact analysis can be very helpful in setting the right expectations and doing a proper cost-benefit analysis (which may result in postponement of the change, as happened in this project).
4. The defect removal efficiencies of code reviews and unit testing are very low. Processes for both, and implementation of these processes, need to be reviewed to improve these numbers. In this project, the system/integration testing compensated for the poor performance of reviews and unit testing. However, for larger projects, this may not be possible and poor performance in reviews and unit testing can have adverse effects on quality.

11. PROCESS ASSETS SUBMITTED

Project management plan, project schedule, configuration management plan, Java coding standards, code review checklist, integration plan review checklist, impact analysis checklist, causal analysis reports for defect prevention.

12. REFERENCES

Omitted.

12.3 SUMMARY

A project does not end with the delivery and installation of the software; before it is closed, it must be used for learning. Project closure analysis is one method to achieve this goal.

Following are some of the key takeaways from the Infosys approach to project closure:

- Keep the project closure analysis metrics-based. Analyze the data to understand the performance of the project and the causes for any major deviations. These causes can serve as a source of improvement initiatives.
- The metrics analysis should report the final quality delivered, the productivity achieved, the distribution of effort, the distribution of defects, the defect removal efficiency of various quality activities, and the cost of quality.
- Collect reusable process assets such as plans, checklists, standards, and guidelines, and make them available for others.

With respect to the CMM, project closure is not a direct requirement of the KPAs dealing with project management. However, the closure report provides the data for the process database and process capability baseline, which are necessary to satisfy many of the requirements of the Project Planning KPA and the Integrated Software Management KPA. They also aid in learning and recordkeeping, which are required at level 3.

12.4 REFERENCES

1. S. Brady and T. DeMarco. Management-aided software engineering. *IEEE Software,* Nov. 1994.

2. E.J. Chikofsky. Changing your endgame strategy. *IEEE Software,* Nov. 1990.

3. B. Collier, T. DeMarco, and P. Fearey. A defined process for project postmortem review. *IEEE Software,* July 1996.

4. R. Grady. *Successful Software Process Improvement.* Prentice Hall PTR, 1997.

5. K. Caputo. *CMM Implementation Guide: Choreographing Software Process Improvement.* Addison-Wesley, 1998.

6. V.R. Basili and H.D. Rombach. The experience factory. In *The Encyclopedia of Software Engineering, John J. Marciniak, editor.* John Wiley and Sons, 1994.

7. K. Kumar. Post implementation evaluation of computer-based information systems: Current practices. *Communications of the ACM,* Feb. 1990.

Index

Also Available from Addison-Wesley

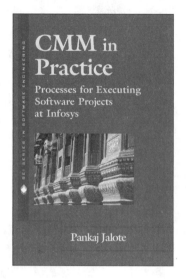

CMM in Practice
Processes for Executing Software Projects at Infosys

Pankaj Jalote

0-201-61626-2
Hardcover
400 pages
©2000

This book describes the implementation of CMM at Infosys Technologies, and illustrates in detail how software projects are executed at this highly mature software development organization. The book examines the various stages in the life cycle of an actual Infosys project as a running example throughout the book, describing the technical and management processes used to initiate, plan, and execute it.

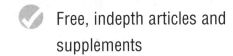
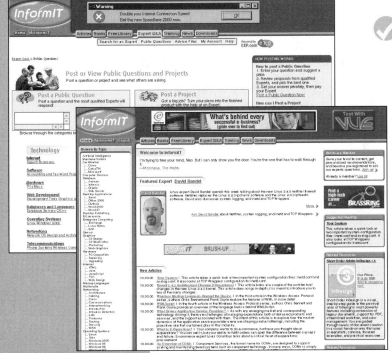